THE PAST, PRESENT, AND FUTURE OF LIBRARIES

THE PAST, PRESENT, AND FUTURE OF LIBRARIES

Cosponsored by the American Philosophical Society, the Gladys Krieble Delmas Foundation, and the Association of Research Libraries

Edited by the
American Philosophical Society

American Philosophical Society Press
Philadelphia

> Transactions of the
> American Philosophical Society
> Held at Philadelphia
> for Promoting Useful Knowledge
> Volume 110, Part 3

Copyright © 2022 by the American Philosophical Society for its Transactions series.

All rights reserved.

ISBN: 978-1-60618-103-4

Ebook ISBN: 978-1-60618-108-9

U.S. ISSN: 0065-9746

The publisher has no responsibility for the persistence or accuracy of URLs for external or third-party Internet websites referred to in this publication and does not guarantee that any content on such websites is, or will remain, accurate or appropriate.

Library of Congress Cataloging-in-Publication Data

Names: Past, Present, and Future of Libraries (Conference) (2018 : Philadelphia, Pa.), author. | American Philosophical Society, sponsoring body, editor. | Gladys Krieble Delmas Foundation, sponsoring body. | Association of Research Libraries, sponsoring body.

Title: The Past, Present, and Future of Libraries / cosponsored by the American Philosophical Society, the Gladys Krieble Delmas Foundation, and the Association of Research Libraries ; The American Philosophical Society, editors.

Description: Philadelphia : American Philosophical Society Press, 2021. | Series: Transactions of the American Philosophical Society, 0065-9746 ; v. 110, pt. 3 | "The Past, Present, and Future of Libraries" was held from September 27-29, 2018 in Philadelphia, PA. | Includes bibliographical references and index. | Summary: "In commemoration of the American Philosophical Society's 275th anniversary, the Society's Library, along with the Gladys Krieble Delmas Foundation and the Association of Research Libraries (ARL), hosted an interdisciplinary and international conference that explored the history of libraries, the present opportunities for libraries (especially independent research libraries and those with special collections), and the potential future for libraries as they continue to evolve in the 21st century"—Provided by publisher.

Identifiers: LCCN 2021040895 (print) | LCCN 2021040896 (ebook) | ISBN 9781606181034 (paperback) | ISBN 9781606181089 (mobi)

Subjects: LCSH: Libraries--United States—Congresses. | Libraries—United States—History—Congresses. | Research libraries—Congresses. | Libraries—Special collections—Congresses. | LCGFT: Conference papers and proceedings.

Classification: LCC Z731 .P337 2018 (print) | LCC Z731 (ebook) | DDC 027.073—dc23

LC record available at https://lccn.loc.gov/2021040895

LC ebook record available at https://lccn.loc.gov/2021040896

Cover design by Eugenia B. González.

Contents

Librarian's Note ix
    Patrick Spero

I. Reading Communities

1 From Literary Salon to Library: The Female Mind and the Art of Reading Across the Color Line 3
    Ariel Clark Silver

2 Women of the Roxburghe Club: Bibliomania, Country Houses, and Bridges to the Twenty-First Century 25
    Sharon S. Prado

II. Building Collections

3 Ushering in the Era of Expansion: Academic Libraries Supporting Change in American Higher Education, 1860–1920 75
    Katy B. Mathuews

4 Decolonizing Special Collections: Building the Native American Literature Collection at Amherst College 93
    Mike Kelly

III. Access and Accessibility

5 Take Me into the Library and Show Me Myself: Toward Authentic Accessibility in Digital Libraries 111
    Dorothy Berry

6   Changing Attitudes Toward Access to Special Collections 127
    Jae Jennifer Rossman

7   Preservation of Electric Government Information: An Urgent
    National Priority..151
    Scott Matheson

IV. Tools and Technologies

8   The Schoenberg Database of Manuscripts: A Special Collections
    Research Tool for the Twenty-First Century....................................167
    Emma Cawlfield Thomson

9   Virtual Reality and the Academic Library of the Future.................185
    Zack Lischer-Katz and Matt Cook

10 The New Wave of Digital Collections: Speculating on the Future
    of Library Curation 211
    Alex Wermer-Colan and James Kopaczewski

V. Networks, Collaboration, Community

11 The Collection Is the Network: Collection, Collaboration, and
    Cooperation at Network Scale..245
    Daniel Dollar, Jeff Kosokoff, and Sarah Tudesco

12 Refworld: Future Frontiers for Special Collections Libraries.......257
    Rachael Dreyer

Index..*275*

Contributors

Dorothy Berry, MA, MLS, Houghton Library, Harvard University, Cambridge, Massachusetts

Matt Cook, MA, MLIS, Digital Scholarship Program Manager, Harvard Library, Cambridge, Massachusetts

Daniel Dollar, MLS, Associate University Librarian for Scholarly Resources, Yale University Library, New Haven, Connecticut

Rachael Dreyer, MSI, Eberly Family Special Collections Library, Pennsylvania State University, University Park, Pennsylvania

Mike Kelly, MA, MLS, Head, Archives & Special Collections, Amherst College, Amherst, Massachusetts

James Kopaczewski, PhD candidate, Department of History, Temple University, Philadelphia, Pennsylvania

Jeff Kosokoff, MA, MLS, Strategic Projects Consultant, University of Washington Libraries, Seattle, Washington

Zack Lischer-Katz, PhD, Assistant Professor, School of Information, University of Arizona, Tucson, Arizona

Scott Matheson, JD, MLIS, MPA, Associate Law Librarian for Technical Services, Lillian Goldman Law Library, Yale Law School, New Haven, Connecticut

Katy Mathuews, PhD, Vernon R. Alden Library, Ohio University, Athens, Ohio

Sharon S. Prado, BM, MM, PhD, Office of the Deputy President for Academic Affairs, University College Dublin, Dublin, Ireland

Jae Jennifer Rossman, MA, MSLIS, Yale University Library, New Haven, Connecticut; **PhD candidate**, School of Library and Information Science, Simmons University, Boston, Massachusetts

Ariel Clark Silver, PhD, Faculty member, Columbus OH LDS Institute of Religion, Columbus, Ohio; President-elect, Nathaniel Hawthorne Society

Patrick Spero, PhD, Librarian and Director of the American Philosophical Society Library, Philadelphia, Pennsylvania

Emma Cawlfield Thomson, MLIS, Schoenberg Institute for Manuscript Studies, University of Pennsylvania Libraries, Philadelphia, Pennsylvania

Sarah Tudesco, MLS, Program Director, Assessment and User Experience Research, Yale University Library, New Haven, Connecticut

Alex Wermer-Colan, PhD, Digital Scholarship Coordinator, Temple University, Loretta C. Duckworth Scholars Studio, Philadelphia, Pennsylvania

Librarian's Note

The Past, Present, and Future of Libraries

In October 2018, the American Philosophical Society gathered a group of scholars, library professionals, and thought leaders to discuss the past, present, and future of the library. The occasion for the gathering was also to mark the 275th anniversary of the APS. Founded by Benjamin Franklin and several of his fellow civic-minded friends in 1743, the APS was created "to promote useful knowledge." Franklin's original proposal outlined four ways it was to do so. First, it would elect the "virtuosi" to be members. These were meant to be the leading thinkers dispersed throughout North America. Second, it would hold regular meetings of these members, who could share what they were learning with each other either in person or through correspondence that was read to other members at the meeting. Third, it would disseminate this knowledge through a publications program. And fourth, it would use the dues of members to fund promising research. Remarkably, the vision outlined in Franklin's proposal still stands. The Society today supports each of these programs.

    A library, however, was not a part of this original proposal. It was, though, implicit in what was written and soon became a key part of the APS. Since the APS was meant to be an organization that connected members from disparate parts of North America together, letters became the chief medium through which ideas were exchanged and relationships forged. As a result, the APS soon became a repository of scientific correspondence from its members. As the institution became more active in the 1760s and 1770s, members soon began donating books and artifacts, the latter forming the foundations for a "cabinet of curiosities." In 1799, as the institution experienced a burst of new energy in the Early Republic, the APS formed a committee charged with overseeing the formal and strategic growth of its collections. They authored a call for donations that was sent to colleagues throughout the nation and published in several newspapers. Material soon streamed into the institution. Today, this initial foundation has expanded to include over 14 million pages of manuscripts, 300,000 books, thousands of hours of audio material, and several thousand artifacts.

As the Society marked its momentous anniversary and reflected upon its own institutional history, it decided to organize a conference that would explore the wider history of libraries. But it wanted to do more than just reflect on the past. It wanted to talk about what is happening today in libraries and among librarians, and, perhaps more important, what the future of libraries and librarianship might look like. To do so, the conference's program committee wanted to bring together people who rarely gather in one place but share many common interests and goals. We had scholars who studied the history of libraries and of cataloguing. We had professionals who lead small public libraries, large university libraries, and independent research libraries, like the APS's. And we had people on the forefront of change, talking about new cataloguing methods and the ways new technology is reshaping library spaces and uses. The APS, as an organization that aims to bring people together to have important conversations, was well positioned to hold this gathering. But there was some self-interest at play as well. We thought this convening could also help the APS think about the future of its own research library as it charts its way through its third century.

The chapters that follow show the range of topics covered—and the vitality of libraries, past, present, and future. There are essays on the expansion of libraries and access to knowledge with the rise of large universities, the role of libraries as agents of change, the use of virtual reality to make library catalogues and collections more useable, the digital future of special collections, and the ways technology can encourage new modes of collaboration and service. If there is a common theme among all these essays, it is that libraries have rarely been static institutions. Though to many people who walk through their doors, libraries may seem like places of quiet inertia, these chapters show that libraries are and will remain vibrant institutions that evolve alongside society—and sometimes are at the forefront of innovation.

Like most libraries, the APS has itself been adapting as the world around us changes. The APS Library has embraced a digital future. It founded a Center for Digital Scholarship in 2017, launched an open-data initiative, began digitizing collections on a large scale, and has accepted several "born digital" collections. It has also rethought how it can serve researchers and, perhaps most important with the advent of mass digitization, *where* it can serve people. For special collections, the ease with which material can be digitized and displayed is breaking down some of the largest barriers to access. Researchers from afar no longer need to find the funds and take the time to travel to Philadelphia to consult the material they need. Instead, they can do so from their computer screens in their homes.

There is, of course, another story rooted in the history of libraries—and indeed of the nation itself—that many librarians are confronting with renewed vigor and attention. While libraries strive to provide access to as many people as possible and have a mission of advancing knowledge through the use of their collections, they have often fallen short of their aspirations. We have essays on the need to decolonize Native American collections, on authenticity and access to digital libraries and special collections, on the role of race and gender in libraries, and on the need to preserve digital records.

The APS is among those libraries trying to address many of these issues as well. For instance, for almost two decades, the Society has been working to make its Native American collections more accessible to a wider audience. To better serve Native communities and community-based scholars, it has created a new guide that highlights the communities from which collections originated rather than emphasizing the collector of the material. It has also adopted new descriptive techniques that recognize indigenous contributors to collections and uses indigenous place names in descriptions. Most important of all, the APS—through its Center for Native American and Indigenous Research—has worked directly with Native communities to learn from them the significance and potential uses of the APS's material for their needs. As a result of this work, in 2014, the Society was also among the first institutions to create protocols for handling culturally sensitive material. More recently, the library has begun an audit of its entire catalogue to better understand the descriptive techniques and categories its catalogue has inherited. The goal is to remediate records by identifying and replacing discriminatory words, objectionable phrases, and exclusionary subject headings. These changes, we hope, will be a step toward creating a more inclusive and accessible catalogue.

We hope that this volume will give others a sense of some of the conversations we held in October 2018. Collectively, these chapters touch on many of the most important issues libraries have faced, past, present, and future. And although this book showcases some of the most compelling papers presented, what the printed word cannot share is the discussions that followed each panel. For those who were unable to attend, we've preserved the conference on our website so that you can hear the full sessions, including the question-and-answer period. We also hosted panels that featured leaders of public libraries, research libraries, and university libraries in conversations with each other. These discussion panels are also available online. Our goal with this volume and with these archived videos is not only to preserve what happened but to maintain the dialogue begun in October 2018. We hope this contribution may be of use to libraries and librarians as they continue to reflect on the past, improve what they do in the present, and make libraries, one of the most important institutions in a democratic society, even better in the future.

Patrick Spero
Librarian of the American Philosophical Society
October 2021

I

Reading Communities

1

From Literary Salon to Library: The Female Mind and the Art of Reading Across the Color Line

Ariel Clark Silver

Phillis Wheatley was given access to the personal library of her masters, John and Susanna Wheatley, Margaret Fuller read texts supplied by her father, Timothy Fuller, as did Jane Johnston, an Ojibwa, who read from the library of her Irish father, John Johnston. Louisa May Alcott borrowed books from Ralph Waldo Emerson, a neighbor, and Frances Ellen Watkins Harper was given access to a wide range of literature when she worked as a domestic servant in a Quaker household. Elizabeth Peabody opened a bookstore in Boston that provided access to texts and conversation for both literary women and men even as David Ruggles opened a bookshop in Manhattan stocked with anti-slavery literature that also functioned as a reading room and circulating library for both Black men and women.[1] These private collections and enterprises, along with the advent of the literary salon in the early American republic, provided an educational foundation for some Colonial and antebellum American women.

---

[1] Rosie L. Albritton, "The Founding & Prevalence of African-American Social Libraries & Historical Societies, 1828–1918" in *Untold Stories: Civil Rights, Libraries, and Black Librarianship*, ed. John Mark Tucker (Champaign, IL: University of Illinois Press, 1998), 33–34.

Even when libraries started to appear, some before and some after the Revolution, they were mostly the preserve of wealthy, educated, White men. As private book clubs turned into athenaeums, joint-stock associations, social libraries, and other subscription-based institutions, they could afford to be exclusive, and often they were. As James Raven has noted, early American "library institutions constructed a largely masculine space in which women were publicly marginalized."[2] One such entity, the Library Company of Philadelphia, founded in 1731 by Benjamin Franklin and other members of the Junto, a debating society, represented a degree of transformation, extending the "application of the democratic spirit to the distribution of intellectual advantages"[3] beyond private landed wealth and scholarly association. A century later, in 1833, "The Philadelphia Library Company of Colored Persons" was established as a "counterpart"[4] open to Black men. But these "enlargement[s] of intellectual opportunity for man simply as man,"[5] on both sides of the color line, were just that, remarkable opportunities for men, but not women, in early America.

There were a few subscription lending libraries during the Colonial period where "male hegemony was diluted,"[6] including the Redwood Library in Newport, the New York Society Library, and the Baltimore Library Company, for women related to shareholders could borrow books on the accounts of their husbands or fathers. When the Library Company of Philadelphia merged with three other subscription libraries in 1769, one of which had a few female shareholders, they, too, began to open their stacks to a small but growing cadre of women.[7] Most Colonial female readers, however, turned instead to circulating libraries, where they could subscribe for just shillings, rather than pounds, borrow books six days a week rather than one, and select titles without the supervision of male relatives. After the Revolution and before the Civil War, social libraries and literary societies were established throughout the Northeast

---

[2] James Raven, "Social Libraries and Library Societies in Eighteenth-Century North America," in *Institutions of Reading: The Social Life of Libraries in the United States*, eds. Thomas Augst and Kenneth Carpenter (Amherst, MA: University of Massachusetts Press, 2007), 45.
[3] Moses Coit Tyler, "The Free Public Library in the United States: Evolution and Function," in *Librarianship in Gilded Age America*, eds. Leonard Schlup and Stephen H. Paschen (Jefferson, NC: McFarland & Company, 2009), 82.
[4] Albritton, "The Founding & Prevalence of African-American Social Libraries & Historical Societies," 30.
[5] Tyler, "The Free Public Library in the United States," 82.
[6] Raven, "Social Libraries and Library Societies in Eighteenth-Century North America," 45.
[7] James Green, "Subscription Libraries and Commercial Circulating Libraries in Colonial Philadelphia and New York," in *Institutions of Reading: The Social Life of Libraries in the United States*, eds. Thomas Augst and Kenneth Carpenter (Amherst, MA: University of Massachusetts Press, 2007), 64.

to provide female patrons the kind of access to books from abroad, mostly London, that many male colleagues had already enjoyed for at least half a century. For African American women, several societies were started in New England and in mid-Atlantic cities in the 1830s, including the Female Literary Society and Minerva Literary Society in Philadelphia, the Afric-American Female Intelligence Society in Boston, and the Ladies Literary Society and the Female Literary Society in New York City. But it was not until the Boston Public Library opened in 1854 that a large collection was supported by taxes over subscriptions, making more literary resources more available to more of the population.

Once public lending libraries spread in earnest at the end of secession, these institutions represented broad social change. Like Colonial circulating libraries, they aimed to reach a wide readership, but without commercial interest. Rather, they were held in the common good and supported by the labor of the people. As such, they had the potential to advance faith in the "power of knowledge" and the "civic ideals" of the nation,[8] a secular religion that had special resonance for those who had been denied literacy and the cultural, political, and religious power it affords. Increasingly staffed and run by women, who emerged as librarians in their own right as libraries expanded with the growth of the nation, these institutions still sometimes segregated women to designated reading rooms within the shared space[9] and sometimes resisted integration, failing to fulfill their own educational mission, particularly after the end of Reconstruction in the South. Still, in the midst of the gendered and racialized history of the American library in the nineteenth century, many creative and collaborative efforts were made to teach literacy and establish libraries as educational institutions for the development of the female mind, by both White and Black women, in advance of their acceptance at institutions of higher education, which did not begin until the mid-nineteenth century and, in notable instances, did not occur at all until the later part of the twentieth century. Colonial circulating libraries, antebellum subscription libraries and literary societies, and public libraries were, in many cases, the sole entities that made possible advanced learning for women across the color line both before and after the Civil War and into the twentieth century.

---

[8] Thomas Augst, "Faith in Reading: Public Libraries, Liberalism, and the Civil Religion," in *Institutions of Reading: The Social Life of Libraries in the United States*, eds. Thomas Augst and Kenneth Carpenter (Amherst, MA: University of Massachusetts Press, 2007), 155.
[9] Abigail A. Van Slyck, "The Lady and the Library Loafer: Gender and Public Space in Victorian America," *Winterthur Portfolio* 31 (1996): 223.

Female Readers and the Republic

In the social experiment that evolved into American democracy, the emergence of the library as a site of knowledge held in common constituted Early Republican political purpose comingled with primarily Protestant moral conviction: a "republic of letters" and a "missionary project" that defined the boundaries and reach of civilization in a new world.[10] In manifestations from salons to literary societies, from bookshops to circulating libraries, from summer schools and Sabbath schools to scholars who borrowed books from church and community holdings, from athenaeums to reading rooms, from family collections to public bequests, these early libraries sought to disseminate knowledge and elevate society. For American women, the development of such institutions of learning both circumscribed and expanded their social and educational opportunities, often through unsuspecting means.

The first social libraries in eighteenth-century America were founded by men seeking both to solidify their own status and convert the Colonial enterprise into a structure of culture. But they quickly faced competition from commercial circulating libraries midcentury onward that participated in the expanding production of printed materials by both selling and renting texts, satisfying a demand for the rapid exchange of fashionable titles, such as novels, and catering their services to female readers, who were eager to acquire literature. Social and subscription libraries felt some pressure to become more popular and accessible, forcing institutions that had become "clubby retreats" for gentlemen of business into associations that "challenged boundaries of class, gender, and race that had kept books as the expensive possession of learned elites."[11]

Even as women in Early Republican America were themselves characterized as "circulating libraries"[12] who wore books, blamed for reducing the printed word to a commodity and making texts as abundant and cheap as textiles, such a critique cut in multiple directions. If women stood outside the realm of culture and learning, it was because they had been excluded from it. Furthermore, commodification was coming not just for books, but for them. Much as women and girls would be set to work in mills making fabric for a mass market, they would soon be

---

[10] Thomas Augst, "Introduction," in *Institutions of Reading: The Social Life of Libraries in the United States*, ed. Thomas Augst and Kenneth Carpenter (Amherst, MA: University of Massachusetts Press, 2007), 5–6.
[11] Augst, "Introduction," 8.
[12] Augst, "Introduction," 10.

conscripted to create copy for an insatiable print culture. These scribbling women, as Hawthorne called them, would write stories serialized in weekly newspapers, which were then often reprinted as novels. Later, they became the library card cataloguers whose own education and skill made the acclaimed erudition of others possible. They not only made the textiles and the texts, they consumed them and were also commodified by them.

The emergence of a mass culture that involved and was often marketed to women raised many questions about the scope, content, and purpose of female education. Would reading women who bought cheap novels denigrate this new republic of letters, or would this proliferation of texts denigrate them? Could women be saved instead for a higher purpose in a newly organized free government, that of republican mothers raising virtuous male citizens, "instructing their sons in the principles of liberty and government?"[13] To this maternal end, girls were increasingly given access to formal education beyond the primary level after the Revolution, even in rural areas, at least in New England. But these educated girls not only became republican mothers, they became teachers in the Early Republic as well, signaling a female role in society beyond the domestic sphere, a role that was accepted as a reasonable extension of motherhood. The campaign for "republican motherhood"[14] led to several other important consequences for women in the first half century of a new nation, including an increase in levels of female reading outside urban centers, an increase in female written and printed communication, involvement in civic and cultural activity outside the home, and a desire for greater social and political equity.

The Education of Women and the Advent of Antebellum Activism

The broader publication and circulation of books in American society, primarily through commercial circulating libraries that started in urban centers, soon signaled the "intellectual emancipation of women."[15] The exposure to new ideas and the cultivation of independent thought brought new hopes, possibilities, and expectations. There was real opposition and

---

[13] William J. Gilmore-Lehne, *Reading Becomes a Necessity of Life: Material and Cultural Life in Rural New England, 1780–1835* (Knoxville: University of Tennessee Press, 1989), 43.
[14] Gilmore-Lehne, *Reading Becomes a Necessity of Life*, 43.
[15] Gilmore-Lehne, *Reading Becomes a Necessity of Life*, 42.

resistance to female education in the wake of the Revolution, both because female personhood, particularly in marriage, was not often acknowledged, and because the social and commercial ends of such education for women could not be ascertained or justified. Linguistic capital was required for advancement in antebellum America, something that was difficult for both women and lower-class men, and well-nigh impossible for Blacks, to obtain. Slaves, a "form of capital themselves," were "strictly debarred from obtaining any cultural or monetary capital of their own."[16] After the Revolution, there was a "more permissive spirit and a real interest in educating Blacks," particularly Black females, but as the nation became more involved in an industrial economy, that liberalism gave way to antipathy and hostility that "impeded black schooling efforts."[17] It was not until after the Civil War that "significant energies"[18] were spent on Black literacy and education.

But even in the midst of a prevailing sense of a "certain sexual destiny" for women, and a racial prejudice that deeply affected Black education, a small shift had already begun to occur in the scope of subjects to which at least White (and a very few Black) women were exposed.[19] No longer did they study simply reading, writing, arithmetic, and, of course, religion, but also rhetoric, figures, literature, history, botany, chemistry, geometry, and geography, first in summer schools and then eventually in winter schools. With the advent of female academies that provided more than elementary education, girls often found themselves excluded from schools that catered to boys, though some remained open to both young men and young women.[20] While daughters as well as sons attended school, their mothers organized women's reading clubs, which often met weekly for "reading and criticism,"[21] created and attended literary salons for cultural edification, and supported the lyceum movement, attending lecture series organized at the local level to host writers and thinkers, and increasingly, activists.

From Colonial times, a handful of women had access to private collections, either family holdings or the libraries of others, but the development of more widespread educational forums for both adolescent

---

[16] Dana Nelson Salvino, "The Word in Black and White: Ideologies of Race and Literacy in Antebellum America," in *Reading in America*, ed. Cathy N. Davidson (Baltimore: The Johns Hopkins University Press, 1989), 147.
[17] Salvino, "The Word in Black and White," 147.
[18] Salvino, "The Word in Black and White," 146.
[19] Gilmore-Lehne, *Reading Becomes a Necessity of Life*, 47.
[20] Gilmore-Lehne, *Reading Becomes a Necessity of Life*, 43.
[21] Gilmore-Lehne, *Reading Becomes a Necessity of Life*, 49.

and adult females led to a new kind of freedom, from mothers who could educate others to women who could organize for broad social reform beyond the hearth. Indeed, the first generation of educated women in the American republic led the new nation into antebellum activism, becoming teachers, authors, missionaries, speakers, and advocates for the abolition of slavery and for female suffrage. The emergence of such engaged females intent on cultural improvement for themselves and others symbolized for some men "all the dangers latent in women's intellectual development,"[22] as it challenged their own social and cultural prominence. But the presence of an educated class of women elevated society as a whole and aided even the men who then had to compete with them in the marketplace of ideas.

Reading, Writing, and Desegregation in Anti-Slavery Salem

The seaboard town of Salem, Massachusetts, provides an early and important example of how these intersecting dynamics across lines of gender and race actually played themselves out in the arena of access to knowledge and learning. Home to one of earliest membership libraries outside a major urban center, the Salem Athenaeum was founded in 1810, just three years after the one established in Boston. The Athenaeum in Salem was preceded by the Monday Evening Club, the Philosophical Library, and the Civil Society, which gathered in Mrs. Pratt's Ship Club. Athenaeums, in New York, Boston, Salem, and other cities, brought books out of the private realm and into public and civic life, expanding their reach, but in ways different from commercial circulating libraries. Admission came through membership, rather than purchase of print material outright, and thus such institutions became touchstones for social conflict even as they sought to be instruments of social edification. Some Athenaeums, such as the one founded in New York, were open to men and their families, but women were permitted to attend the lectures, acknowledging that "the ladies of New York will thus be enabled to pursue studies, and investigate subjects, from which, by the present system of education, they are excluded."[23] To join such institutions, one had to be accepted, something money could not always buy. In such places, gender was often a soft divide, race a more absolute one.

---

[22] Gilmore-Lehne, *Reading Becomes a Necessity of Life*, 50.
[23] Austin Baxter Keep, *The History of the New York Society Library* (Boston: Gregg Press, 1972), 322.

The Salem Athenaeum, founded fourteen years before the New York Athenaeum, appeared to be open to White women as well as White men, for Mary Manning, the aunt to Nathaniel Hawthorne, owned a share on which he borrowed books in his youth. His mother, Elizabeth, was also presumably a member. Another well-educated woman, Susan Burley, who read German and French as well as English, established a Saturday-evening literary salon in Salem, which Hawthorne called "Hurley-Burleys" and was loathe to miss. Burley also formed the Salem Book Club, probably for women, which persisted well into the twentieth century, when it finally merged with the Salem Athenaeum. Before her death in 1850, Susan donated to the Athenaeum her personal library, a wealth of books in several foreign languages, including many vintage volumes, and a fund of $1000 for the acquisition of new books on multiple topics. Another female bequest, from Caroline Plummer, brought 30,000 volumes to the Athenaeum in 1854. Even at this early juncture, there were women who not only read books, but collected them, and their private holdings permanently enriched many public collections.

At the moment when the Salem Athenaeum was being established, forces emerged to challenge the racial divide in Salem schools, and thus Salem society, leading to several remarkable cultural and literary developments. John Remond and Nancy Lenox, both prosperous free Blacks, married in 1807 and brought ten children to their union. When their children were subsequently expelled from school because of the color of their skin, the Remonds led the fight to desegregate public education in Salem, well before schools were desegregated throughout the state. Their home, Hamilton Hall, played host to several governors, the East India Marine Society, and the Marquis de Lafayette, even as it sponsored abolitionists such as William Lloyd Garrison and Frederick Douglass. In 1832, Nancy and Sarah Remond, along with other females of color, established the Female Anti-Slavery Society of Salem, the first female abolitionist society in America. Two years after incorporation, they voted to include White women. Sarah and Charles, two of the Remond children, became leading international orators in the abolition movement. When Charles attended the World Anti-Slavery Convention in London with Garrison in 1840, they exiled themselves in protest because American female delegates were excluded from the proceedings. Sarah lectured throughout England against segregation and became a British citizen, determined not to return to her homeland because of the strong prejudice there against persons of African descent.

The social and educational advocacy of the Remonds attracted others to Salem. Charlotte Forten, a young African American girl whose family had been free for four generations, was sent from Philadelphia in the 1840s to live with the Remonds so that she could attend an integrated public school. Charlotte graduated from the Salem Normal School and became the first Black person to teach in the Salem schools. She became a member of the Female Anti-Slavery Society of Salem, published articles and poems in *The Liberator* and *The Atlantic Monthly*, and kept a journal of her experience as teacher to Black students and nurse to Black troops in Port Royal, the South Carolina Sea Islands, which came under the control of the Union Army during the Civil War. She was probably not admitted to the Salem Athenaeum during her lifetime, but the literary works she created during her years in Salem and beyond have been on exhibit there and showcase the ways in which she read and was read by others across the color line. One entry from May 30, 1854, speaks volumes:

> His trial [that of a fugitive slave captured in Boston] is still going on and I can scarcely think of anything else; read again to-day as most suitable to my feelings and to the times, "The Runaway Slave at Pilgrim's Point," by Elizabeth B. Browning; how powerfully it is written! how earnestly and touchingly does the writer portray the bitter anguish of the poor fugitive as she thinks over all the wrongs and sufferings that she has endured, and of the sin to which tyrants have driven her but which they alone must answer for! It seems as if no one could read this poem without having his sympathies roused to the utmost on behalf of the oppressed.[24]

Here is a Black woman reading a White woman writing about a Black woman; that Black female reader then becomes a writer whose words educate readers across the color line about the experience of being a free, Black female seeking to set others, both White and Black, free through the very same process of reading and writing.

Collections Across the Color Line in Boston

The nearby Boston Athenaeum, founded in 1807, the year the Remonds of Salem married, sought in its own way to read across social, racial, and political divides. The Athenaeum in Boston was intent from its inception on becoming a public library, as opposed to the Boston Library Society, which was convened monthly by men and women who dined in each other's homes. Organized as a subscription library, it was frequented

---

[24] Charlotte Forten Grimke, *The Journals of Charlotte Forten Grimke*, ed. Brenda Stevenson (New York: Oxford University Press, 1988), 673.

by both male and female authors, including Nathaniel Hawthorne and Margaret Fuller, as well as salon hostesses, such as Annie Adams Fields and Elizabeth Palmer Peabody, who also ran a bookstore in downtown Boston. During the antebellum period, the Boston Athenaeum sponsored art exhibits, lyceum lectures, and abolition discussions, in addition to lending books and providing space to read, converse, and debate. Immediately after the war, two members, Francis Parkman and Algernon Coolidge, embarked on an ambitious project to amass the Confederate Imprint Collection, "everything printed in the South during the war that goes to illustrate the state and action of the Southern mind,"[25] placing *The Richmond Examiner* right alongside *The Liberator*. Although such material may not have probed the Southern experience from the perspective of the slaves directly, it certainly created a collection that bore evidence to the scope of that peculiar institution and manifested the work of those who perpetuated, maintained, and defended it.

Where early libraries functioned informally out of homes, schools, and churches, more formal institutions, such as the Boston Athenaeum, could bring designated literary documents together to form important holdings that preserved particular histories. In 1871, the Boston Athenaeum reached in another direction across the color line and received a significant Native American collection, created from the papers of Henry Rowe Schoolcraft, who was an explorer, Indian Agent, and cultural anthropologist for forty years. His first wife, Jane Johnston, an Ojibwa, learned oral history and the Ojibwa language from her native mother and written language, history, and European culture from her Irish father, John Johnston. Jane and Henry lived a literary life, often exchanging private letters and poetry, and she became the first known Native American literary writer, producing poems, traditional Ojibwa stories, and translations of Ojibwa songs into English. She had an enormous influence on the ethnological work of her husband, who wrote a six-volume history of the Native Americans, which in turn served as the main source for *The Song of Hiawatha*, by Henry Wadsworth Longfellow.

Female Subscription, Literary Patronage, and Cultural Creation

Even before Salem and Boston, there were subscription libraries in Philadelphia, Charleston, Newport, and New York that attempted to counteract

---

[25] Richard Wendorf, *America's Membership Libraries*, ed. Richard Wendorf (New Castle, DE: Oak Knoll Press, 2007), 99.

From Literary Salon to Library

the perceived low culture of circulating libraries and transform rising literacy rates, especially among women, into a more elevated social experience with books, one that would create a nation of refined and educated readers. These earliest social libraries sought to encourage the connection among literary practice, cultural engagement, and civic responsibility. The Library Company of Philadelphia, which developed out of the Junto, a social cohort turned informal book club, sought to spread knowledge beyond a Colonial aristocracy to an increasingly diverse and daringly new republic. The Charleston Library Society, founded in 1748 by some who had moved there from Philadelphia, expanded its membership by allowing widows to inherit memberships from their husbands and accepted a large bequest of horticultural and botanical books from Edith K. Morris to help establish its collection. The Redwood Library in Newport counted many educated ladies among its patrons, creating compilations, such as "The Ladies Library,"[26] just for them. Later in its history, Mrs. Richard Bliss, wife of the Redwood Librarian, served for twenty-three years as its first card cataloguer, devoting enormous effort and skill to organizing the entire collection and making it readily accessible to patrons.

The New York Society Library, established in 1754, was open to both men and women, free of charge, for research purposes. Memberships, which often endured for generations, were assigned on the basis of household, offering wives and children access through their husbands. Among its founders was Anne Waddell, an early influential businesswoman in New York. Women also built and sustained the collection of the library at critical junctures. The first major bequest, from Elizabeth Demilt in 1851, brought the library out of debt, and a further gift, from Sarah Parker Goodhue in 1936, allowed the library to move to a new home on the Upper East Side, much closer to its patrons. As at the Redwood, the New York Society Library benefitted from the time and talents of female cataloguers. In the late nineteenth century, Grace MacMullen revised the entire collection according to the prevailing dictionary methods.[27] Beginning in the twentieth century, women, such as Marion King and Helen Ruskell, were employed in important capacities at the library, and the library also began to hire female librarians such as Edith Hall Crowell and Sylvia Hilton. The collection, with strengths in biography, literature, history, and travel writing, continually attracted authors, including Emerson, Thoreau, Poe, Dickens, and Melville in the

---

[26] Wendorf, *America's Membership Libraries*, 33.
[27] Wendorf, *America's Membership Libraries*, 71.

nineteenth century. The turn of the century brought female authors, including Willa Cather and her companion Edith Lewis, to the library as well. The charging cards filled by these female writers showed a remarkable breath of reading interests, from Russian fiction to French biography. Their library patronage revealed the important relationship between reading and writing for authors. Women like Wheatley, Johnston, Fuller, Alcott, Forten, Harper, and Cather were able to produce literature in great measure because they were exposed to such a wide range of literature.

From the outset of the abolition movement through the end of Reconstruction, social libraries for African Americans were created to cultivate a race of educated readers well versed in literary culture, mirroring the purpose of literary societies for Whites. But these Black societies also felt compelled to create and preserve a more complete version of that culture that included African American history and literature. It was not just that they were excluded from membership in White literary societies, their stories were excluded as well. In response to this double discrimination, social libraries, such as Reading Room Society in Philadelphia (1828), the New York Philomathean Society (1830), and the Philadelphia Library Company of Colored Persons (1833), became the earliest and most important repositories of Black literature, history, and Americana. These collections and a few others led to the formation of the American Negro Historical Society (1897), which later became the Afro-American Historical Society, and the Negro Society for Historical Research (1911), developing eventually into the Schomburg Center for Research in Black Culture.

Many of these antebellum social libraries remained segregated, both by race and gender. Among African American literary societies, only the Gilbert Lyceum (1841) appears to have admitted both men and women.[28] As discussed earlier, there were also numerous African American social libraries for women, including female literary societies in Philadelphia, Boston, and New York. The development of social libraries made it possible for more members of the Republic, particularly more females, to participate in the culture of reading and to make both White and Black America a nation of readers. Before the Revolution, there were just three hundred subscription libraries. One hundred years later, there were more than three thousand such libraries, libraries that had helped to build a literate class of females who read literary magazines, searched out anthologies, pressed for standard editions of works in print, de-

---

[28] Albritton, "The Founding & Prevalence of African-American Social Libraries & Historical Societies," 32.

manded news they could depend on, and developed themselves as writers. For African American women, these literary societies often served as a springboard, not just to self-improvement and education, but to involvement in the cause of abolition. Their social libraries functioned much as Hamilton Hall did for John and Nancy Remond in Salem, a place from which to advocate for change, in the schools, in the institution of slavery, and in society at large. Thus, these literary societies not only consumed but also created culture, insisting on active engagement in and influence upon society, in education, politics, and the arts. In many ways, these social libraries allowed women to rise above consumption and commodification, but in order to transform a female readership into a united citizenry, they would need to develop integrated institutions that could bring Black and White readers together to impact the burgeoning republic.

Civic Devotion, Sunday School, and Female "Schollars" in New York

Social libraries increased in number over the course of the nineteenth century, often tailoring their services to select, and segregated audiences, such as the Colored Reading Society for Black men or the Female Literary Society for African American women, both in Philadelphia, or the Phoenix Society, a literary association for Blacks in New York.[29] But more public and comprehensive literary movements were required to cultivate a nation that could not only read, but read across the color line. Public libraries, funded by taxes rather than membership fees, began to emerge midcentury, before the war, in cities like Boston, New York, and Philadelphia, and also in some smaller towns and cities, mostly in New England. After the Civil War, public libraries moved increasingly south and west. These libraries derived their existence from government support rather than private bequest or endowment. Still, they were motived by the same civic and cultural consciousness that initially brought social libraries into being.

Even as such private and public literary institutions were developed to counter the commercialism of the circulating libraries and deliver canonical literature to populations marginalized in Colonial America, other efforts emerged in the Early Republic to encourage White and

---

[29] Elizabeth McHenry, "'An Association of Kindred Spirits': Black Readers and Their Reading Rooms" in *Institutions of Reading: The Social Life of Libraries in the United States*, eds. Thomas Augst and Kenneth Carpenter (Amherst, MA: University of Massachusetts Press, 2007), 99.

Black female literacy. In more rural, agrarian areas in antebellum America, summer schools were started to serve the educational needs of girls. Eventually they took their place in winter schools with boys after the harvest was over, and also in female academies that could extend their academic exposure beyond grammar school. But in early urban centers, women, both old and young, worked six days a week, all year long. The appearance of Sabbath schools at the outset of the nineteenth century, particularly in New York, offered a remarkable example of intellectual opportunity and integrated education for females across age, class, and color lines, as well as a plausible model for subsequent large-scale public education efforts.

These Sunday schools began as common school education in the major cities of the new republic for the poorest and most vulnerable residents, White and African American female children. In New York City, between 1800 and 1830, "Sunday schooling became an important matrix for the acquisition of literacy and for the use of libraries and books, particularly for African-American females. Of equal importance, Sunday school became a de facto agent of gradual emancipation due to the mandated relationship between full emancipation and the ability to read."[30] Their purpose was to provide for many female students what public education could not, that is, classes in reading and writing at a time when they were not working. They also filled a need for illiterate learners who were too old for common schools. Indeed, they became common schools for these girls and women. Sabbath schools were established to teach young people, then adults, to read and write so that they could become morally literate, but in the process, the religious purpose extended to a more comprehensive education that included geography, account-keeping, and other subjects that would fit them for business, as well as domestic arts such as knitting and sewing. In short order, these Sunday schools also established lending libraries where female students, both young and old, deemed "schollars," earned the privilege to borrow or purchase books by making progress in their studies.[31] Such early religious schools, generally open to students of any denomination, "provided a library for urban women and girls who had limited access to books and schooling due to status, class, race, language, the demands of labor, or social isolation" and, in the process, elevated their both their educational and social status.[32]

---

[30] Marilyn H. Pettit, "Liberty & Literacy: Sunday Schools and Reading for African American Females in New York City, 1799–1826," in *Untold Stories: Civil Rights. Libraries, and Black Librarianship*, ed. John Mark Tucker (Champaign, IL: University of Illinois Press, 1998), 11.
[31] Pettit, "Liberty & Literacy," 14.
[32] Pettit, "Liberty & Literacy," 15.

These Sabbath schools offered an interesting and important alternative to segregated literary and educational activity, accepting children of any race, age, and church affiliation. By 1817, just five years after the War of 1812, there were 25 female schools with over 5,000 students and over 300 teachers operating under the aegis of the New York Female Union Society to Promote Sabbath Schools. Many of these schools, including School No. 2 and School No. 6, enrolled just about equal numbers of White and Black girls. Most included adult female students as well, sometimes more Black than White, but seldom only one group or the other. The classes were taught by female teachers, both Black and White, sometimes females who themselves had been Sabbath school "schollars." Classes were offered in reading and writing and "other standard elements of a common school education according to the ability of the teacher."[33] By 1820, there were already 40 such schools in New York City, each one with an enrollment of over 100 students. Flexible attendance made it possible for many more girls and women to participate around their demanding work schedules. They were encouraged in their presence and not punished for their absence. Despite the large numbers, the learning experience was carefully conceived to pair two teachers with eight to ten students, far more of a tutorial then boys of that era received in common one-room school rooms or houses. So successful was this approach to learning, many young men pleaded to be admitted to the female Sunday schools, resulting in the formation of some schools for "female adults and youth of both sexes,"[34] who continued to be taught by women. Another measure of the success of such schools can be found in the 1816 New York City census records. The numbers demonstrate that nearly three quarters of all Black women living in the city at that time were enrolled in Sunday schools.[35]

Female schools, as they developed in antebellum New York, offered "an entire culture of schooling, books, and library to a working and dependent population of black and white women and girls."[36] Reading and writing also allowed these women to read "handbills, newspapers, letters, accounts, bank drafts, wills, and contracts of labor and indenture" and the classroom experience provided exposure to "structured learning" and pedagogical methods, along with opportunities for intellectual and financial advancement.[37] The move to literacy and learning across a

---

[33] Pettit, "Liberty & Literacy," 12.
[34] Pettit, "Liberty & Literacy," 13–14.
[35] Pettit, "Liberty & Literacy," 13.
[36] Pettit, "Liberty & Literacy," 15.
[37] Pettit, "Liberty & Literacy," 15.

range of subjects made these females socially mobile and prepared them, through education and manumission, to participate more freely, actively, and independently in civil society. Sabbath schools for Black and White working-class women in New York and other cities in the Early Republic accomplished what Saturday schools, literary salons, and women's clubs sought to achieve for middle-class and agrarian women in antebellum America.

Public Libraries, Public Education, and the Elevation of the Female Mind

This early cooperative model of Black and White females working together to create schools and libraries for Black and White females, both young and old, paved the way for the development of public schools and libraries that aspired to similar ends: education, socialization, and citizenship. These Sabbath schools, sponsored by churches, enjoyed financial support from the city of New York. Local government minutes confirmed that this educational enterprise among the "poorer classes of society" both "diminish[ed] the demand for taxation [and] increase[d] the supply from which Taxes are to be drawn."[38] But when the Constitution was interpreted to restrict governments from contributing their tax revenues to religious institutions, even when they received a terrific return on their investment, funding from the city was lost and such schools eventually gave way to public, state-funded institutions. Both public schools and public libraries after the war descended from such enlightened educational efforts and carried with them many of the same hopes for literacy, enlightenment, and acculturation, but often lacked the organizational model or "unexpected absence of racism"[39] that these early urban antebellum Sunday schools achieved.

Public libraries, as stand-alone entities, enjoyed greater continuing support from private counterparts as they built their own collections and found their own footing. Many social libraries endured well past the end of the Civil War. When these subscription libraries began to decline in the latter part of the nineteenth century, their collections became the point of origin for many public libraries. But public libraries, even post emancipation, were very often segregated in terms of race and gender. For this reason alone, many African American social libraries persisted

---
[38] Pettit, "Liberty & Literacy," 19.
[39] Pettit, "Liberty & Literacy," 20.

through the end of the nineteenth and into the twentieth century. Through Reconstruction and in the face of later political compromises that justified social codes of separation and exclusion, African Americans held fast to the institutions of intellectual improvement they had created, both because they were not given access to public libraries but also because their narratives were not often represented there. Where many social libraries for Whites served to build public library collections, the holdings in social libraries for Blacks became "the nuclei of rich resources in black literature and history"[40] for historically Black institutions and other research institutions devoted to African American studies.

The social library movement, in its many manifestations both before and after the Civil War, had done so much to educate and elevate the intellectual life, social standing, and cultural influence of many American women. Social libraries were able to successfully reach across the gender line, first through household and widowhood subscriptions, then through appeals to and involvement of female readers, tailoring collections to their interests and accepting their gifts of time and talent, and finally through direct engagement with and employment of women in their ranks. Other social and subscription libraries were created directly for and by women, both White and Black, and promoted their education and civic engagement, even activism. But these literate women, who helped organize and often led the fight for abolition, had not been able to accomplish for themselves what they had helped accomplish for African American men—full citizenship in the form of suffrage.

The ratification of the Fourteenth Amendment in 1868 was a year of "particular significance for American women, [who were] shocked with the recognition that civil equality would not be granted by a beneficent male power structure."[41] Once women discovered in the wake of the war that literacy and opportunities for education did not lead directly to their own emancipation in society, they transformed their anti-slavery societies into suffrage societies and sought other means to achieve equality. During Reconstruction and the Gilded Age, women often pursued education, influence, and independence through institutions designed for women—the advent of women's colleges, the development of women's clubs, and the emergence of women's professions, including work as librarians.[42]

---

[40] Albritton, "The Founding & Prevalence of African-American Social Libraries & Historical Societies," 38.
[41] Clare Beck, "Adelaide Hasse: The New Woman as Librarian," in *Reclaiming the American Library Past: Writing the Women In*, ed. Suzanne Hildenbrand (Norwood, NJ: Ablex Publishing, 1996), 99.
[42] Beck, "Adelaide Hasse," 99.

But these new roles they realized for themselves, in which they "remained apart from the male spheres of power in business, the professions, and electoral politics,"[43] may have done more to uphold rather than defy convention. As Dee Garrison notes in *Apostles of Culture*, "The most striking point to be made about women's adaptation to library work between 1876 and 1920 is the extent to which they supported the traditional female concern for altruism and high-mindedness. They invoked the Victorian definition of proper female endeavors at the same time as they struggled to widen it. Librarianship, when defined as self-denying and spiritual, offered women the opportunity not to change their status but to confirm it, not to fulfill the self but to perpetuate a limited self-image."[44] Indeed, even women who simply sought presence as patrons in public libraries after the war were, at times, expected to confine their patronage to reading rooms designated for "ladies," a "sex-segregated public space" that delimited their public presence and engagement.[45]

The arrival of the new American woman who announced her intention to live in, and contribute to, the public sphere certainly "constituted a revolutionary demographic and political phenomenon" that "challenged existing gender relations and the distribution of power."[46] The "social and sexual legitimacy"[47] of such a woman was deeply contested for several generations, much as the "sexual destiny"[48] of early American women had once been debated. But women did carve out a space for themselves professionally as librarians in the wake of the Civil War, building on the achievements of post-Revolutionary and antebellum female teachers, and further extending the range of their social and intellectual reach. As the public library movement spread south and west in the midst of the postbellum "profusion of print,"[49] women often did more than accept positions as librarians: they created them. Social libraries, literary societies, and women's clubs "took their cultural mission seriously" and gave "high

---

[43] Beck, "Adelaide Hasse," 99.

[44] Dee Garrison, *Apostles of Culture: The Public Librarian and American Society, 1876–1920* (New York: Free Press, 1979), xv.

[45] Abigail A. Van Slyck, "The Lady and the Library Loafer: Gender and Public Space in Victorian America," *Winterthur Portfolio* 31 (1996): 223.

[46] Caroll Smith-Rosenberg, "The New Woman as Androgyne: Social Disorder and Gender Crisis, 1870–1936," in *Disorderly Conduct: Visions of Gender in Victorian America*, ed. Carroll Smith-Rosenberg (New York: Oxford University Press, 1986), 245.

[47] Smith-Rosenburg, "The New Woman as Androgyne," 245.

[48] Gilmore-Lehne, *Reading Becomes a Necessity of Life*, 47.

[49] Barbara Sicherman, "Sense and Sensibility: A Case Study in Women's Reading in Late-Victorian America," in *Reading in America*, ed. Cathy N. Davidson (Baltimore: Johns Hopkins University Press, 1989), 201.

priority to establishing libraries"[50] by contributing volumes and raising funds to build libraries in their own communities, then hired women to run them. Indeed, it is estimated that women founded 75 percent of all public libraries in America.[51]

This female library movement, which flourished during the Progressive Era, "forged parallel power structures to those used by men"[52] as it created new public institutions and new public roles for women as professionals. Determined to build on the antebellum spirit of female activism that had inadvertently grown out of "republican motherhood,"[53] these late-Victorian women founded public libraries to contribute to civic education and refinement, but also to encourage intellectual activity among women over the course of their lives. While the establishment of both White and Black women's colleges provided an educational experience for some young and single females, libraries could feed intellectual curiosity and fuel self-enlightenment for women in the midst of many other responsibilities and demands on their time. The "self-interest"[54] that spawned such widespread institutions of literacy and life-long education across America through the end of the nineteenth century provided a powerful response to the restrictions implied in the Fourteenth Amendment, even as it paved the way for the passage of the Nineteenth Amendment at the conclusion of the First World War, which finally granted full citizenship to women in the form of the vote.

Securing female suffrage in the aftermath of the First World War softened the gender divide in American life, but the more absolute divide of race remained in place for several subsequent decades. As Dana Salvino suggests, "a black might be able to read Aeschylus and Homer, yet be able to procure a job no better than one as domestic help."[55] The racial segregation that was encoded and enforced during the eighty years between the end of Reconstruction and the conclusion of the conflict in Korea, particularly in education, allowed Black educators to pass on Black culture to their students, much as Black literary societies in the nineteenth century had done, but it could not confer any kind of "status authority"

---

[50] Sicherman, "Sense and Sensibility," 201.
[51] Sicherman, "Sense and Sensibility," 201.
[52] Kathleen D. McCarthy, "Parallel Power Structures: Women and the Voluntary Sphere," in *Lady Bountiful Revisited: Women, Philanthropy, and Power*, ed. Kathleen D. McCarthy (New Brunswick, NJ: Rutgers University Press, 1990), 1.
[53] Gilmore-Lehne, *Reading Becomes a Necessity of Life*, 43.
[54] Cheryl Knott Malone, "Women's Unpaid Labor in Libraries: Change and Continuity," in *Reclaiming the American Library Past: Writing the Women In*, ed. Suzanne Hildenbrand (Norwood, NJ: Ablex Publishing Company, 1996), 280.
[55] Salvino, "The Word in Black and White," 152.

within the "white social economy" to its students.[56] Both White and Black female (and male) students during these years read about the color line, but did not have many opportunities to read across the color line, either in school or in a library setting. In *Black Boy*, Richard Wright tells of his own experience in the 1920s using a White female alibi to obtain a book by H. L. Mencken from the local public library:

> The white librarian looked at me. "What do you want, boy?" As though I did not possess the power of speech, I stepped forward and simply handed her the forged note, not parting my lips. "What books by Mencken does she want?" she asked. "I don't know, ma'am," I said, avoiding her eyes. "You're not using these books, are you?" she asked pointedly. "Oh no, ma'am, I can't read."

The advent of school desegregation that began with the *Brown vs. Board of Education* decision in 1954 propelled desegregation in other educational settings, including libraries, though intense effort was required to end the "hegemony of the white ideology of literacy."[57] The acquisition of both knowledge and power across divides of gender and race is intricately bound up with beliefs about and access to literacy, as demonstrated by the ways in which libraries in America developed and evolved throughout the nineteenth and into the twentieth century. From literary salons to libraries, females contributed significantly to the cause of intellectual, cultural, and economic freedom that literacy came to represent by working creatively to educate and liberate themselves and their fellow citizens, helping to create a republic of letters that could read richly, productively, and compassionately across the color line.

Bibliography

Albritton, Rosie L. "The Founding & Prevalence of African-American Social Libraries & Historical Societies, 1828–1918." In *Untold Stories: Civil Rights. Libraries, and Black Librarianship*, edited by John Mark Tucker. Champaign, IL: University of Illinois Press, 1998.

Augst, Thomas. "Introduction." In *Institutions of Reading: The Social Life of Libraries in the United States*, edited by Thomas Augst and Kenneth Carpenter. Amherst, MA: University of Massachusetts Press, 2007.

———. "Faith in Reading: Public Libraries, Liberalism, and the Civil Religion." In *Institutions of Reading: The Social Life of Libraries in*

---

[56] Salvino, "The Word in Black and White," 153.
[57] Salvino, "The Word in Black and White," 153.

the United States, edited by Thomas Augst and Kenneth Carpenter. Amherst, MA: University of Massachusetts Press, 2007.

Beck, Clare. "Adelaide Hasse: The New Woman as Librarian." In *Reclaiming the American Library Past: Writing the Women In*, edited by Suzanne Hildenbrand. Norwood, NJ: Ablex Publishing Company, 1996.

Garrison, Dee. *Apostles of Culture: The Public Librarian and American Society, 1876–1920*. New York: Free Press, 1979.

Gilmore-Lehne, William J. *Reading Becomes a Necessity of Life: Material and Cultural Life in Rural New England, 1780–1835*. Knoxville: University of Tennessee Press, 1989.

Green, James. "Subscription Libraries and Commercial Circulating Libraries in Colonial Philadelphia and New York." In *Institutions of Reading: The Social Life of Libraries in the United States*, edited by Thomas Augst and Kenneth Carpenter. Amherst, MA: University of Massachusetts Press, 2007.

Grimke, Charlotte Forten. *The Journals of Charlotte Forten Grimke*, edited by Brenda Stevenson. New York: Oxford University Press, 1988.

Keep, Austin Baxter. *The History of the New York Society Library*. Boston: Gregg Press, 1972.

Malone, Cheryl Knott. "Women's Unpaid Labor in Libraries: Change and Continuity." In *Reclaiming the American Library Past: Writing the Women In*, edited by Suzanne Hildenbrand. Norwood, NJ: Ablex Publishing Company, 1996.

McCarthy, Kathleen D. "Parallel Power Structures: Women and the Voluntary Sphere." In *Lady Bountiful Revisited: Women, Philanthropy, and Power*, edited by Kathleen D. McCarthy. New Brunswick, NJ: Rutgers University Press, 1990.

McHenry, Elizabeth. "'An Association of Kindred Spirits': Black Readers and Their Reading Rooms." In *Institutions of Reading: The Social Life of Libraries in the United States*, edited by Thomas Augst and Kenneth Carpenter. Amherst, MA: University of Massachusetts Press, 2007.

Pettit, Marilyn H. "Liberty & Literacy: Sunday Schools and Reading for African American Females in New York City, 1799–1826." In *Untold Stories: Civil Rights, Libraries, and Black Librarianship*, edited by John Mark Tucker. Champaign, IL: University of Illinois Press, 1998.

Raven, James. "Social Libraries and Library Societies in Eighteenth-Century North America." In *Institutions of Reading: The Social Life of Libraries in the United States*, edited by Thomas Augst and Kenneth Carpenter. Amherst, MA: University of Massachusetts Press, 2007.

Salvino, Dana Nelson. "The Word in Black and White: Ideologies of Race and Literacy in Antebellum America." In *Reading in America*, edited by Cathy N. Davidson. Baltimore: The Johns Hopkins University Press, 1989.

Sicherman, Barbara. "Sense and Sensibility: A Case Study in Women's Reading in Late-Victorian America." In *Reading in America*, edited by Cathy N. Davidson. Baltimore: The Johns Hopkins University Press, 1989.

Smith-Rosenberg, Caroll. "The New Woman as Androgyne: Social Disorder and Gender Crisis, 1870–1936." In *Disorderly Conduct: Visions of Gender in Victorian America*, edited by Carroll Smith-Rosenberg. New York: Oxford University Press, 1986.

Tyler, Moses Coit. "The Free Public Library in the United States: Evolution and Function." In *Librarianship in Gilded Age America*, edited by Leonard Schlup and Stephen H. Paschen. Jefferson, NC: McFarland & Company, 2009.

Van Slyck, Abigail A. "The Lady and the Library Loafer: Gender and Public Space in Victorian America." *Winterthur Portfolio* 31 (1996): 221–42.

Wendorf, Richard, ed. *America's Membership Libraries*. New Castle, DE: Oak Knoll Press, 2007.

2

Women of The Roxburghe Club: Bibliomania, Country Houses, and Bridges to the Twenty-First Century

Sharon S. Prado

> Never fear. *Bibliomania* is, of all species of insanity, the most rational and praise-worthy.—Thomas Frognall Dibdin, *Bibliomania*[1]

The Republic of Ireland is rich in different types of libraries whose origins are equally varied. Across the country there are more than sixty public libraries built by the generosity of Andrew Carnegie.[2] There are many Irish libraries with ties to the Roxburghe Club and the history of private libraries in Britain and Ireland is told through a complex set of stories.[3] The country house libraries in Britain and Ireland are tied to land ownership, inheritance, and wealth creation, enabling the building of vast estates and beautiful rooms in which to house books and manuscripts.[4]

---

[1] Thomas Frognall Dibdin, *The Bibliomania; or, Book-madness; Containing Some Account of the History, Symptoms, and Cure of This Fatal Disease* (London: Printed by W. Savage, 1809), 94.
[2] Brendan Grimes, *Irish Carnegie Libraries: A Catalogue and Architectural History* (Newbridge, Ireland: Irish Academic Press, 1998).
[3] *The Cambridge History of Libraries in Britain and Ireland*. eds. Elisabeth Leedham-Green and Teresa Webber, vol. 1, to 1640; eds. Giles Mandelbrote and K. A. Manley, vol. 2, 1640–1850; eds. Alistair Black and Peter Hoare, vol. 3, 1850–2000 (Cambridge, UK: Cambridge University Press, 2006).
[4] Mark Purcell, *The Country House Library* (New Haven, CT: Yale University Press, 2017) and *The Big House Library in Ireland: Books in Ulster Country Houses* (Swindon, Wiltshire: National Trust, 2011).

Why collect books? Because you can touch them and experience them as physical objects. Because you can experience them independent of proximity to an electrical socket. Because electronic facsimiles, although great at creating wider access to materials, fall short when experiencing the full materiality of the book. Without the activities of bibliophiles prior to the widespread use of electricity, rare books and manuscripts would not be available now for digital preservation in the twenty-first century.

The Roxburghe Club, as the first private membership society devoted to private collecting and the publishing of limited editions of books from their own collections, made unwitting contributions to later public institutions' ability to preserve rare manuscripts and first editions, making them more widely available. Twenty-first-century beneficiaries of the Roxburghe Club's collecting include the Houghton Library at Harvard University, the British Library, the University of Manchester John Rylands Library, the Pierpont Morgan Library and Museum (the Morgan), the Beinecke Rare Book and Manuscript Library at Yale, the Huntington Library in California, and many others. Digitizing these collections creates wider access to beautiful objects that are books, but also to rare materials, otherwise available only to the few.[5]

Individuals spend the first half of their lives acquiring possessions only to spend their later years figuring out how best to dispose of them. Sometimes collections grow to own the collector, and sometimes inheriting is too burdensome, requiring book sales and even the demolition of architecturally important estate houses.[6] Are the reasons for collecting that motivated the early Roxburghe Club members in 1812 the same as for those members currently engaged in the club? What were the motivations for collecting for the women members? Were the expansive libraries (books) status symbols used to fill the country estate houses, also in their grandeur, symbols of wealth and power, or did they confer more meaning? For the female Roxburghe Club members, not all were responsible for building or acquiring the collections that they owned (or managed).

Alaine de Botton, writing in *Status Anxiety*, notes that "our sense of identity is held captive by the judgement of those we live among,"[7]

---

[5] For a recent treatment on the concept of what constitutes value and rarity in book collecting, see David McKitterick, *The Invention of Rare Books: Private Interest and Public Memory, 1600–1840* (Cambridge: Cambridge University Press, 2018).

[6] Purcell, *The Country House Library*, 2017, "Between 1900 and 2000 probably 1,700 British country houses–about a sixth of the total—were demolished," citing G. Worsley, "Beyond the Powerhouse: Understanding the Country House in the Twenty-First Century," *Historical Research* 78, no. 201 (August 2005): 429.

[7] Alain de Botton, *Status Anxiety* (New York: Pantheon Books, 2004), 8.

and that we look to others "to settle the question of our significance." He goes on to say, that "the place we occupy in the world determines how much love we are offered ... a love without which we will be unable to trust."[8] French philosophers in the eighteenth century defended the usefulness of the affluent as providing employment. Individuals decide how much is enough to acquire by comparing themselves to a group that most closely resembles themselves. Status can be conferred through inherited privilege or through individual achievement, but in each case, the accretion of material goods is the visible sign to the world that one has value. If one does not overcome poverty, then economic meritocracy assigns shame and loss of respect by others who have achieved the accumulation of unnecessary symbols of wealth.[9] Belonging and status created wonderful private libraries, which now confer status upon universities, archives, and private/public spaces that now act as beneficent stewards.

The histories of the term *bibliomania* and of the Roxburghe Club are often linked. The third Duke of Roxburghe, John Ker (1740–1804), was an unmarried book collector in Scotland whose title passed in 1804 to a relative, William Bellenden-Ker (1728–1805), seventh Lord Bellenden. Lord Bellenden died just one year after inheriting the title, also leaving no heir. The succession of the estate would remain undecided until 1812, when once settled, prompted the forty-two-day auction of the third Duke's library, forming the impetus for the founding of the Roxburghe Club, which took his name in memory of the Duke.[10] The seat of the Duke of Roxburghe is Floors Castle in Scotland[11] and the auction catalogue for the sale of his library, printed at the time, is now available in digitized format, providing a view into an eighteenth-century book collector's tastes as well as into the organization of his library, which was sold at his London residence seven years after his death.[12]

---

[8] de Botton, *Status Anxiety*, 10.
[9] de Botton, *Status Anxiety*, passim.
[10] Graeme D. Eddie, *Papers of the Dukes and Dukedom of Roxburghe, 1806–1924*, administrative/biographical information compiled by Graeme D, Eddie, Edinburgh University Library, Special Collections Division. https://archiveshub.jisc.ac.uk/search/archives/cbc949db-72ba-3f29-9859-c79a739c1ab8/.
[11] Floors Castle may be visited today and is an estate in the Historic Houses Association, see https://www.floorscastle.com/visit-us/floors-castle/ accessed August 17, 2018.
[12] Robert Harding Evans, *A catalogue of the library of the late John Duke of Roxburghe; which will be sold by auction, 18th May 1812, and the [blank] following days, by R.H. Evans. [With] A suppl. The books will be sold 13 July, 1812, and the 3 following days [and] The prices of the Roxburghe library* (London: George and William Nichol, Printed by W. Bulmer and Co, 1812). Accessed August 17, 2018. https://books.google.ie/books/about/A_catalogue_of_the_library_of_John_duke.html?id=B1EVAAAAQAAJ&redir_esc=; https://books.google.ie/books/content?id=B1EVAAAAQAAJ&pg=PA40&img=1&zoom=3&hl=en&sig=ACfU3U3TMDvzook9iYzSc-jDaudOQrhTGw&ci=0%2C3%2C997%2C1653&edge=0; https://books.google.ie/books/content?id=B1EVAAAAQAAJ&pg=PA41&img=1&zoom=3&hl=en&sig=ACfU3U0m6kORnDsjb5I0__WVJHCSw-m49A&ci=1%2C11%2C991%2C1358&edge=0/.

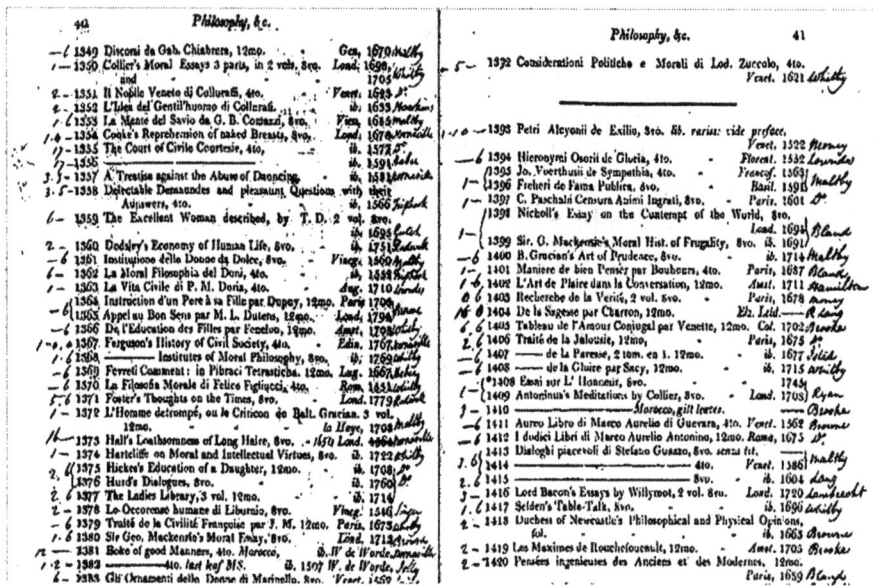

Figure 2.1 G. and W. Nichol, John Ker, Third Duke of Roxburghe, *A catalogue of the library of ... John duke of Roxburghe*.

Robert Harding Evans, *A catalogue of the library of the late John, Duke of Roxburghe* (London: G. and W. Nichol, Wilmer Bulmer & Co.), 40–41.

The booksellers apologize in the preface of the sale catalogue for the fact that books of "common occurrence" occur next to items of greater value, noting that this was not the collector's approach to housing his collection, with items of lesser importance being housed upstairs. The preface also notes that the Duke of Roxburghe "valued philosophical writers, in proportion as they improved the morals of mankind."[13] Of the 9,353 titles auctioned between 18 May and 4 July 1812, ninety-eight titles appear in the category "Philosophy, Morals, etc."

Figure 2.1 excerpts pages from the online digital facsimile of the auction catalogue illustrating some of the philosophy books collected by the Duke. The catalogue has annotations in the margin identifying who purchased which book at the auction. Philosophical titles include *The Court of Civil Courtesie* (1577), *The Excellent Woman* (1695 in 2 volumes), *Hartcliffe on Moral and Intellectual Virtues* (1722), a three-volume set, *The Ladies Library* (1714), and *Boke of Good Manners*, (n.d. but printed

---

[13] Ibid., 17.

by Wynken de Worde, a sixteenth-century printer).

"But to know what books are valuable and what are worthless; their intrinsic and extrinsic merits; their rarity, beauty, and particularities of various kinds; and the estimation in which they are consequently held by knowing men—these things add a zest to the gratification we feel in even looking upon and handling certain volumes.[14] Thus wrote Thomas Frognall Dibdin (1776–1847) about the book madness, or bibliomania, that gripped the co-founders of the Roxburghe Club.

Recent publications (Husbands 2017; McKitterick 2018; Purcell 2017) and Barker's (2012) bicentenary history of the Roxburghe Club discussed the club's founding in 1812. Common among its members were large estates and an interest in acquiring private libraries to fill them along with the beginnings of valuing the rarity of books for rarity's sake. Thomas Frognall Dibdin was a bibliographer and librarian for the 2nd Earl Spencer, who collected a fine private library at Althorp with his assistance. Dibdin published two catalogues about the Spencer library: *Bibliotheca Spenceriana* (1814–15) and *Aedes Althorpianae* (1822).[15] Dibdin's 1809 publication *Bibliomania* addresses owning books as physical artifacts, that is, for the purpose of ownership for ownership's sake and for how they look and not necessarily for their content. Earl Spencer's collection of over 40,000 volumes included fine and rare copies, including the earliest known example of printing, dated 1423, pasted inside a manuscript titled *Laus Virginis*, which now resides with approximately 2,000 other incunabula printed prior to 1480 at the John Rylands Library at the University of Manchester.[16]

The term and concept of bibliomania predate the Roxburghe Club.[17] In 1494 Sebastian Brant printed a popular book, *Das Narrenschiff* (*Ship of Fools*), which was translated into Latin and adapted in an English translation by Alexander Barclay, a Devonshire priest, in a 1509 edition printed by Richard Pynson. A reprint of the 1509 edition in 1874 indicates

---

[14] Thomas Frognall Dibdin, *Bibliomania* (London: Henry G. Bohn, 1842 ed.), 24.
[15] Purcell, *The Country House Library*, 166. The Althorp Library was sold in 1892 and currently is core to the collection at the University of Manchester John Rylands Library. See https://spencerofalthorp.com/rooms/library/ cited on 21 August 2018.
[16] "The John Rylands Library, Manchester," *The British Medical Journal* 2, no. 2169 (1902): 258–60. http://www.jstor.org/stable/20273077/.
[17] David McKitterick discusses the history of the term and attributes its adoption primarily to eighteenth-century publications and early nineteenth-century newspapers and journals, among them Dibdin's *Bibliomania*.

that the 1509 book was extremely rare.[18] The Jamieson 1874 reprint edition includes a Barclay prologue, which admonishes readers in sermon-like fashion to avoid the behaviors and attitudes of those on the ship. The book begins with a long poem about owning unprofitable or useless books. As an incunabula, it may have warned against the spread of knowledge through books and satirized the notion of buying books that an illiterate populace could not read. The poems serve to warn against behaviors (procrastination, leaping and dancing, greed, bad manners, etc.) and present a cautionary morality tome of more than one hundred poems enhanced with novel illustrations. The woodcut shown in Figure 2.2 is by Albrecht Dürer's studio and appeared on the cover of the 1809 edition of Dibdin's *Bibliomania*.

> I am the first fool [19] of all the whole navy
> To keep the pump,[20] the helm and also the sail
> For this is my mind, this one pleasure have I
> Of books to have great plenty and apparel [not equipped or prepared][21]
> I take no wisdom by them: nor yet avail[22]
> Nor perceive them not: And then I them despise
> Thus am I a fool and all that to sew that guise

David McKitterick attributes *bibliomania*'s entrance as a term of common usage in the eighteenth century to the author Edward Harwood's *View of the various editions of the Greek and Roman classics*, first published in 1775.

"Some, indeed, whom God has blessed with more opulence than understanding, burn with an insatiable ardour of enjoying every beauteous form of a favorite book that hath ever been exhibited in any country since the invention of the typographical art; and others have the Biblioma-

---

[18] "The book is extremely rare. There is a fine copy in the Bodleian Library among Selden's books, another in the British Museum, Grenville Collection, and another in the Library of John's College, Oxford." Sebastian Brant, Alexander Barclay and Thomas Hill Jamieson, *The Ship of Fools* (Edinburgh: W. Paterson; London: Henry Sotheran & Co, 1874) xcix. [Brant, Sebastian, 1458–1521; Barclay, Alexander, 1475–1552; Jamieson, T. H. (Thomas Hill), 1843–1876], accessed July 19, 2018. https://archive.org/details/theshipoffools01barcuoft. The Pynson 1509 is titled, *The Shyp of Folys of the Worlde*. Cf. xcviii. A Latin translation is titled *Stultifera Nauis ... The Ship of Fooles*. Alexander Barclay was a priest in Devonshire, so perhaps this adaptation is not intended as satire but rather a sermon for readers to avoid the types of individuals that float aboard the Ship of Fools.
[19] "fool, n.1 and adj." *OED Online*. June 2018. Oxford University Press. http://www.oed.com/view/Entry/72642?rskey=MUhGcS&result=1&isAdvanced=false (accessed August 22, 2018).
[20] "pump, v.". *OED Online*. June 2018. Oxford University Press. http://www.oed.com/view/Entry/154517?rskey=8SGWNp&result=20 (accessed August 22, 2018).
[21] "apparel, v." *OED Online*. June 2018. Oxford University Press. http://www.oed.com/view/Entry/9511?rskey=uaRgMC&result=2&isAdvanced=false (accessed August 22, 2018).
[22] "avail, v." *OED Online*. June 2018. Oxford University Press. http://www.oed.com/view/Entry/13581?rskey=jixXEh&result=2&isAdvanced=false (accessed August 20, 2018).

Figure 2.2 *The Ship of Fools*, 1874 reprint of 1509 edition 19, p. 147.

nia in so dire and frantic a degree, that those rare Editions, which they despair of securing by their wealth, they will not hesitate about secreting from libraries by their ingenuity."[23]

Dibdin's *Bibliomania* was published in several expanded editions and reflects an obsessive pursuit by wealthy men to catalogue, collect, and to fill beautiful rooms in their country estates. In *Bibliomania* there is a category of collectors, Book Auction Bibliomaniacs, for whom auctions as a mechanism for acquiring books created a competitive innovation and drove the price of acquisitions beyond what a bookshop keeper might receive. Although the early founders and subsequent historians refer to the zealous attention to the acquisition of books as *bibliomania*, Nicolas Barker (himself a Roxburghe Club member), writing in celebration of the Club's bicentennial, underscores the importance of the club and the prominence of its membership to politics, scholarship, and the preservation of important rare books and manuscripts. In addition to Dibdin, Earl Spencer, Earl Gower, William Bolland, Sir Egerton Brydges, Sir Francis Freeling, Edward Vernon Utterson, John Delafield Phelps, William Bentham, George Henry Heber, George Isted, John Dent, Robert Lang, the Revered Thomas Heber, and Joseph Haslewood all met at the first gathering on 17 June 1812. The Roxburghe toast offered annually at their usual dinner gathering included a litany of people and organizations important to books and to "the Cause of Bibliomania all over the world."[24] Over time the primary purpose was to dine together, not as a literary society, but as a club of like-minded men (until 1984) who enjoyed memorializing the Duke of Roxburghe with fellow elected members who shared a love of books.

Although the Roxburghe Club was foremost a club, the indirect outcome of its book-collecting activities encouraged advances in book production. During the nineteenth century the Club contributed to changes in book making: It gave rise to three-color printing, the development of technologies to render facsimiles, the concept of limited editions versus mass printing, re-binding and use of elegant book bindings, initiated a new illustration process of letter-press photographic relief engraving, and furthered the practice of holding auctions for private collectors and those in the book trade.

---

[23] David McKitterick, *The Invention of Rare Books: Private Interest and Public Memory, 1600–1840* (Cambridge: Cambridge University Press, 2018), 252, quoting Harwood, *View of the various editions of the Greek and Roman classics*, (1775), vii–viii. McKitterick notes that midcentury the term lost its negative connotations and instead became a badge of honor, 300.

[24] Nicolas Barker, *The Roxburghe Club: A Bicentenary History* (London: Roxburghe Club, 2012), 30–31.

As the life cycle of most organizations involves change, in 1884 when the president of the club died after leading it for thirty years, the membership selection process began to favor those who had political influence and industrialist wealth. The fifth Earl of Rosebery, Philip Archibald Primrose (7 May 1847–21 May 1929), became Prime Minister while amassing an important library about Scottish history, assisted by his heiress wife, Hannah de Rothschild (27 July 1851–19 November 1890).[25] American James Russell Lowell was elected in 1887 while serving as ambassador in London, and the Club voted to send copies of all books published by the Roxburghe Club to the Library of Congress. In 1891 the Club sent copies of earlier published works as well. From Ireland, Charles Brinsley Marlay, High Sheriff of Westmeath, Louth and County Cavan, joined in 1896 and later served as Vice President of the Royal Botanical Society and Treasurer of the Benevolent Society of St. Patrick. Lieutenant-Colonel Henry William Edmund Petty-Fitzmaurice, the sixth Marquess of Lansdowne, joined in 1920 and was one of the first senators of the Irish Free State in 1922 and a fellow of the Society of Antiquaries.[26] A total of twelve Americans have been members, including: James Russell Lowell; Sir Alfred Chester Beatty; John Pierpont Morgan; John Pierpont Morgan, Jr.; Donald Frizell Hyde; William Jackson; Paul Mellon; Frederick B. Adams; Sir Paul Getty; Robert S. Pirie (1934–2015; member from 1984); Mary Hyde Eccles; and Jayne Wrightsman.

In 2001 the Roxburghe Club traveled to Dublin, Ireland, to visit several libraries of note: The National Library of Ireland, The Library of Trinity College Dublin, Archbishop Marsh's Library, the Chester Beatty Library, and the Worth Library at Dr. Steevens's Hospital.[27] Sir Alfred Chester Beatty was an American geologist of Irish descent who later acquired British citizenship and became an honorary citizen of Ireland. While working for the Guggenheim Company he traveled to Serbia, Siberia, and Rhodesia, collecting Asian manuscripts, papyri, and European medieval manuscripts. His library, The Chester Beatty Library, holds an East Asian Collection, Islamic Collections of manuscripts (Arabic, Qur'an, Persian, Turkish, and Mughal-Era Indian), early examples of the Bible on papyri, as well as rare books from the Western tradition, which

---

[25] Jennifer Breger, "Hannah de Rothschild, Countess of Rosebery" *Jewish Women: A Comprehensive Historical Encyclopedia* (1 March 2009. Jewish Women's Archive.) Accessed August 14, 2018. https://jwa.org/encyclopedia/article/rothschild-hannah-de-countess-of-rosebery/. This is not the same Hannah Rothschild who is currently a Roxburghe Club member.
[26] Barker, *Bicentenary*, 145ff.
[27] Elizabethanne Boran, ed., *Book Collecting in Ireland and Britain, 1650–1850* (Dublin, Ireland: Four Courts Press, 2018).

he donated to Ireland. He presented to the Roxburghe Club the heavily illustrated manuscript *Chronicle of Akbar the Great: a description of a manuscript of the Akbar-Nama illustrated by the Court painters* (Roxburghe Club editions, no. 202; presented by A. Chester Beatty). The Worth Library at Dr. Steevens's Hospital, also on the 2001 club tour, was collected by Edward Worth (1676–1733), a Dublin physician and book collector interested in beautifully bound books. His well-preserved library of 4,400 volumes features many examples of early European modern bookbinding.[28] Archbishop Narcissus Marsh (1638–1715), like Edward Worth, studied at Oxford and later became the Provost (President) of Trinity College in Dublin. An excellent synopsis by the librarian of Marsh's Library, a purpose-built structure with public access as intended by Archbishop Marsh when he designed it, notes that of the 25,000 volumes, eighty are incunabula and that the Library serves as a "major centre for seventeenth-century studies."[29]

The Roxburghe Club archives and books are located in the Society of Antiquaries at Burlington House in London. Dr. John Martin Robinson, an architectural historian and Roxburghe Club member, is archivist at Arundel Castle in Norfolk, UK, the seat of the Duke of Norfolk (the Howard family). Dr. Robinson is secretary of the Roxburghe Club and prolific author about country houses in Britain and, in particular, writes about the loss of cultural heritage when estates are no longer maintained or are even destroyed.[30]

An initial exploration into the gender distribution within the Roxburghe Club membership revealed that women book collectors were not members of the club until late into the twentieth century. The women of the Roxburghe Club comprise only six of the 350 individuals (in aggregate) who have made up the club's membership over the two hundred-and-nine years of its existence. The term *bibliomania* applied to men collectors primarily and by the time women were first admitted as members, it had lost its negative overtones and mainly fallen out of use. The criteria for club admittance largely follows the pattern of inherited wealth, with links to the British peerage, with ownership of a large library

---

[28] Ibid., Elizabethanne Boran, "Dr. Edward Worth: A Connoisseur Book Collector in Early Eighteenth-Century Dublin," 80–103. See also http://edwardworthlibrary.ie/history-of-the-library/the-enigma-of-worth/ accessed August 22, 2018.

[29] Muriel McCarthy, "Narcissus Marsh & his Library," *History Ireland* Early Modern History (1500–1700), Features, 3, no. 4 (Autumn 1996). Accessed August 22, 2018., https://www.historyireland.com/early-modern-history-1500-1700/narcissus-marsh-his-library/.

[30] J. Robinson, *Felling the Ancient Oaks: How England Lost Its Great Country Estates* (London: Aurum Press, 2011).

and estates, and also having the means to reproduce books for the membership and to entertain in those social circles. Of these six women, two earned PhDs, several are authors of numerous publications, as well as editors, scholarly collaborators, and a documentary filmmaker (among other literary and philanthropic pursuits).

Two of the American Roxburghe Club women built bridges between their collections and activities between Europe and the United States in influential ways. The contents of their libraries vary widely in scope and focus. Three have presented limited-edition copies from their own libraries to the club. All are connected to large country houses or estates and some to the history of the country house library. Each of the Roxburghe Club women was either born into wealth or married men whose career success enabled them to acquire books, manuscripts, art, properties, and experiences not unlike the men who first established the Club. Table 2.1 indicates the year that each became a member; the estate libraries associated with each; their spouse(s) and their titles (if any); the titles of books that they presented to the Roxburghe Club; and institutional libraries, archives, or editions that are beneficiaries of their activities.[31] All but two had children of their own. This table summarizes at a glance the places where their collections first resided and where the materials now reside in libraries and archival collections where efforts to digitize books offer wider access to the public.

Women of the Roxburghe Club[32]

Mary Morley (née Crapo) Hyde Eccles, Viscountess Eccles (July 8, 1912–August 26, 2003)

Christian ("Kisty") Mary (née McEwen), Dowager Lady Hesketh, Officer of the Order of the British Empire, office of Deputy Lieutenant (July 17, 1929–April 7, 2006)

---

[31] For further reading about women who would have influenced the nature of libraries preceding the establishment of the Roxburghe Club in 1812, see J. Marschner, D. Bindman, L. Ford, Yale Center for British Art, & Historic Royal Palaces, *Enlightened Princesses: Caroline, Augusta, Charlotte, and the Shaping of the Modern World* (New Haven, CT: Yale Center for British Art; Historic Royal Palaces; Yale University Press, 2017 [which includes a contribution by Jane Roberts, a Roxburghe Club member]).

[32] See Table 2.1, which offers information on each of the women Roxburghe Club members, the date of election to the Club, their homes and spouse(s), the title of any book produced for the club, and contributions to present library or archival collections.

Table 2.1 Women of the Roxburghe Club, 1985 to Present

Roxburghe Club Member	Country House(s)	Spouse(s) and Title	Book Published for the Roxburghe Club	Bridge to Universities, Libraries, Archives, Museums
Mary Morley (née Crapo [Crapeau]) Hyde Eccles, PhD (July 8, 1912–August 26, 2003) First female member; joined on November 7, 1985.	Four Oaks Farm, Branchburg, NJ, USA Dean Farm, Upper Chute, Wiltshire, UK	1. Donald Hyde (1909–66) 2. Viscountess Eccles, married to David Eccles, 1st Viscount Eccles (1904–99)	*James Boswell's Book of Company at Auchinleck*. Edited by Mary, Viscountess Eccles, and Gordon Turnbull, presented 1995.	Donald and Mary Hyde Collection of Dr. Johnson and Early Modern Books and Manuscripts at Houghton Library, Harvard University David and Mary Eccles Centre for American Studies, British Library Lady Eccles Oscar Wilde Collection, British Library *Samuel Johnson Letters* (5 vols.) Hyde Edition, Princeton University Press and Oxford University Press Mary Eccles Collection, Grolier Club Archives Mary Hyde Eccles, donor and trustee at Pierpont Morgan Library and Museum
Frances Mary Richardson Currer (March 3, 1785–April 28, 1861) **Not a club member**, but a contemporary of nineteenth-century club founders and recognized as first English female	Eshton Hall, Craven, Yorkshire, UK[a]	Not married, but good friends with Richard Heber, club member (1812–33)	Sotheby's auctions in 1862, 1916, 1979, 1994 of library.	University of Leeds Special Collections Eshton Hall Estate Archive MS 417[b] Bradford Public Library

Christian (Kisty) Mary (née McEwen), Dowager Lady Hesketh, OBE, DL, PhD (July 17, 1929– April 7, 2006) Member from 1991–2006.	Easton Neston, Northhamptonshire and Pomfret Lodge	Frederick Fermor-Hesketh, 2nd Baron Hesketh (8 April 8, 1916– June 10, 1955)	University of Pennsylvania Kislak Center for Special Collections, Rare Books and Manuscripts has 41 boxes of Sotheby's auction catalogues, 1931–2016 inclusive.[c] Sotheby's auctions in 1999, 2005, 2010	Lancaster University Ruskin Library; then withdrawn and library sold at auction(s)
Jane (née Low) Roberts, The Honorable Lady Roberts, Dame Commander of the Royal Victorian Order (September 4, 1949–June 29, 2021) Joined as member in 2003.	Resided formerly at Adelaide Cottage, Windsor Home Park; Cottage in South Oxfordshire	Sir Hugh Roberts (1948–), Director of the Royal Collection and Surveyor of the Queen's Works of Art The Honorable Lady Roberts, DCVO	Author of many books about Windsor, the Royal Collection, and specific artists represented there (Leonardo, Holbein, Sandby).	Royal Library at Windsor Castle

(continued)

Table 2.1 Women of the Roxburghe Club, 1985 to Present (continued)

Roxburghe Club Member	Country House(s)	Spouse(s) and Title	Book Published for the Roxburghe Club	Bridge to Universities, Libraries, Archives, Museums
Jayne (née Larkin) Wrightsman (October 21, 1919–April 20, 2019) Joined as member in 2006.	Palm Beach, FL, Manhattan, London	Charles Bierer Wrightsman (1895–1986)[d]	*Placets de l'officier Desbans*. Presented 2007.	Pierpont Morgan Library and Museum Metropolitan Museum of Art Wrightsman Galleries
Lady Victoria (née Holdsworth) Getty (b. 1949). Joined as member in 2007.	Wormsley Estate	1. James Bertram Lionel Brooke (August 16, 1940–May 27, 2017) 2. Sir J. Paul Getty Jr., KBE (1932–2003) Lady Victoria Getty	Inglis, Esther. (2012). *Esther Inglis's Les Proverbes de Salomon* a facsimile with an introduction by Nicolas Barker.	Wormsley Library is still housed at the Wormsley Estate

The Honourable Hannah Mary Rothschild, CBE (May 22, 1962–) Joined as member in 2017.	Waddesdon Manor, Aylesbury, Buckinghamshire	William Lord Brookfield (former spouse) The Honourable Hannah Mary Rothschild, CBE	Rothschild Foundation Archives Waddesdon Manor Archives

[a] Emiko Hastings, curator of books at the William L. Clements Library at the University of Michigan, is working on a project about women book collectors. See her blog posting about Currer, April 30, 2016, accessed July 31, 2018. https://librarianofbabel.wordpress.com/2016/04/30/the-library-of-frances-mary-richardson-currer/. Dibdin estimated that Currer's library exceeded 15,000 volumes and two printed catalogues were produced. The second one from 1833 (more than 500 pages) is available in the California Digital Library: C. J. Stewart, F. Mackenzie, and S. Rawle, *A Catalogue of the Library Collected by Miss Richardson Currer, at Eshton Hall, Craven, Yorkshire.* London: Printed for private circulation only [by J. Moyes], 1833. https://archive.org/details/catalogueoflibra00rich/. Frances "was the posthumous daughter and sole heir of the Revd Henry Richardson (1758–84) who, shortly before his death, took the name of Currer on succeeding to the estates of Sarah Currer. Her mother was Margaret Clive Wilson, the only surviving child and heir of Matthew Wilson of Eshton Hall" Colin Lee, "Currer, Frances Mary Richardson (1785–1861), Book Collector." *Oxford Dictionary of National Biography* (Oxford: Oxford University Press, 2004).
[b] "Eshton Hall Estate Archive." https://explore.library.leeds.ac.uk/special-collections-explore/5111/.
[c] Sotheby's. *Books and manuscripts from the Fermor-Hesketh library at Easton Neston: Auction: Wednesday 15 December 1999; sale L09223* (London: Sotheby's, 1999); Sotheby's *Easton Neston, Towcester Northamptonshire: Selected contents sold on the instructions of the Lord and Lady Hesketh and the Trustees of Frederick, 2nd Baron Hesketh, deceased.* London: Sotheby's. [*Easton Neston, Towcester, Northamptonshire:* Sotheby's, Tuesday 17, 18 & 19 May 2005 (London: Sotheby's, 2005); Sotheby's *Magnificent Books, Manuscripts and Drawings From the Collection of Frederick 2nd Lord Hesketh 07 December 2010* (London: Sotheby's, 2010).
[d] Christopher Masters, "Wrightsman, Charles Bierer," *Grove Art Online* (2003). https://doi.org/10.1093/gao/9781884446054.article.T092360/.

Jane Stephanie (née Low), Lady Roberts (September 4, 1949–June 29, 2021), art historian

Jayne (née Larkin) Wrightsman (October 21, 1919–April 20, 2019)

Lady Victoria (née Holdsworth) Getty (1949–)

The Honourable Hannah Mary Rothschild, Commander of the Order of the British Empire (22 May 1962–)

Frances Mary Richardson Currer (1785–1861) has been included in Table 2.1, not because she was a Roxburghe Club member, but because she was the first recognized female bibliophile in the nineteenth century. She was a contemporary of the founding Roxburghe Club members and good friends with Richard Heber, who was an early member who owned libraries scattered across Europe in eight different estates. Although her library at Eshton Hall and her inherited wealth would have qualified her equally with other founding members, she was not an elected member of the Club.

Mary Morley (née Crapo) Hyde Eccles, Viscountess Eccles

The first female member of the Roxburghe Club, Mary Morley Hyde Eccles, Viscountess Eccles, was an American collector, scholar and philanthropist, born July 8, 1912, in Detroit, Michigan, and died August 26, 2003, in Branchburg, New Jersey (Figure 2.3). Her father, Stanford Tappan Crapo (1865–1939), and her mother, Emma Caroline Morley (1872–1937), originally from Fort Scott, Kansas, married in 1894 in Plainsville, Ohio.[33] Mary Morley Hyde Eccles was from an entrepreneurial family whose wealth was derived from shipping, railroads, and the sale of construction materials. Her undergraduate education at Vassar (then an all-women's college), which she completed in 1934, and later a PhD in English literature from Columbia University in 1947, prepared her for

---

[33] Stanford Tappan Crapo, accessed February 5, 2019. https://www.findagrave.com/memorial/97651369/stanford-tappan-crapo/.

Figure 2.3 Mary Hyde Eccles.
https://iiif.lib.harvard.edu/manifests/view/ids:460351617$1i/.

a life of serious scholarship. Her early interest in rare books emanated from her scholarly examination of early editions of Elizabethan drama.[34] Many of her publications were based on the rare books, manuscripts, letters, photographs, and other literary works she procured in partnership with her first husband, Donald Frizell Hyde (1909–66), who served as president of the Bibliographical Society of America and as president of the Grolier Club.[35]

Bruce Redford's "Biographical Memoir" in 2008 for the American Philosophical Society's *Proceedings*, notes that Mary Hyde Eccles enjoyed the benefits of her wealth and connections by collecting eighteenth-century English literature focused on Samuel Johnson, James Boswell, and on an important collection of Oscar Wilde printed and primary sources. Professor Redford spent lengthy research visits at her Four Oaks Farm and library, producing the five-volume edition of the Samuel Johnson Letters. In a conversation with Dr. Redford, who knew her well, I learned that she was proud to have been elected a member of the American Philosophical Society in 1978 as a leader in the arts, professions, and private and public affairs.[36] She generously shared her collections with other Johnson scholars, encouraging publications by many authors who acknowledged and benefited from her ready largesse.

Although the French Impressionist painter Mary Cassatt believed that "Women should be some**one** and not some**thing**," it is difficult to disassociate the female Roxburghe Club members from their significant others' involvement in the club. In Mary Hyde Eccles's case, her first husband, Donald Frizell Hyde, was among only a handful of other Americans elected to the club in its two hundred-and-nine-year history, and his membership preceded hers by more than twenty years. Donald Hyde became a club member in 1964 until his death in 1966. Mary Hyde's membership in 1985 was prompted only by her second husband's query to the Roxburghe Club about women's eligibility to stand for election

---

[34] Bruce Redford, "Obituary: Mary, Viscountess Eccles: Anglophile Scholar and Benefactor who Amassed the World's Finest Collection of 18th-century English Literature," *The Guardian* ([London (UK)] 16 Sep 2003): 1.25. See also Bruce Redford, "Mary Hyde Eccles" *Proceedings of the American Philosophical Society* 152, no. 2 (2008): 239–41; Bruce Redford, 2007, Eccles [née Crapo; other married name Hyde], Mary Morley, Viscountess Eccles (1912–2003), literary collector and scholar," *Oxford Dictionary of National Biography*.

[35] "In Memoriam: Donald F. Hyde." *The Bulletin of the American Society of Papyrologists* 3, no. 2 (1966): 53–55. http://www.jstor.org/stable/24519514/.

[36] Bruce Redford worked extensively at the Hyde's Four Oaks estate as sole editor of the five-volume edition of *The Letters of Samuel Johnson* (known as *The Hyde Edition*), published by Princeton University Press. See Samuel Johnson, and Bruce Redford, *The Letters of Samuel Johnson* (Princeton, NJ: Princeton University Press, 1992). I would like to thank and acknowledge the time that Dr. Redford offered me in a conversation about the Hydes in preparing the preconference version of this chapter.

as members. David McAdam Eccles, first Baron Viscount Eccles, Privy Counsellor, Order of the Companions of Honour, Kight Commander of the Royal Victorian Order, had joined in 1966.

It was at the June 26, 1984 meeting of the Roxburghe Club, hosted by Edmund Brudenell at Deene Park, Northamptonshire, that Lord David Eccles asked whether the club rules excluded women from membership.

> There was an appalled silence, broken by Lord De L'Isle, who had not won the VC without more than ordinary courage, saying, "But we don't want to be lectured to by some blue-stocking", echoing a thought that had occurred to most present. In the discussion that followed, it was agreed that to admit one only would be a mistake, Lord Perth going so far as to suggest six.... The secretary confirmed, otiosely, that the Rules of the Club did not debar women; in fact, they did not mention the opposite sex. It was clear that by no means all the twenty-two members present agreed with Lord Eccles's proposal, and it was agreed that the Secretary should circulate a paper to all members to seek their opinion; by 1 August thirty-four members had replied, seventeen supporting the proposal, sixteen against, with one abstention.[37]

The patriarchal group begrudgingly admitted its first woman the next year, the same year that David Eccles, first Viscount Eccles, married Mary Hyde on September 26, 1985, with her election date to the club occurring six weeks later on November 7. It was perhaps her interest in eighteenth-century literature that prompted the "bluestocking" objection to admitting women—a term that originated during the life of Samuel Johnson (1709–84) to describe a women's society that met for intellectual and philosophical exchange, led by Elizabeth Montagu and Elizabeth Vesey in literary salons that did include men. The term *bluestockings* could derisively refer to women who were too learned or too intellectual, an interesting vestigial meaning lingering into the twentieth century, which may have influenced the results of the vote to admit women into the club in 1985.

Mary Hyde Eccles's own publications reflect her interest in poetry, theater, and the literature by and about Samuel Johnson and James Boswell.[38] She also edited the letters between Bernard Shaw and Alfred Douglas, while building her Oscar Wilde collection. The Grolier Club, the preeminent bibliophile society in New York, published her select essays and lectures in a 2002 commemorative edition. Her importance

---

[37] Quoting the Roxburghe Club Meeting Minutes of 26 June 1984 in footnote 1 on page 255 of Barker, *Bicentenary* 254–55, 255n1.

[38] See Appendix for list of publications by women who were Roxburghe Club members.

to twentieth- and twenty-first-century scholarship is memorialized in the collections bequeathed to various libraries, bridging the transatlantic divide as she and her second husband did in life throughout their literary travels, splitting their time among her estate at Four Oaks Farm, an apartment in Manhattan, and Lord Eccles's estate at Dean Farm, Upper Chute, Wiltshire (UK), and an apartment at Barton Place near Parliament.

At Houghton Library (the primary repository for rare books and manuscripts) at Harvard University, the Hydes established the Donald and Mary Hyde Collection of Dr. Johnson and Early Modern Books and Manuscripts.[39] The majority of the Hyde Collection is housed in the Hyde Rooms at Houghton and contains more than 4,000 volumes, approximately 5,500 manuscripts and letters, and more than 5,000 prints, drawings, and objects bequeathed by Mary Hyde Eccles (Figure 2.4).[40]

The finding aid for MS Hyde 98 at Houghton describes the Mary Hyde Eccles papers, which span the years 1939–2003 (1853–2003 inclusive) and comprise 88 linear feet in 84 boxes of correspondence and other of her personal papers.[41] Eight boxes of materials about her membership in the Grolier Club are found in the Grolier Club Archive and include travel diaries and photo albums.[42] The Hydes also collected Japanese prints and illustrated books and traveled the globe, their destinations included China, Haiti, Jamaica, India, Singapore, Sri Lanka, Italy, Ireland, Egypt, as well as other places, serving as informal cujy/ltural ambassadors.

The book that Mary Hyde Eccles published from her collection for the Roxburghe Club has ties to Ireland. In 1995 she presented to the Club, *James Boswell's Book of Company at Auchinleck*, which she edited together with Gordon Turnbull.[43] Auchinleck is the Boswell estate in Scotland, which was inherited by the Talbots through marriage in the nineteenth century. The Talbots moved the Boswell materials to Malahide Castle, just north of Dublin. It was the Hydes who assisted Ralph Isham, also a rare book collector, with the procurement of the Boswell papers

---

[39] Adam Kirsch, "The Hack as Genius: Dr. Samuel Johnson Arrives at Harvard," *Harvard Magazine* (November–December 2004), accessed August 16, 2018. https://harvardmagazine.com/2004/11/the-hack-as-genius.html/.
[40] Accessed August 13, 2018. http://hcl.harvard.edu/libraries/houghton/collections/hyde.cfm/.
[41] Mary Hyde Eccles Papers, 1853–2005 (MS Hyde 98). Houghton Library, Harvard University. This guide provides biographical/historical information as well as detailed description of the contents: personal papers, financial records, visual material, diaries, travel diaries, etc.
[42] Hyde Eccles collection, 1903–2002 (bulk 1959–2002). Grolier Club, New York.
[43] J. Boswell, M. H. E. Eccles, G. Turnbull, D. Buchanan, Roxburghe Club, & Stinehour Press. (1995). *James Boswell's Book of Company at Auchinleck, 1782–1795*, eds. Viscountess Eccles and Gordon Turnbull (Somerville, NJ: Viscountess Eccles, 1995). http://id.lib.harvard.edu/alma/990076300650203941/catalog/.

Figure 2.4 One of the Hyde Rooms at Houghton Library, Harvard University.

Harvard Public Affairs and Communications, Harvard University. https://commons.wikimedia.org/wiki/File:Houghton_Hyde_Room.jpg/.

at Malahide Castle. Mary's account of her acquisition of the black ebony cabinet, once housed first at Auchinleck, then Malahide Castle, details how the Samuel Johnson letters and the James Boswell diaries made their way from Scotland, to Dublin, to the United States, and ultimately to Yale University.[44] The auction catalogue (which belonged to the Hydes) of the 1893 sale at Auchinleck has been digitized in IIIF (International Image Interoperability Framework) format at Houghton and demonstrates in hand-written marginal annotations who bought which items

---

[44] William Zachs, ed., *Mary Hyde Eccles: A Miscellany of Her Essays and Addresses* (New York: The Grolier Club, 2002); "Boswell's Ebony Cabinet," 113ff (first published in *Studies in the Eighteenth Century III*, eds. R. F. Brissenden and J. C. Eade [Toronto: University of Toronto Press, 1976]). This volume of essays, from the Third David Nichol Smith Memorial Seminar, continues the valuable and lively tradition established in the two earlier seminars and volumes. The Mary Hyde essay, "Boswell's Ebony Cabinet" was first published in David Nichol Smith Memorial Seminar, R. F. Brissenden and J. C. Eade, *Studies in the Eighteenth Century, III: Papers presented at the Third David Nichol Smith Memorial Seminar, Canberra, 1973* (Toronto: University of Toronto Press, 1976).

at the sale.⁴⁵ Ralph Isham visited Malahide Castle and Fettercairn House (in Scotland and owned by the Forbes family of Aberdeenshire) to collect, assemble, and publish the *Private Papers of James Boswell*, eventually selling the collection to Yale University in 1949. Boswell's sons, James Boswell (1778–1822) and Sir Alexander Boswell (1775–1822), were early members of the Roxburghe Club.⁴⁶

The Book of Company at Auchinleck reflects the daily life of James Boswell beginning in 1782 until 1795, the year of his death. It records with his annotations the guests who visited Auchinleck, how they dined, and other personal commentary by Boswell, reproduced in a facsimile edition for the Roxburghe Club.⁴⁷ Auchinleck House, built between 1755 and 1760 by James Boswell's father, Alexander Boswell, eighth Laird of Auchinleck, has been preserved by the Landmark Trust in Scotland and may be booked now for holidays.⁴⁸ The restoration of the house used records in the Boswell Papers at the Beinecke Rare Books and Manuscripts Library at Yale, an indirect outcome of the Hyde's assistance to Ralph Isham to acquire and preserve the Boswell collection, now at Yale.⁴⁹ The current house library at Auchinleck holds copies of the Yale Edition of Boswell Papers, reconstituting in part the library's original contents and providing a repatriation of cultural heritage in a published modern edition.

The Lady Eccles Oscar Wilde Collection at the British Library contains over two thousand items collected over many years by Mary and Donald Hyde. It was augmented when the Hydes purchased H. Montgomery Hyde's Wilde collection in 1962. Mary's interest in playwriting motivated her to seek out the Irish playwright Oscar Wilde's successes in the form of first editions. She built what is considered to be the best private collection of his manuscripts, books, and ephemera.⁵⁰ She ultimately bequeathed her collection to the British Library, where her second husband, David McAdam Eccles, had played an important role. Viscount Eccles served under three prime ministers, including Minister Churchill's

---

⁴⁵ Sotheby, Wilkinson & Hodge, *Catalogue of the Selected Portion of the Celebrated Auchinleck Library* (London: Dryden Press: J. Davy and Sons, 1893). EC75.B6578.Y895s. Houghton Library, Harvard University, Cambridge, MA. For more on IIIF, see, https://iiif.io/.

⁴⁶ Barker, *Bicentenary*, 50.

⁴⁷ This book is still available through Quaritch, last listed for sale for 260 British sterling. See note 43.

⁴⁸ Auchinleck House, Ochiltree, Ayrshire. https://www.landmarktrust.org.uk/search-and-book/properties/auchinleck-house-4834#Overview/.

⁴⁹ Caroline Stanford, 2001 and 2015, Auchinleck House History Album, The Landmark Trust: Shottesbrooke, Maidenhead, Berkshire SL6 3SW. Accessed August 14, 2018. www.landmarktrust.org.uk/.

⁵⁰ Lloyd, Andrea. "The Lady Eccles Oscar Wilde Collection," *The Electronic British Library Journal* 10 (2010): 1–13.

Figure 2.5 Eccles 293, British Library, example of Riviere bookbinding of Oscar Wilde's *Salome*, 1894, front and back cover and spine.

https://www.bl.uk/catalogues/bookbindings/FullImage.aspx?&ImageId=ImageId=53788&Copyright=BL/.

cabinet, was Minister for Education, and also organized the British Library into an entity separate from the British Museum. In addition to becoming the first chairman of the British Library Board, he and his wife established the David and Mary Eccles Centre for American Studies at the British Library.

Figure 2.5, from the Lady Eccles Oscar Wilde Collection in the British Library database of bookbindings, exemplifies the Roxburghe Club interest in exquisite bookbindings and the book as a beautiful object. The bookbinder for this Oscar Wilde edition of *Salome* is Riviere & Sons (Robert Riviere, d. 1882) of London. The onlaid green goatskin binding has been gold-tooled.

The Pierpont Morgan Library and Museum benefited from Mary Hyde Eccles's collecting interests and philanthropy for almost forty years. She was a member of the board of trustees from 1966 until her death in 2003 and her contributions appear variously in the Morgan library catalogue as either *Eccles, Mary Hyde, donor (343 items)*, or *Viscountess Eccles*. For the Morgan's seventy-fifth anniversary and the fiftieth anniversary of the Association of Fellows, she presented a nine-volume first edition of *The Life and Opinions of Tristam Shandy, Gentleman*, printed between 1760–67.[51] Other items donated included numerous letters from Samuel Taylor Coleridge to various recipients.

Christian ("Kisty") Mary (née McEwen), Dowager Lady Hesketh, Officer of the Order of the British Empire, Deputy Lieutenant (1929–2006)

Like Mary Hyde Eccles, Christian (nicknamed "Kisty") Mary, Dowager Lady Hesketh also earned a PhD. Her King's College, London thesis, "The Political Opposition to the Government of Charles I in Scotland," was published in 1999. She grew up in Scotland at Marchmont, a Palladian estate purchased by her grandfather Robert Finnie McEwen from the Hume Campbell family. Her grandfather, with the assistance of Sir Robert Lorimer, expanded the original house built in 1750 and Marchmont is recognized as one of the finest houses of its kind in Scotland.[52] Her parents were Sir John McEwen and Bridget Lindley, four of whose children predeceased them.[53]

She married Frederick Fermor-Hesketh, second Baron Hesketh (1916–55), at the private chapel of Marchmont House, Berwickshire, on November 22, 1949. Beginning in the 1950s, Lord Hesketh began collecting rare books at his estate, Easton Neston, in Northhamptonshire, which also included the Towcester Racecourse, a private Formula One racing track. The estate had been in his family since 1535, and the main house, designed by architect Nicholas Hawksmoor, was completed in 1702.

The Sotheby auction catalogues of 1999 and 2005 describe two auctions of books and manuscripts from the Fermor-Hesketh estates.[54]

---

[51] Laurence Sterne, *The Life and Opinions of Tristam Shandy, Gentleman*, 9 vols. (York: printed by Ann Ward, 1760–67).

[52] Marchmont Estate has undergone recent renovation, completed in 2016 and is among those listed in the Historic Houses Association. https://www.historichouses.org/houses/house-listing/marchmont.html/. See also Roger White, "Marchmont: The Scottish expertise and craftsmanship behind the revival," *Country Life*, 27 August 2017. https://www.countrylife.co.uk/architecture/marchmont-the-scottish-expertise-and-craftsmanship-behind-the-revival-164354#2I7cs8oJ30lzAH2d.99/.

[53] Obituary, Allan Massie, "The Dowager Lady Hesketh: Historian and Rugby Fan Whose Bold Spirit Defied Tragedies," *The Guardian* (25 April 2006).

[54] Sotheby's. London, *Books and manuscripts from the Fermor-Hesketh library at Easton Neston: Auction: Wednesday 15 December 1999; sale L09223* (London: Sotheby's, 1999). Sotheby's (Firm), *Easton Neston, Towcester Northamptonshire: Selected contents sold on the instructions of the Lord and Lady Hesketh and the Trustees of Frederick, 2nd Baron Hesketh, deceased* (London: Sotheby's, 2005). *[Easton Neston, Towcester, Northamptonshire: Sotheby's, Tuesday 17, 18 & 19 May 2005.* London: Sotheby's Sotheby's. London, *Magnificent Books, Manuscripts and Drawings From the Collection of Frederick 2nd Lord Hesketh 07 December 2010* (London: Sotheby's, 2010).

A portion of the library had been donated to Lancaster University in 2006, but later withdrawn and sold at auction in 2010. The entire 2010 auction of the Hesketh collection in 2010 consisted of ninety-one lots of manuscripts, books, and drawings, rendering a total sales price of £14,925,100.00. Items sold included beautiful illuminated French manuscripts on vellum, the first edition of the whole Bible in English, a collection of letters from Queen Elizabeth I concerning the custody of Mary Queen of Scots, the First Folio of Shakespeare's plays, and ornithology and botanical drawings.

The highest price of the sale went for Lot 50, the large-format *Birds of America* in four volumes, which sold for £7,321,250 (Figure 2.6).[55] The dimensions of the book, known as *double elephant* (39 × 29 inches) would be representative of the interest in books for display or of extreme size, and the rarity of this set is attributed to the limited number now in existence.[56] This particular four-volume set had been acquired by Frederick, second Lord Hesketh, in 1951, purchased by William H. Robinson for £7000. The return on investment to his estate cannot be overstated. In 2005 Easton Neston was sold and subsequently refurbished by Leon Max, and was the subject of an hour-long BBC history documentary.[57]

Although Lady Hesketh did not publish a book for the Roxburghe Club, she was author of several publications, including *For King and Conscience: John Graham of Claverhouse; Viscount Dundee, 1648–1689*; and *The Country House Cookery Book*. In addition to serving as Deputy Lieutenant and High Sheriff of Northhamptonshire, she enjoyed writing about rugby as a journalist, commissioned a new library at Easton Neston in 1967, and had four children, two of whom died—one not long after

---

[55] Audubon, John James. *The Birds of America; From Original Drawings by John James Audubon* (London: Published by the author, 1827–38). "World Record as Book Sells for £7m," *The Telegraph*, 8 December 2010. Sotheby's. London, *Magnificent Books, Manuscripts and Drawings From the Collection of Frederick, 2nd Lord Hesketh. 3 Volumes Complete Set. Part I; Part II: Audubon the Birds of America; Part III: Redoute's Les Roses* (London: Sotheby's, 2010.). Three-volume set of auction catalogs for a sale of 91 lots held at Sotheby's London, December 7, 2010. Sale code: L10413. Accessed February 11, 2019. http://www.sothebys.com/en/auctions/ecatalogue/2010/magnificent-books-manuscripts-and-drawings-from-the-collection-of-frederick-2nd-lord-hesketh-l10413/lot.50.html/.

[56] These books and their rarity are further described in a 2012 Christie's catalogue, Audubon, John James (1785–1851). *The Birds of America; from Original Drawings* (London: Published by the Author, 1827–1838), 4 volumes, "double-elephant" broadsheets (979/975 × 650/632 mm). Engraved title page in each volume and 435 hand-colored, etched and aquatint plates by William H. Lizars (Edinburgh), Robert Havell, Sr., and Robert Havell, Jr. (London), after Audubon's original life-size watercolor drawings, on J. Whatman and J. Whatman Turkey Mill paper with watermarks dated 1827–1838. Accessed August 20, 2018. See https://www.christies.com/lotfinder/Lot/audubon-john-james-1785-1851-the-birds-of-5525248-details.aspx/.

[57] Dan Cruickshank, "The Country House Revealed," BBC (2011). Accessed August 20, 2018. https://youtu.be/Q4eK-NeLxpI/.

Figure 2.6 From John James Audubon, *Birds of America* (1827–38).
Photo credit Sothebys. Reprinted with permission.

her husband's death and another son in a car accident. She notably was not responsible for amassing the vast library, which was her husband's pursuit, and ultimately the responsibility of dispersing the library fell to her son.

Jane (née Low), Lady Roberts, Dame Commander of the Royal Victorian Order [58]

Jane Roberts was elected to the Roxburghe Club in 2003, the year after her appointment as Royal Librarian. Both she and her husband, Sir Hugh Ashley Roberts, were art historians who, until their retirement, worked for Her Majesty Queen Elizabeth II at Windsor Castle. In 1975, as Jane Low, she was appointed Curator of the Print Room at Windsor Castle; in addition, from 2002–13 she served as Royal Librarian. She was the daughter of Toby Low, first Baron Aldington, and Araminta (née Mac-Michael; daughter of Sir Harold MacMichael and great-niece of George Nathaniel Curzon). Her father qualified as a barrister but served in the army throughout World War 2 before entering Parliament in 1945; he served in the House of Commons from 1945–62 (and was a Minister under Churchill in 1954–55) and was also active in the House of Lords from 1962, combining his public service with careers in banking, industry, and insurance. His papers are now in the Bodleian Library. He married Felicité Anne Araminta Bowman (1920–2012) in 1947 and had three children.[59]

As author Jane Roberts wrote extensively about the Royal Library, editing many exhibition catalogues, books, and academic papers, including *Queen Elizabeth II: A Birthday Souvenir Album*; *Five Gold Rings, a Royal Wedding Souvenir Album* (2007); and *Charles, Prince of Wales: A Birthday Souvenir Album* (2008).[60] Her early publications relate to her role as Curator of the Print Room. For an exhibit at the Metropolitan Museum in New York she prepared the catalogue (with Kenneth Keele, 1983), *Leonardo da Vinci: Anatomical Drawings from the Royal Library, Windsor Castle*. For an exhibit at the Museum of Houston, she published

---

[58] Since this chapter was written in 2018, I am sad to report that Jane Roberts died on June 29, 2021. Her obituary profiles her long service to the Royal household. Accessed on September 17, 2021. https://www.msn.com/en-gb/news/uknews/jane-roberts-curator-of-the-print-room-at-windsor-castle-and-the-first-woman-to-be-made-royal-librarian-obituary/ar-AALSSFG/.

[59] John Ure, "Low, Austin Richard William [Toby], 1st Baron Aldington, (1914–2000)," *Oxford Dictionary of National Biography*. https://doi.org/10.1093/ref:odnb/74952/.

[60] See the Appendix for a more complete list of her publications.

Drawings by Holbein from the Court of Henry VIII: Fifty Drawings from the Collection of Her Majesty Queen Elizabeth II, Windsor Castle: The Museum of Fine Arts, Houston, 17 May–16 August 1987 (1st ed.), and both published catalogues serve as examples of her work that bridge the United Kingdom and the United States. She contributed a chapter about the Royal Library at Windsor to a recent publication by McKendrick and Doyle (2013): *1000 Years of Royal Books and Manuscripts*, which discusses other royal libraries and the transfer of the Old Library from a palace to a museum.[61] She also contributed to the 2017 publication that accompanied the exhibition *Enlightened Princesses: Caroline, Augusta, Charlotte, and the Shaping of the Modern World*, co-organized by the Yale Center for British Art and Historic Royal Palaces, on view at the Yale Center for British Art, New Haven, from February 2 to April 30, 2017, and at Kensington Palace, London, from June 22 to November 12, 2017, which examines how women in courtly roles influenced an array of cultural activities, including the development of royal libraries and art collections.[62]

Jayne (née Larkin) Wrightsman

Mrs. Jayne Wrightsman became a Roxburghe Club member in 2006, twenty years after the death of her husband, Charles Bierer Wrightsman (June 13, 1895–May 27, 1986). She was born in Flint, Michigan, October 21, 1919, and spent her high school years in Los Angeles. Charles was an oil executive and president of Standard Oil of Kansas and attended Philips Exeter Academy, Stanford, and Columbia Universities. His patronage of the Metropolitan Museum, where he served as trustee, and the renowned art collection that he and Jayne together created, resulted in nine French period rooms at the Museum and three galleries named for the Wrightsmans, along with paintings by Vermeer, Rubens, El Greco, Georges de la Tour, Jacques-Louis David, and Giovanni Battista Tiepolo.[63] In this age of concern for privacy, this chapter confines comments mostly to her contributions to the Roxburghe Club. As noted in a 2003 article

---

[61] For a brief history of the Royal Collection Trust, see https://www.royalcollection.org.uk/collection/about-the-collection/the-royal-library-and-royal-archives/a-history-of-the-royal-library/. Accessed August 20, 2018.

[62] J. Marschner, D. Bindman, L. Ford, and Yale Center for British Art, & Historic Royal Palaces. *Enlightened Princesses: Caroline, Augusta, Charlotte, and the Shaping of the Modern World* (New Haven, CT: Yale Center for British Art; Historic Royal Palaces; Yale University Press, 2017).

[63] Obituary, "Charles Bierer Wrightsman, Philanthropist, Is Dead at 90," *New York Times*, May 28, 1986.

for *Vanity Fair*, Mrs. Wrightsman declined to be interviewed for that article, writing the author, "I feel over-honoured, but it has been an ironclad rule of mine never to grant interviews either about my friends or myself. I cannot make an exception, even for you."[64] Her friends included Jacqueline Kennedy, who enlisted her assistance with the redecoration of the White House, and many others in New York's upper echelons of society. She married Mr. Wrightsman in 1944 and they lived in Palm Beach, Florida, in a house designed by Maurice Fatio, owned a London property, and an apartment in Manhattan at 820 Fifth Avenue.

Director Emeritus John Walker (1906–95) of the National Gallery, Washington, DC, spent much time with the Wrightsmans on trips abroad and wrote this about Jayne's self-taught expertise on French art and furniture:

> I found in my files letters written by her in 1957 inquiring about a correspondence course in French eighteenth-century art, which was being offered by the University of Chicago. Was it worthwhile for her to take it? I replied, after investigating the course, that it was far too elementary. By that time, I felt, she knew as much as most curators. I sent her, instead, a very thorough and professional bibliography. I have no doubt that she procured and read nearly every article I suggested. Today she has become one of the best connoisseurs in America of the art of the *ancien regime*.[65]

Although the Wrightsman's primary collecting focus was on European paintings and eighteenth-century French furniture belonging to the French monarchy, after her husband's death she produced a facsimile for the Roxburghe Club in 2007 from her collection of books and manuscripts.[66] The *Placets de l'officier Desbans* ("Petitions of the Officer Desbans") manuscript was originally created in 1775 by a French army officer, Edme-Louis Desbans.[67] The choice of book offered an eighteenth-century view into how one asked the ruling aristocracy for a raise. If one is writing to Marie-Antoinette and King Louis XVI, the request or petition involved employing the Parisian artist Gabriel Jacques de Saint-Aubin to create fifteen illustrations and text bound in red silk to appeal properly

---

[64] Francesa Stanfill, "Jayne's World," *Vanity Fair* (January 2003): 103–18, 111.
[65] Charles Bierer Wrightsman, Jayne Wrightsman, F. J. B. Watson, C. C. Dauterman, & E. Fahy, *The Wrightsman Collection*, 5 vols. (New York: Metropolitan Museum of Art, 1966). Quoting John Walker, 7.
[66] Edme Louis Desbans, Gabriel Jacques de Saint-Aubin, Neil MacGregor, and Jayne Wrightsman, *Placets de l'officier Desbans* (New York: Privately printed for members of the Roxburghe Club, 2007).
[67] The original manuscript is described in Everett Fahy, ed., *The Wrightsman Pictures*. (New York: Metropolitan Museum of Art, 2005). Accessed February 15, 2019. https://libmma.contentdm.oclc.org/digital/collection/p15324coll10/id/123973/.

Figure 2.7 Gabriel Jacques de Saint-Aubin. *Placets de officier Desbans*, Desbans presenting his petition to Queen Marie Antoinette, illustration 3 [color image excerpted from Cone, Polly, ed. *A Guide to the Wrightsman Galleries at the Metropolitan Museum of Art*, entries by James Parker, curator, and Clare LeCorbeiller, associate curator, Dept. of European Sculpture and Decorative Arts (New York: Metropolitan Museum of Art, 1979)].

to royal tastes (Figure 2.7). The officer Desbans presented two petitions, one to the queen and one to the king, featuring various aspects of their activities like attending a Gluck opera and the king's coronation. In optimistic anticipation of receiving the promotion, the fifteenth illustration in the petitions shows Edme-Louis Desbans at Versailles in the Hall of Mirrors, triumphant in his quest for the recognition he deserves.[68] This Roxburghe presentation book is described by Nicolas Barker as a convincing facsimile: "The book is bound in red morocco with the arms of Marie-Antoinette, and is so close a facsimile of every part, drawings,

---

[68] A full description of the facsimile is available in C. Wrightsman et al., *Wrightsman Collection*. vol. 5, 340–44.

binding, nette, that only Neil MacGregor's introduction, itself an elegant expose of book and purpose, destroys the illusion. It was designed by Bruce Campbell and printed by Santiago Saavedra, Ediciones El Viso, Madrid."[69]

The Morgan Library and Museum is also a beneficiary of Mrs. Wrightsman's philanthropy. Not only did she serve on the board from 1983–86, she is an honorary member of the Fairfax Murray Society for the Department of Drawings and Prints. Among the donations offered from her own collection(s) are literary and historical manuscripts, drawings and prints, and a seventeenth-century illuminated manuscript describing Louis XIV's navy. Autographed letters from John Quincy Adams and Thomas Jefferson and from the French aristocracy to George III, once in her library, are now at the Morgan. There is a two-page receipt dated July 26, 1757, from Jeanne Antoinette Poisson de Pompadour, Marquise de (1721–64), selling her Chateau of Bellevue to Louis XV for 300,000 livres, with her signature. Other rare materials have been added through a gift fund from Mrs. Wrightsman established for that purpose.

Lady Victoria (née Holdsworth) Getty

Lady Victoria Getty would have been introduced to Roxburghe Club members when she entertained them at Wormsley Estate with her husband, Sir J. Paul Getty (1932–2003; member from 1988). After Sir Paul Getty purchased Wormsley Estate, he added a purpose-built library to house his book collection with construction beginning after 1971. Nicolas Barker in *The Bookman* (2003) describes the space. In 2009 the Bodelian Library exhibit, "An Artful Craft: Historic Bookbindings from the Broxbourne Library and Other Collections," featured books from the collection which represents, "the world's most comprehensive private collection of bookbindings."[70] The Wormsley Library was described first in a publication by Sir Paul Getty in 1999.[71] Victoria Getty's father-in-law, John Paul Getty, Sr., established the Getty Museum and Research Institute in Los Angeles, CA.

---

[69] Barker, *Bicentenary*, 277.
[70] Bodelian Library, University of Oxford, news 11 June 2009, "Judging Books by their cover: a history of bookbinding at the Bodelian." Accessed July 25, 2018. https://www.bodleian.ox.ac.uk/news/2009/2009_jun_11/.
[71] Sir Paul Getty, *The Wormsley Library: A Personal Selection*, ed. H. George Fletcher (Maggs Bros & Pierpont Morgan Library, 1999). Catalogue compiled by H. George Fletcher, Robert J. D. Harding, Brywn Maggs, William Voelkel, and Roger Wieck. *Catalogue of the Antiquarian Booksellers Association*, June 2003, 17.

Figure 2.8 Title page of *Esther Inglis's Les Proverbes de Salomon*.

After her husband's death, Lady Getty joined the Roxburghe Club in 2007 and presented a facsimile manuscript with an introduction by Nicolas Barker, originally created in 1601 by Esther Inglis for Catherine de Bourbon, King Henry IV's sister (Figure 2.8). Titled *Esther Inglis's Les Proverbes de Salomon*, it represents the calligraphy of Esther Inglis, who made similar beautiful examples of religious texts for other royalty and important persons in Edinburgh (Figure 2.9).[72] Notably, the presentation book features the manuscript production of a female calligrapher who most likely was paid for her work.

The Wormsley Library is still housed within a private home and as such does not offer ready public access to the magnificent library there. Lady Getty's stepson, Mark Getty, an Irish businessman, owns Wormsley. He joined the Roxburghe Club in 2008.

---

[72] This volume is described in greater detail and is available for sale at the Maggs bookseller. Accessed August 21, 2018. https://www.maggs.com/departments/roxburghe_club/authors/inglis/esther-inglis andrsquos-les-proverbes-de-salomon-a-facsimile-with-an-introduction-by-nicolas-barker/230334/.

Facsimile of a calligraphic manuscript of *Les Proverbes de Salomon* written by Esther Inglis in Edinburgh in 1601 originally for Catherine de Bourbon (1558–1604), sister of King Henri IV, altered probably for Sir Thomas and Lady Hayes. The manuscript was acquired by the late Sir Paul Getty, K.B.E. in 1977 and is now in The Wormsley Library.

Figure 2.9 Esther Inglis, 1571–1624. Calligrapher and miniaturist.

Scottish National Portrait Gallery. Artist Unknown. 1595. Gifted by the Society of Antiquaries of Scotland in 2009. Photography by Antonia Reeve.

The Honourable Hannah Mary Rothschild, Commander of the Order of the British Empire

Hannah Mary Rothschild, the most recently elected female member of the Roxburghe Club, is the daughter and granddaughter of Roxburghe members—Jacob Rothschild (born 1936; member from 1995) is her father[73] and Victor Rothschild is her grandfather(1910–90; member from 1936 to his death).[74] She is a writer; filmmaker; company director; and assists with the estate, Waddesdon Manor, where she is a trustee. She is also a trustee of the Rothschild Foundation and of the Tate Gallery in London. She holds the distinction of serving as the first woman chair of the Board of Trustees for the National Gallery in London, where she has been on the board since 2009. Hannah married William Lord Brookfield in 1994 and has three daughters. Her creative output and biographical information appear on her website.[75]

In addition to documentary films and other publications, Hannah Rothschild is the author of a biographical article and book, and has created a film about her great aunt Kathleen Annie Pannonica de Koenigswarter, Baroness de Koenigswarter.[76] Her great aunt "Nica" supported the work of jazz artists, in particular, Thelonious Monk, and led a life quite different from what one might expect given her upbringing at Waddeson Manor. Hannah's documentary film about Nica's life, *The Jazz Baroness* (2009), explores her move to New York in 1951, where she abandons her former life and family to immerse herself in the jazz scene.

Waddesdon Manor represents but one of the many Rothschild family estates and was built for Baron Ferdinand de Rothschild in the nineteenth century. In addition to the rare books, collections include Sèvres porcelain; eighteenth-century French furniture, paintings, prints, and drawings; and illuminated manuscripts.[77] The library materials are being digitized and selections from the collection are displayed on the website as Hidden Treasures.[78] The web content offers a wealth of information, including provenance, description of manuscripts, bibliography, and so on. The estate has a new purpose-built archival building to care for the collections.

---

[73] Barker, *Bicentenary*, 300.

[74] Barker, *Bicentenary*, 199.

[75] For a list of articles, books, and screenplays written by Hannah Rothschild, accessed February 12, 2019, see http://www.hannahrothschild.com/writing.html/.

[76] Hannah Rothschild, "Koenigswarter [née Rothschild], (Kathleen Annie) Pannonica [Nica] de, baroness de Koenigswarter [known as the Jazz Baroness] (1913–1988), musical patron," *Oxford Dictionary of National Biography*. Accessed 1 August 1, 2018. http://www.oxforddnb.com/view/10.1093/ref:odnb/9780198614128.001.0001/odnb-9780198614128-e-101125/.

[77] Eriksen, S. *Waddeson Manor: The James A. Rothschild bequest to the National Trust: a guide to the house and its contents* (Freiburg: Freiburg, Office du Livre, 1973). See also http://waddesdon.org.uk/the-collection/item/?id=1771/. This example's provenance indicates that it was acquired by Bernard Quaritch, a dealer who also acquired part of the Frances Currer library.

[78] "Waddesdon. Hidden Treasures." Accessed February 13, 2019. https://waddesdon.org.uk/highlights/hidden-treasures/.

Each of the women in the Roxburghe Club enjoyed the benefits of access to things beautiful, to knowledge, travel, privilege, and persons of influence. Although they may have inherited books or entertained their husband's book-collecting friends and interests, some did guide the selection of books and manuscripts acquired for their libraries according to their own interests. The Appendix lists publications written by these women. Fortunately, through their unique contributions to Roxburghe Club activities and through their generous philanthropy, their collections enrich the lives of others and offer somewhat wider access to rarities from once-rarified settings.

Appendix
Publications by Women of the Roxburghe Club

Mary Morley (née Crapo) Hyde Eccles, Viscountess Eccles

Eccles, Mary Hyde. *The Impossible Friendship; Boswell and Mrs. Thrale.* London: Chatto & Windus, 1973.

———. *Julian Boyd & the Battlefield of Hastings: The Robert L. Nikirk Lecture, 2002.* New York: Grolier Club, 2003.

———. *Levée at Fifty-Third Street [play].* Cambridge, UK: University Printing House, 1972.

———. *Playwriting for Elizabethans, 1600–1605* (Columbia University Studies in English and Comparative Literature; no. 167). New York: Columbia University Press, 1949.

———. *Playwriting for Elizabethans, 1600–1605.* New York: Octagon Books, 1973.

———. *Shakespeare, Jr.* Philadelphia: [publisher not identified], 1946.

Eccles, Mary Hyde, Bruce Redford, and Johnsonians (Sociey). *"Dr. Johnson's Life in scenes": A Reproduction of Those Leaves from James Boswell's Manuscript of the Life (Houghton fMS Eng 1386) in Which Dr. Johnson Dines with Mr. Wilkes.* New York: The Johnsonians, 2003.

Eccles, Mary Hyde, and William Zachs. *Mary Hyde Eccles: A Miscellany of Her Essays and Addresses.* New York: Grolier Club, 2002.

Eccles, Stoddard, Mary Hyde Eccles, and Roger E. Stoddard. *Levée at Fifty-Third Street.* Cambridge UK: University Printing House, 1972.

Houghton Library, D. Hyde, M. H. E. Eccles, and S. Ives. *An Exhibit of Books and Manuscripts from the Johnsonian Collection formed by Mr. and Mrs. Donald F. Hyde at Four Oaks Farm.* Cambridge, MA: Houghton Library, 1966.

Hyde, Mary. *The Impossible Friendship: Boswell and Mrs. Thrale.* Cambridge, MA: Harvard University Press, 1972.

Hyde, Mary Morley. (1965). *"Not in Chapman."* Oxford: Clarendon Press.

McAdam, E. L., Donald F. Hyde, and Mary Hyde. *Samuel Johnson: Diaries, Prayers and Annals.* Vol 1. New Haven, CT: Yale University Press, 1958. http://www.yalejohnson.com/frontend/sda_viewer?n=106841

Piozzi, Hester Lynch, Mary Hyde Eccles, and Edith Goodkind Rosenwald. *The Thrales of Streatham Park.* Cambridge, MA: Harvard University Press, 1977.

Shaw, Bernard, Alfred Bruce Douglas, and Mary Hyde Eccles. *Bernard Shaw and Alfred Douglas, a correspondence.* New Haven, CT: Ticknor & Fields, 1982.

Auction Catalogue

Eccles, Mary. *Fine Printed Books and Manuscripts Including Americana: Property from the Estate of Mary, Viscountess Eccles, Illinois Institute of Technology, The Western Reserve Historical Society ...* ; Thursday 16 December 2004; auction.

Autograph Collection at Houghton

Eccles, Mary Hyde. *Mary Hyde Eccles Papers, 1853–2005: Guide.* Cambridge, MA: Houghton Library, Harvard Library, Harvard University.

Graff, Robert D., and Marjorie S. Graff. *Mary Hyde Eccles Papers, Ca. 1953–1983.* Unprocessed letters at Houghton, requires permission of curator to access, 1953. http://id.lib.harvard.edu/alma/990115420960203941/catalog.

Christian Mary McEwen, Dowager Lady Hesketh, OBE, DL, PhD

Hesketh, Christian. "The Political Opposition to the Government of Charles I in Scotland." PhD diss., University of London, 1999.

Hesketh, Christian, Elisabeth Luard, and Laura Blond. *The Country House Cookery Book.* 1st U.S. ed. New York: St. Martin's Press, 1985.

Hesketh, Christian, and Royal Stuart Society. *Charles I's Coronation Visit to Scotland in 1633* [Paper], 52. London: Royal Stuart Society, 1998.

Linklater, Magnus, and Christian Hesketh. *For King and Conscience: John Graham of Claverhouse, Viscount Dundee, 1648–1689.* London: Weidenfeld and Nicolson, 1989.

Lady Jane Roberts, DCVO (1949–2021)

Doyle, K., and S. McKendrick. *1000 Years of Royal Books and Manuscripts.* London: The British Library, 2013. http://id.lib.harvard.edu/alma/990139429690203941/catalog

Keele, Kenneth D., Jane Roberts, Windsor Castle Royal Library, & Metropolitan Museum of Art. (1983). *Leonardo da Vinci: Anatomical drawings from the Royal Library, Windsor Castle* [catalogue]. New York: Metropolitan Museum of Art, 1983.

Marschner, J., D. Bindman, L. Ford, Yale Center for British Art, and Historic Royal Palaces. *Enlightened Princesses: Caroline, Augusta, Charlotte, and the Shaping of the Modern World.* New Haven, CT: Yale University Press, 2017. http://id.lib.harvard.edu/alma/990149292970203941/catalog

Marshal, A., J. Fisher, & Windsor Castle Royal Library. *Mr. Marshal's flower album: From the Royal Library at Windsor Castle.* London: Victor Gollancz, 1985. [Preface by Jane Roberts.]

Pedretti, Carlo. *Leonardo's Horses: Studies of Horses and Other Animals by Leonardo da Vinci from the Royal Library at Windsor Castle: Florence, Palazzo Vecchio, 19 May–30 September 1984.* Firenze: Giunti Barbèra, 1984. [Preface by H.R.H. the Duke of Edinburgh; catalogue by Carlo Pedretti; introduction by Jane Roberts.]

Roberts, J., "Edward Harding and Queen Charlotte," in *Burning Bright: Essays in Honour of David Bindman*, eds. Diana Dethloff, Tessa, and Kim Sloan. London: UCL Press, 2015.

———, ed., *George III & Queen Charlotte. Patronage, Collecting and Court Taste.* London: Royal Collection Trust, 2002.

———. *Queen Elizabeth II: A Birthday Souvenir Album.* London: Royal Collection, 2006.

———. *Queen's Gallery, & Buckingham Palace. Royal Treasures: A Golden Jubilee Celebration.* London: Royal Collection, 2002.

———. *Royal Artists: From Mary Queen of Scots to the Present Day.* London: Grafton, 1987.

———. *Royal Landscape: The Gardens and Parks of Windsor.* New Haven, CT: Yale University Press, 1997.

———, ed., *Royal Treasures: A Golden Jubilee Celebration.* London: Royal Collection Trust, 2002.

———. *Treasures: The Royal Collection.* London: Royal Collection Publications and Scala, 2008.

Roberts, J., M. Hirst, and National Gallery of Art. *A Dictionary of Michelangelo's Watermarks.* Milan: Olivetti, 1988. ["This book is published by Olivetti on the occasion of the exhibition 'Michelangelo Draftsman' presented at the National Gallery of Art, Washington, 9 Oct.–11 Dec. 1988," 4.]

Roberts, J., J. Marsden, Queen's Gallery, Palace of Holyroodhouse, and Royal Collection Trust. *The King's Head: Charles I, King and Martyr.* London: Royal Collection Enterprises Limited, 1999. [exhibition catalogue].

Roberts, J., and Palazzo Vecchio. *The Codex Hammer of Leonardo da Vinci: The Waters, the Earth, the Universe* [exhibition] Florence. Palazzo Vecchio, Los Angeles: Armand Hammer Foundation, 1982.

Roberts, J., T. Sandby, Paul Sandby, and Rijksmuseum. *Views of Windsor: Watercolours by Thomas and Paul Sandby: From the Collection of Her Majesty Queen Elizabeth II.* London: Merrell Holberton, 1995.

Roberts, J., P. Sutcliffe, and S. Mayor *Unfolding Pictures: Fans in the Royal Collection*. London: Royal Collection, 2005.

Roberts, J., Windsor Castle Royal Library and Queen's Gallery. *Master Drawings in the Royal Collection: From Leonardo da Vinci to the Present Day*. London: Collins Harvill in association with The Queen's Gallery, 1986.

Roberts, J., and R. Wong. *Charles, Prince of Wales: A Birthday Souvenir Album*. London: Royal Collection Publications, 2008.

Roberts, Jane, and Hans Holbein. *Holbein*. London: Chaucer, 2005.

Roberts, Jane, Hans Holbein, and Museum of Fine Arts, Houston. *Drawings by Holbein from the Court of Henry VIII: Fifty Drawings from the Collection of Her Majesty Queen Elizabeth II, Windsor Castle: The Museum of Fine Arts, Houston, 17 May–16 August 1987* (1st ed.). New York: Johnson Reprint, 1987.

Roberts, Jane, and Queen's Gallery. *George III and Queen Charlotte: Patronage, Collecting and Court Taste*. London: Royal Collection Publication, 2004s.

Roberts, Jane, Queen's Gallery, and Buckingham Palace. *Royal Treasures: A Golden Jubilee Celebration*. London: Royal Collection, 2002.

Honourable Hannah Rothschild, CBE

Arthur, Olivia, and Hannah Rothschild. "The A-List: Looking Back." *Harper's Bazaar* (London) (February 2013): 128–37.

Auerbach, J., H. Rothschild, R. McNab, Jake Auerbach Films Ltd., and Arts Council of England. *Kitaj: In the Picture*. Academic Video Online: Premium. London: Arts Council England, 1994.

———. *Sickert's London*. Academic Video Online: Premium. Manchester, England: Arts Council England, 1992.

Fairweather, Catherine, and Hannah Rothschild. "The King and I." *Harper's Bazaar* (2013): 165–69.

Lee, Helena, and Hannah Rothschild. "Picture This." *Harper's Bazaar* (2015): 124.

Patalay, Ajesh, and Hannah Rothschild. "The Director Uncut." *Harper's Bazaar* (2013): 133–35.

———. "Dream Machines." *Harper's Bazaar* (2013): 104–05.

Rothschild, Hannah. "Amazing Grayson." *Harper's Bazaar* (London) (November 2014): 232–37.

———. "The Art of War." *Harper's Bazaar* (November 2013): 52–59.

———. "The Baroness." *Harper's Bazaar* (London) (2012): 109.

———. *The Baroness: The Search for Nica, the Rebellious Rothschild*. First American ed. New York: Alfred A. Knopf, 2013.

———. Brights of Spring." *Harper's Bazaar* (London) (March 2013): 241.

———. "Costume Drama." *Harper's Bazaar* (London) (November 2013): 214–17, 254.

———. "Fabrics of Time." *Harper's Bazaar* (London) (March 2013): 312–17.

———. "Georgia on My Mind." *Spectator* April 28, 2007.

———. "Handle With Care." *Harper's Bazaar* (London) (April 2013): 144.

———. *The Improbability of Love: A Novel* London, UK: Bloomsbury, 2015.

———. "The Jazz Baroness." *Jewish Quarterly* 55, no. 2 (2008): 60–65.

———. "Koenigswarter [née Rothschild], (Kathleen Annie) Pannonica [Nica] De, Baroness De Koenigswarter [known as the Jazz Baroness] (1913–1988), Musical Patron." *Oxford Dictionary of National Biography*, Oxford: Oxford University Press, September 23, 2010.

———. "The New Season Starts Here." *Harper's Bazaar* (London) (June 2013): 115–17.

———. "Lord in the Wings." *Harper's Bazaar* (2010): 132.

———. "Making Your Mark." *Harper's Bazaar* (London) (October 2013): 210–11.

———. "On a Roll." *Harper's Bazaar* (London) no. 91 (2013): 310–11.

———. "1 An English Country Garden." *Harper's Bazaar* (London) (August 2013): 95–96.

———. "Silver Screen Dream Team." *Harper's Bazaar* (London) (February 2013): 138–41.

———. "The Titian Detective Story." *Harper's Bazaar* (London) (January 2013): 126–29, 172.

Rothschild, Hannah, and Leslie Megahey. *Keeping Up with the Medici. Vol. 2*. Academic Video Online: Premium. London: British Broadcasting Corporation, 1991.

Select Bibliography

Attar, Karen, ed., and Chartered Institute of Library Information Professionals. Rare Books Special Collections Group, Issuing Body. *Directory of Rare Book and Special Collections in the United Kingdom and the*

Republic of Ireland. 3rd ed. London: Facet Publishing, 2016.

Austin, Gabriel, and Donald Frizell Hyde. *Four Oaks Library.* Somerville, NJ: Thistle Press, 1967. [Vol. 2 has *Four Oaks Farm.*

Barber, Brian. "Working in 'The Cause of Bibliomania throughout the World': Sir Thomas Brooke (1830–1908), a Yorkshire Businessman-Bibliophile." *Yorkshire Archaeological Journal* 90, no. 1 (2018): 158–77.

Barker, Nicolas. *The Publications of the Roxburghe Club, 1814–1962.* Cambridge: Roxburghe Club, 1964. [Nicholas John Barker is himself a Roxburghe Club member, elected in 1970.]

———. "Mary, Viscountess Eccles." *Independent,* 20 (5 September 2003). Retrieved from https://ucd.idm.oclc.org/login?url=https://search.-proquest.com/docview/1035726501?accountid=14507.

———. *The Roxburghe Club: A Bicentenary History.* [London]: Roxburghe Club, 2012.

———. "Sir Paul Getty, Contemporary Collectors LVI." *Book Collector,* 53(2) (2004): 181–212.

Beros, M. "Bibliomania: Thomas Frognall Dibdin and Early 19th Century Book Collecting." TXT I, no. 1 (Boom Uitgevers 2014): 140–45.

Bigham, Clive. *The Roxburghe Club: Its History and Its Members 1812–1927.* Oxford: Printed for the Roxburghe Club at the University Press, 1928. [Bigham was a member of the Roxburghe Club.]

Black, Alistair, and Peter Hoare, eds. *The Cambridge History of Libraries in Britain and Ireland.* Vol. 3, 1850–2000. Cambridge, UK: Cambridge University Press.

Bloomfield, B. C., and Library Association. Rare Books Group. *A Directory of Rare Book and Special Collections in the United Kingdom and the Republic of Ireland.* 2nd ed. London: Library Association Publishing in Association with Rare Books Group of the Library Association, 1997.

Boran, Elizabeth, ed. *Book Collecting in Ireland and Britain, 1650–1850.* Dublin, Ireland: Four Courts Press, 2018.

Brant, S., A. Barclay, and T. H. Jamieson (1874). *The Ship of Fools. Translated by Alexander Barclay. [Reprinted from Pynson's edition of 1509; with introduction, "Notice of the Life and Writings of A. Barclay," and "A Bibliographical Catalogue of Barclay's Works." by T.H. Jamieson. With woodcuts.].* 2 vols. (Edinburgh: William Paterson; London: Henry Sotheran & Co., 1874. Reprint of 1509 Pynson edition.

Cone, Polly, ed. *A Guide to the Wrightsman Galleries at the Metropolitan Museum of Art /* entries by James Parker, curator and Clare LeCorbeiller, associate curator, Dept. of European Sculpture and Decorative

Arts. New York: Metropolitan Museum of Art, 1979.

Dawson, George E., and Grabhorn Press. *Chronology of Twenty-five Years: The Roxburghe Club of San Francisco, 1928–1953*. San Francisco: Grabhorn Press, 1954.

Desbans, Edme Louis, Gabriel Jacques de Saint-Aubin, Neil MacGregor, and Jayne Wrightsman. *Placets de l'officier Desbans*. New York: Privately printed for members of the Roxburghe Club, 2007.

Dibdin, Thomas Frognall. *The Bibliomania; or, Book-madness; Containing Some Account of the History, Symptoms, and Cure of This Fatal Disease. In an Epistle Addressed to Richard Heber, Esq*. London, Printed by W. Savage, 1809.

———. Londres: Longman, Hurst, Rees and Orme, 1809.

———. London: Printed for the author, and sold by Messrs. Longman, Hurst, Rees, Orme, and Brown, 1811.

———. *New ... edition to which are now added preliminary observations, and a supplement including a key to the assumed characters in the drama*. London: H. G. Bohn, 1842.

———. London: Chatto and Windus, 1886.

———. *Bibliotheca Spenceriana, or a descriptive catalogue of the books printed in the fifteenth century and of many valuable first editions in the library of Georg John, earl Spencer ... - Aedes Althorpianae, or an account of the mansion, books and pictures at Althorp, the residence of George John, earl Spencer. To which is added a supplement to the Bibliotheca Spenceriana, ... - A Descriptive Catalogue of the books printed in the fifteenth century, lately forming part of the library of the duke di Cassano Serra and now the property of George John, earl Spencer, ... with a general Index of authors and editions, contained in the present volume and in the Bibliotheca Spenceriana and Aedes Althorpianae*. London, 1814–23.

"Donald Frizell Hyde 1909–1966," *The Papers of the Bibliographical Society of America* 60, no. 1 (1966): 101. https://doi.org/10.1086/pbsa.60.1.24300912

Doyle, Kathleen, and Scot McKendrick, eds. *1000 Years of Royal Books and Manuscripts*. London: The British Library, 2013.

Eccles, Mary Hyde & Zachs, William & Grolier Club. *Mary Hyde Eccles: A Miscellany of Her Essays and Addresses*. New York: Grolier Club, 2002.

Elliott, I. 2004 "Parsons, Laurence, Fourth Earl of Rosse (1840–1908), Astronomer and Engineer." *Oxford Dictionary of National Biography*. Accessed August 10, 2018. http://www.oxforddnb.com/view/10.1093/ref:odnb/9780198614128.001.0001/odnb-9780198614128-e-35398.

Eriksen, S. *Waddeson Manor: The James A. Rothschild Bequest to the National Trust: A Guide to the House and Its Contents.* Freiburg: Office du Livre, 1973.

Evans, R. *A Catalogue of the Library of the Late John, Duke of Roxburghe.* Cambridge, UK: Cambridge University Press, 2014. https://play.google.com/books/reader?id=B1EVAAAAQAAJ&printsec=frontcover&output=reader&hl=en_GB&pg=GBS.PP7

Evans, Robert H., John Ker, Duke of Roxburghe, George Nicol, and William Nicol. *A Catalogue of the Library of the Late John, Duke of Roxburghe.* London: Robert H. Evans, 1812.

Evans, Roxburghe, & John Ker Roxburghe. *A Supplement to the Catalogue of the Library of the Late John, Duke of Roxburghe: The Books Will Be Sold ... the 13th of July 1812 and Three Following Days by Robert H. Evans.* London: Robert H. Evans, 1812.

Fahy, Everett, ed. *The Wrightsman Pictures.* New York: Metropolitan Museum of Art, 2005.

Husbands, S. *The Early Roxburghe Club, 1812–1835: Book Club Pioneers and the Advancement of English Literature.* London, UK: Anthem Press, 2017.

Hyde Eccles collection, 1903–2002 (bulk 1959–2002). Grolier Club, New York.

Inglis, Esther. (2012.) Esther Inglis's *Les Proverbes de Salomon* a facsimile with an introduction by Nicolas Barker.

"In Memorium: Donald F. Hyde." *The Bulletin of the American Society of Papyrologists* 3, no. 2 (1966): 53–55. https://www.jstor.org/stable/24519514.

Jerdan, William. "Roxburghe Club." *The Literary Gazette: A Weekly Journal of Literature, Science, and the Fine Arts* 2, no. 74 (1818): 393.

Johnson, S., & Bruce Redford. *The Letters of Samuel Johnson.* Princeton, NJ: Princeton University Press, 1992.

Lagorio, Valerie M. "The Roxburghe Club Collection." *Books at Iowa,* no. 35 (1981): 14–18. https://doi.org/10.17077/0006-7474.1427

Lee, Colin. "Currer, Frances Mary Richardson (1785–1861), Book Collector." *Oxford Dictionary of National Biography.* Oxford: Oxford University Press, 2004.

Leedham-Green, Elisabeth, and Teresa Webber, eds. *The Cambridge History of Libraries in Britain and Ireland.* Vol. 1, to 1640. Cambridge, UK: Cambridge University Press.

Lloyd, Andrea. "The Lady Eccles Oscar Wilde Collection." *The Electronic British Library Journal* 10 (2010): 1–13.

Mandelbrote, Giles, and K. A. Manley, eds. *The Cambridge History of Libraries in Britain and Ireland* Vol. 2, 1640–1850. Cambridge, UK: Cambridge University Press, 2006.

Mary Hyde Eccles Papers, 1853–2005 (MS Hyde 98). Cambridge, MA: Houghton Library, Harvard University.

Masters, C. "Wrightsman, Charles B(ierer)." *Grove Art Online* (2003). Accessed July 16, 2018. http:////www.oxfordartonline.com/groveart/view/10.1093/gao/9781884446054.001.0001/oao-9781884446054-e-7000092360.

McKenna, N. "A Great Archive Finally Finds Its Rightful Place." *The Times* (4 Feb 2005). Retrieved from https://ucd.idm.oclc.org/login?url=https://search.proquest.com/docview/319260812?accountid=14507

McKitterick, David. "Books in Turmoil." In *The Invention of Rare Books: Private Interest and Public Memory, 1600–1840*, 250–68. Cambridge, UK: Cambridge University Press, 2018.

Overholt, John. *A Monument More Durable than Brass: The Donald & Mary Hyde Collection of Dr. Samuel Johnson: An Exhibition.* Cambridge, MA: Houghton Library, Harvard University, 2009.

Papers of the Dukes and Dukedom of Roxburghe, 1806–1924, administrative/biographical information compiled by Graeme D Eddie. Edinburgh University Library, Special Collections Division. https://archiveshub.jisc.ac.uk/search/archives/cbc949db-72ba-3f29-9859-c79a739c1ab8.

Parker, James, and Clare Le Corbeiller. *A Guide to the Wrightsman Galleries at The Metropolitan Museum of Art.* New York: Metropolitan Museum of Art, 1979.

Pugh, Martin. "Eccles, David McAdam, first Viscount Eccles (1904–1999), businessman and politician." *Oxford Dictionary of National Biography.* Oxford: Oxford University Press, 2009. Accessed August 14, 2018. http://www.oxforddnb.com/view/10.1093/ref:odnb/9780198614128.001.0001/odnb-9780198614128-e-71965.

Purcell, Mark. *The Big House Library in Ireland: Books in Ulster Country Houses.* Swindon, Wiltshire: National Trust, 2011.

———. *The Country House Library.* New Haven, CT: Yale University Press, 2017. Published for National Trust. Chapter 7 is about the Roxburghe Club.

Quaritch, Bernard. *List of Roxburghe Club Publications. Offered at the Net Prices Affixed by Bernard Quaritch.* London: B. Quaritch, 1927.

Redford, B. "Mary Hyde Eccles." *Proceedings of the American Philosophical Society* 152, no. 2 (2008): 239–41. Retrieved from https://ucd.idm.

oclc.org/login?url=https://search.proquest.com/docview/220898840?accountid=145

———. "Obituary: Mary, Viscountess Eccles: Anglophile Scholar and Benefactor Who Amassed the World's Finest Collection of 18th-Century English Literature." *The Guardian* [London (UK)] (16 Sep 2003): 1.25.

———. "Eccles [née Crapo; Other Married Name Hyde], Mary Morley, Viscountess Eccles (1912–2003), Literary Collector and Scholar." *Oxford Dictionary of National Biography*. Oxford: Oxford University Press, 2007. Accessed August 14, 2018. http://www.oxforddnb.com/view/10.1093/ref:odnb/9780198614128.001.0001/odnb-9780198614128-e-92856.

———. "Mary Hyde Eccles (1912–2003)". *The Princeton University Library Chronicle* 65, no. 1 (2003): 124–27. http://www.jstor.org/stable/10.25290/prinunivlibrchro.65.1.0124

Redford, B., Mary Hyde Eccles, Princeton University Press, & The Donald & Mary Hyde Collection of Dr. Samuel Johnson (Houghton Library). (1983). Bruce Redford Papers Concerning The Letters of Samuel Johnson, 1983–1992 (MS Hyde 99) Houghton Library, Harvard University.

Richardson Currer, Miss, 1785–1861; Stewart, Charles James, 1799–1883. *A Catalogue of the Library Collected by Miss Richardson Currer, at Eshton Hall, Craven, Yorkshire*. London: Printed for private circulation only [by J. Moyes], 1833.

Richardson, John V. 2004; 2015. "Thomas Frognall Dibin." *Oxford Dictionary of National Biography*. Oxford: Oxford University Press. Accessed July 20, 2018. https://doi.org/10.1093/ref:odnb/7588.

Robinson, J. *Felling the Ancient Oaks: How England Lost Its Great Country Estates*. London: Aurum Press, 2011.

Roxburghe, J., William Nicol, and George Nicol. *A Catalogue of the Library of the Late John: Duke of Roxburghe, Arranged by G. and W. Nicol ... Which Will Be Sold by auction ... 18th May, 1812, and the Forty-One Following Days, Sundays Excepted ...* London: Printed by W. Bulmer and Co, 1812.

"The Roxburghe Club." *The Quarterly Review* 82, no. 164 (1848): 309.

Rothschild, H. (2017, September 01). "Koenigswarter [née Rothschild], (Kathleen Annie) Pannonica [Nica] de, baroness de Koenigswarter [known as the Jazz Baroness] (1913–1988), Musical Patron." *Oxford Dictionary of National Biography*. Oxford: Oxford University Press. Accessed August 1, 2018. http://www.oxforddnb.com/view/10.1093/ref:odnb/9780198614128.001.0001/odnb-9780198614128-e-101125.

Schreyer, Alice D. *Elective Affinities: Private Collectors & Special Collections in Libraries.* Chicago: The University of Chicago Library, 2001.

Shaw, Bernard, Alfred Bruce Douglas, and Mary Hyde Eccles. *Bernard Shaw and Alfred Douglas: a correspondence.* Oxford: Oxford University Press, 1989.

Shirley, Evelyn Philip. *Catalogue of the library at Lough Fea, in illustration of the history and antiquities of Ireland.* London: Chiswick Press, 1872. Privately printed.

Sotheby's (Firm). *Easton Neston, Towcester Northamptonshire: Selected contents sold on the instructions of the Lord and Lady Hesketh and the Trustees of Frederick, 2nd Baron Hesketh, deceased.* London: Sotheby's, 2005.

———. *Books and Manuscripts from the Fermor-Hesketh Library at Easton Neston: Auction: Wednesday 15 December 1999; Sale L09223.* London: Sotheby's, 1999.

———. *Magnificent Books, Manuscripts and Drawings From the Collection of Frederick, 2nd Lord Hesketh. 3 Volumes Complete Set. Part I; Part II: Audubon the Birds of America; Part III: Redoute's Les Roses.* London: Sotheby's, 2010.

"Sotheby's auction catalogs. Print Collection 42." Finding aid prepared by Isabel Gendler. University of Pennsylvania, Kislak Center for Special Collections, Rare Books and Manuscripts. Accessed January 17, 2018. http://hdl.library.upenn.edu/1017/d/ead/upenn_rbml_PUSpPrintCollection42.

Stanfill, Francesca. "Jayne's World." *Vanity Fair* (January 2003): 105–18. [Blog], accessed July 16, 2018. http://francescastanfill.squarespace.com/jaynes-world.

Turnbull, Gordon. "Boswell, James (1740–1795), Lawyer, Diarist, and Biographer of Samuel Johnson." *Oxford Dictionary of National Biography.* Oxford: Oxford University Press, 2006. Accessed August 14, 2018. http://www.oxforddnb.com/view/10.1093/ref:odnb/9780198614128.001.0001/odnb-9780198614128-e-2950.

Watson, F. J. B., Carl Christian Dauterman, and Everett Fahy. *The Wrightsman Collection. Vols. 3 and 4, Furniture, Snuffboxes, Silver, Bookbindings, Porcelain.* New York: Metropolitan Museum of Art, 1970.

Wheat, C. "Joseph Haslewood and the Roxburghe Club." *Huntington Library Quarterly* 11, no. 1 (1947): 37–49.

Wrightsman, Charles B., Jayne Wrightsman, F. J. B. Watson, Carl Christian Dauterman, and Everett Fahy. *The Wrightsman Collection.* New York: Metropolitan Museum of Art, 1966.

Zachs, William. *Re-collecting Donald and Mary Hyde: Untold Stories from Their Private Archive.* New York: American Trust for the British Library, 2009.

II

Building Collections

3

Ushering in the Era of Expansion: Academic Libraries Supporting Change in American Higher Education, 1860–1920

Katy B. Mathuews

Academic libraries are complex institutions that have evolved with the changing ideals of American higher education. Taking on the culture and politics of the parent institution, academic libraries have been at the forefront of growth and innovation in American higher education, supporting the goals of the profession, the institution, the curriculum, and the research agenda. From the Colonial college to the multiversity,[1] the library remains a steadfast, yet flexible, pillar of support on the college campus. This is particularly true in the decades surrounding the turn of the twentieth century as the American academy expanded in scope and scale.

This chapter includes a broad explanation of how academic libraries evolved to support the changing needs and ideals of American higher education. Focusing on the years 1860–1920, the trends of increased access to higher education, expanded curriculum, and specialized research agendas are highlighted. The accompanying changes in academic libraries are also highlighted, including the professionalization of librarianship

---

[1] Clark Kerr, *The Uses of the University* (Cambridge, MA: Harvard University Press, 1964).

and expanding access, collections, and services using Ohio University's library as a brief case study. As these trends are complex, it is beyond the scope of this chapter to thoroughly examine each in depth. Instead, this chapter provides foundational knowledge and context to better understand the proliferation of the academy and academic libraries at a notable time in the history of American higher education. Before proceeding with this task, however, a brief history of American higher education up to 1860 is presented.

Historical Background

Libraries have long supported scholarly pursuits and cultural preservation. Written records indicate that as far back as 3000 BC, libraries in Sumeria and Egypt served as archives for the business of the day and as caretakers of the written knowledge of such fields as medicine, law, mathematics, and religion. The Sumerian and Egyptian libraries were often paired with religious or cultural institutions. The scope of libraries evolved when the eighth-century Assyrian king Ashurbanipal expanded his extensive family library to serve not just as an archive of records, but to also support educational growth. Dubbed the *Royal Library*, this collection is believed to be the first with the primary mission of education and research. The collection included works on a wide range of topics from all over the known world.[2]

Beginning in the fifth century BC, the Greeks extended the educational role of libraries so they became repositories for new knowledge and the teachings of scholars such as Socrates, Plato, and Aristotle. The work of such scholars began to be recorded through the written word during this time, rather than transmitted using the oral tradition as in preceding years. The mission of the Greek Alexandrian Library was to collect the entire body of written work from the known world. Used primarily by scholars, the collection may have contained as many as 500,000 items on an array of subjects. Unfortunately, it is believed that by AD 270–275 the library was destroyed by fire. Fortunately, the Byzantine and Moslem libraries thrived from AD 450 to AD 1,000. These expansive libraries continued the mission of collecting a wide range of materials to support education and innovation. During the Middle Ages,

---

[2] Richard E. Rubin, *Foundations of Library and Information Science* (New York: Neal-Schuman Publishers, 2004), 260–62.

libraries in the Western world were embedded within religious institutions to support religious education.³

The first university library was established at the University of Paris in the mid-thirteenth century, followed by libraries at Oxford and Cambridge. Though the collections of these libraries were typically small, with less than 1,000 items, the books helped sustain the Renaissance. By the seventeenth century, the notion of preserving knowledge expanded to the creation of national libraries, often partnered with university libraries, such as the Bodleian Library at Oxford University, based on a depository system with limited circulation privileges.⁴

Academic libraries appeared in America during the Colonial era with nine libraries established by 1792, although they had not yet taken on the level of prominence in the campus ecology that they would a century later. The primary mission of the academic library during the Colonial era was to keep the records of the institution, support the curriculum, and protect the books and apparatus owned by the institution.⁵ Academic library collections of Colonial colleges were usually small and housed in one room within a main, multifunctional building.⁶

The curriculum of Colonial colleges, based in the classic liberal arts and heavily dependent on the model of lectures and recitations, did not require an extensive collection of books. Often established by wealthy donors from private collections, academic libraries of the Colonial colleges were also necessarily small as books were quite expensive due to limited production, access, and the available body of work at the time. For example, the libraries at Harvard and Yale contained only approximately 5,000 and 1,700 items, respectively, by the mid-1700s. Typically, Colonial college collections included only religious and language texts primarily donated by wealthy travelers who could afford books from European presses. Indeed, it is believed that less than 10 percent of the Colonial college library collection was the result of intentional spending by the university. Further, the Colonial college libraries were usually open a few hours a week, when daylight could light the space and when the library custodian, a secondary role of an assigned faculty member, was available to tend the space.⁷

---

³ Ibid., 263–69.
⁴ Ibid., 269–71.
⁵ Roger L. Geiger, *The History of American Higher Education: Learning and Culture from the Founding to World War II* (Princeton, NJ: Princeton University Press, 2015), 50.
⁶ Rubin, *Foundations*, 269–71.
⁷ Stephen E. Atkins, *The Academic Library in the American University* (Chicago: American Library Association, 1991), 3–5; John M. Budd, *The Changing Academic Library: Operations, Culture, Environments* (Chicago: Association of College and Research Libraries, 2012), 20; Rubin, *Foundations*, 273–74.

During the westward expansion of the post-Revolutionary War period, state governments supported rebuilding existing and creating new colleges and academic libraries. The curriculum also began to expand in the post-Revolutionary War period. Influenced by the likes of Benjamin Franklin and Thomas Jefferson, the curriculum began to slowly expand to include science, modern literature, agriculture, and more practical studies to spur the growth of the new republic.[8] During the Colonial era of higher education, the college curriculum was devoted to maintaining moral piety and developing leaders of government from among the privileged class. In the post-Revolutionary War period, the curriculum expanded to include the study of classical and modern languages, history, and science.[9]

At this time, the young nation was committed to building a successful republic. Institutions of higher learning were viewed as the cornerstone of a strong republic, shifting from religious aspirations to the ambition of unifying the young nation. Viewing the Colonial colleges as too tightly controlled by specific, mostly religious groups, the ideology of the new republic viewed higher education as a public good that could support the growth of the new nation. Thus, governmental officials began to serve on college governing boards and state governments began to seek authority over higher education institutions. Thus, the first state universities were founded as American higher education expanded its geographic reach. The curriculum also expanded during this time to emphasize morality and expanded professional studies, including navigation, architecture, and agriculture.[10]

The growth of state universities at the turn of the nineteenth century was accompanied by the growth of graduate and professional schools. This era in American higher education also saw a shift away from unifying and strengthening the republic to instead spur the expanding American economy, grounded in regional pride and prestige. During the Civil War, however, many schools, particularly those in the South, were destroyed. As the country began to revive in the aftermath of the Civil War, several winds of change blew through the landscape of American higher education.[11]

Until the Civil War, however, the geographic and ideologic expansion of American higher education did not emphasize the academic

---

[8] Budd, *The Changing Academic Library*, 21.
[9] Geiger, *The History of American Higher Education*, 42–48.
[10] Ibid., 91–92.
[11] Ibid., 123–269.

library. Though the library was often one of the first and most cherished components of an institution, building the system of higher education in America overshadowed the prominence of the library. The scarcity and high cost of books also contributed to the marginal role played by libraries as institutions struggled to maintain operating budgets. In fact, bankruptcy was the cause of over 67 percent of college failures in the 1840s.[12] The position of the academic library during this time in American history is best captured in a quote from then Harvard professor George Ticknor, "We have not yet learnt that the Library is not only the first convenience of a University, but that it is the very first necessity,—that is the life and spirit—and that all other considerations must yield to the prevalent one of increasing and opening it, and opening it on the most liberal terms to all who are disposed to make use of it."[13]

Changes in American Higher Education, 1860–1920

In the years following the Civil War, the landscape of American higher education shifted to accommodate new perspectives. Indeed, as Melvil Dewey asserted: "The colleges are awakening to the fact that the work of every professor and every department is necessarily based on the library; textbooks constantly yield their exalted places to wiser and broader methods; professor after professor sends his classes, or goes with them, to the library and teaches them to investigate for themselves, and to use books, getting beyond the method of primary school with its parrot-like recitations from a single text."[14] The era of change in libraries described by Dewey mirrored the changes faced by the broader higher education system, including increasing access to higher education, changes to the traditional liberal arts curriculum and pedagogy, and changing faculty research needs. These trends are explored in the text that follows.

Practical Studies and Increased Access

Following the practice of state governments supporting higher education, the federal government began to see value in supporting the growth of the higher education landscape. Initially, the federal government's involvement in higher education granted federal land to states to establish

---

[12] Atkins, *The Academic Library in the American University*, 5–8.
[13] Dale Allen Gyure, "The Heart of the University: A History of the Library as an Architectural Symbol of American Higher Education," *Winterthur Portfolio*, 42 no. 2/3 (2008): 9.
[14] Rubin, *Foundations*, 279.

education institutions.[15] Championed by Vermont Congressman Justin Morrill, the Morrill Land Grant Act of 1862 was signed by President Lincoln on July 2, 1862. The Act offered each state thirty-thousand acres of federal land per representative to develop institutions of higher education that, in addition to the classic liberal arts subjects, offered courses related to agriculture and the mechanical arts to support the professions needed in the growing republic.[16]

Morrill intended to open higher education to members of the so-called industrial classes. This would provide greater educational access to Americans who may not have been born into the privilege of the upper class. Morrill also intended for the Act to promote an educational curriculum that included agriculture and mechanical arts in addition to the traditional liberal arts education. It was believed this approach would provide students with an adaptable set of skills to participate in a variety of practical pursuits and to gain social footing. Morrill asserted that a citizenry educated with practical knowledge in addition to the liberal arts would help drive social and economic development as the United States approached the twentieth century. Particularly, Morrill wanted to encourage agricultural research to help the United States keep pace with European agricultural innovation.[17]

Curriculum Changes

Although the Morrill Land Grant Act of 1862 expanded the curriculum to include agriculture and mechanical arts, the general curriculum in higher education underwent several other major changes at the turn of the twentieth century. These changes included the new role research played and the initiation of the elective and major systems. These new components further increased the breadth and depth of American higher education.

The founding of Johns Hopkins University in 1876 sparked the effort to make research prominent in American institutions of higher education. The Johns Hopkins model was grounded in the German style of education in which research supported the foundation of the curriculum and pedagogy. The German-influenced method emphasized investigation and problem solving to search for truth. This new goal helped shift the pedagogy from one that is lecture and recitation based,

---

[15] Rubin, *Foundations*, 280.
[16] Geiger, *The History of American Higher Education*, 281–87.
[17] Geiger, *The History of American Higher Education*, 282.

to one that required the consultation of sources beyond the course textbook. This new research model blended nicely with the practical and applied methods of the land grant institutions and increased the importance of faculty research activities. Alongside this development, the offering of doctoral programs and fellowship opportunities increased the number of doctoral degrees granted from just three in 1861 to 382 in 1900.[18]

The importance of research in American higher education was bolstered by the idea of the professional scholar and the learned societies their disciplines created. The professional scholar was one who maintained teaching responsibilities while also engaging in research and innovation. The founding of professional societies, such as the American Historical Association and the Modern Language Association, among others, encouraged the production of journals to disseminate their members' research. Given the proliferation of research activities, institutions began to advocate for increased funding for the research as well as the facilities and resources required to conduct it. By 1900, the US federal government had allocated $11 million to support research.[19]

C. W. Eliot, Harvard president from 1869 to 1909, also ushered in important changes to the curriculum, shifting to an elective system of course offerings. In order for higher education to adapt to the increasing demand for practical and technical education, Eliot supported a more flexible curriculum, removing many of the subject requirements and incorporating an elective system before the turn of the twentieth century. This change expanded the number of departments and specializations of faculty on college campuses, shifting from narrow curriculum content to a greater flexibility in pursuing individual interests.[20]

The elective model was embraced by Cornell University, a land grant institution that opened in 1868. The Cornell philosophy blended the practical and technical spirit with the flexibility of the elective system, establishing a core of required classes for the first two years of study and electives beyond the first two years. This structure provided a foundation in liberal arts with the flexibility of specialization in practical and technical fields. By 1880, Cornell employed forty-seven professors, among the largest faculty roster in the country. The faculty worked in an array of disciplines with an environment ripe for cross-pollination.[21]

---

[18] Atkins, *The Academic Library in the American University*, 14–16; Budd, *The Changing Academic Library*, 26.
[19] Budd, *The Changing Academic Library*, 29.
[20] Atkins, *The Academic Library in the American University*, 13.
[21] Geiger, *The History of American Higher Education*, 288–90.

Thus, the academy moved from having a narrow focus on a core of required courses to an increasingly diverse, specialized, and flexible ecology. The increasing scope and expanding research agenda of American higher education depended on the academic library to support research and curriculum needs. Indeed, the academic library mimicked the expansion of the academy to support the creation, preservation, and dissemination of knowledge to drive teaching and learning.

Academic Libraries Respond to Change

As the academy expanded to include electives, practical studies, and a renewed commitment to specialized research, the academic library followed suit. Moving beyond serving as simple guardians of the university's collection of books, librarianship was professionalized to provide expert service to support teaching, learning, and research. Academic librarians helped usher in expanded access, collections, and services to meet the needs of an increasingly diverse and complex higher education environment.

Professionalization of Librarianship

The increased importance of research ushered in the values of academic freedom and professional scholarship. The creation of professional associations accelerated in the late 1880s to support specialized fields and to publish the cutting-edge research of the day. As previously mentioned, professional academic associations at this time prompted the establishment of journals to propagate the work of their members. The proliferation of professional and scholarly associations extended to the library world with the founding of the American Library Association (ALA) and its *Library Journal* in 1876.[22] The founding charter of ALA outlined:

> ... the intention of forming a corporation under the name of the American Library Association for the purpose of promoting [the] library interests [of the country] *throughout the world* by exchanging views, reaching conclusions, and inducing cooperation in all departments of bibliothecal science and economy; by disposing the public mind to the founding and improving of libraries; and by cultivating good will among its own members.[23]

---

[22] John M. Budd, *The Academic Library: Its Context, its Purpose, and Its Operation* (Englewood, CO: Libraries Unlimited, 1998) 36, 81.
[23] American Library Association, "Charter of 1879." http://www.ala.org/aboutala/charter-1879-revised-1942/.

Library Journal provided a foundation of communication for librarians to share a common body of professional thought and an arena to share ideas to push the profession forward. Indeed, in its first issue, an editorial called for a profession supported by a course of study. The professionalization of librarianship, it was argued, was necessary to help patrons effectively use the growing collections faced by libraries at the turn of the century. It was considered not just the job of a librarian to amass books, but also to help users access and responsibly use the information contained within their covers.[24]

Thus, the profession was formalized with the development of academic training in *library science*. Formerly known as *library economy*, even the shift in name marked the beginning of the professionalization of librarianship.[25] Dewey began the first library school at Columbia University in 1887. Many schools followed suit, developing master and doctoral degrees in library science. By the 1900s, the standard library school curriculum included cataloging and classification, bibliography, reference work, selection and accession of books, bookbinding, shelf department, loan department, library buildings, and organization and governance.[26]

As the profession developed, those practicing in the field began to advocate for uniform codes of practice. For example, this era saw the introduction of Dewey's classification system in 1876, followed by Charles Cutter's classification system, which served as a basis for the Library of Congress Classification system.[27] These uniform codes helped support the creation of textbooks for use in the library school curriculum. Such textbooks included Cutter's *Rules for a Dictionary Catalog*, ALA's *Condensed Rules for an Author and Title Catalog*, and Dewey's *Library School Accession Rules* and *Library School Shelflist Rules*.[28]

Expanded Collections and Buildings

The professionalization of scholarship that developed by the twentieth century generated a wealth of new books and academic journals, which were acquired by academic libraries to enhance their collections. For example, the University of Illinois grew its periodical subscription from

---

[24] C. M. White, *The Origins of the American Library School* (New York: Scarecrow Press, 1961), 66–67.
[25] Ibid., 12.
[26] Ibid., 90–94.
[27] Patrick M. Valentine, "The Origin of College Libraries in North Carolina: A Social History, 1890–1920," *Information and Culture* 41 no. 1 (2012): 79–112.
[28] Ibid., 98.

414 titles in 1900 to 9,943 in 1924. In addition, scholars required materials to support their research, thus library collections grew to accommodate their needs. Through faculty support, libraries of the early twentieth century were often allocated a substantial portion of the institutional budget to fund the growth of library collections.[29]

The goal of developing library collections at the turn of the twentieth century, then, was to collect an exhaustive breadth and depth of scholarly material. The size of collections was a bragging right for universities, so it was essential to amass expansive collections. The need for a sizable collection was also a practical one because academic libraries needed to have materials appropriate for a variety of undergraduate students and specialized faculty alike. The collections of the library mimicked the scholarly pursuits and degree offerings of the parent institution. The expansion of library collections is evident in inventory counts of the day. In 1876, for example, Harvard had 212,000 books, Yale had 95,200 books, Princeton had 29,500, and the University of Wisconsin had 6,670 books, with most other academic libraries holding about 6,715 books, on average.[30] Within 20 years, Harvard had grown to 452,500, Princeton had 171,000, and the University of Wisconsin had 135,000 books.[31] By 1920, Harvard had 2,028,100, Yale had 1,250,000, and other libraries, such as Cornell University and the University of Michigan, experienced a 600 percent growth in collections.[32]

Expanding collections required larger buildings. The decades surrounding the turn of the twentieth century saw a move from libraries housed in a single room of a multifunction building to buildings solely dedicated to housing library collections and services. The library buildings served as a status symbol and signaled the growing importance of the library on the college campus. Libraries became cathedral-like edifices that stood out in architecture and placement from other campus buildings. Although the trend of having a separate library had already been implemented at the University of Virginia, South Carolina College, and Harvard College, the proliferation of separate library buildings is evident from 1860–1920.[33]

Indeed, the number of academic libraries built in the United States grew from approximately three libraries in the 1860s to 116 in the first

---

[29] Budd, *The Academic Library*, 42.
[30] Gyure, "The Heart of the University," 115.
[31] Ibid., 121.
[32] Ibid., 107–11.
[33] Ibid., 107–32.

decade of the 1900s.[34] Library collections were growing so rapidly during this time period, in fact, that many collections outgrew their library buildings as quickly as they were built. This led architects to design libraries that allowed for future growth, often by building on additional wings. By the early 1900s, as stand-alone library buildings were constructed to accommodate ballooning collections, separate areas for reading, book storage, book processing, and reference and user services were in vogue.[35]

Expanded Access and Services

With more fields of study and increased emphasis on research, students and faculty needed more flexible access to library buildings and collections. No longer would the rules followed by the Colonial colleges support the increasingly active and varied curriculum. Library as place also became important as scholars wanted space to read and research. In the Colonial college era, academic libraries were often open only a few hours per week and severely restricted the amount of materials that could be used by a patron at one time. The reasons for restricted access were varied, including lack of natural light, high cost of materials, and the fact that the lecture and recitation method did not require extensive use of books.[36] By 1876, however, though still quite restrictive by modern standards, access to the library expanded with Harvard's library open forty-eight hours per week, Yale's library open thirty-six hours per week, and most other academic libraries open on average five hours per week.[37]

With a learning model based more in inquiry and increased faculty research activity, library services also expanded. Departmentalization occurred with departments focusing on the acquisition and cataloging of items, public services, and the new reference model. Reference services evolved between 1860 and 1920 and helped spur the growth of the library school curriculum.[38] As research needs became more specialized, reference services were developed to assist patrons with the interpretation of the collections. Reference librarians helped patrons find the appropriate material for their research pursuits, taking seriously the responsibility that they were aiding in the creation of knowledge. Dewey advocated

---

[34] David Kaser, *The Evolution of the American Academic Library Building* (Landham, MD: The Scarecrow Press, 1997), 79.
[35] Gyure, "The Heart of the University," 111–21.
[36] Ibid., 108.
[37] Ibid., 109.
[38] White, *The Origins of the American Library School*, 67.

that specialized reference staff be trained specifically to assist faculty and students in academic libraries, with special reference collections accompanied by a reference service desk that was separate from the circulating collection.[39]

In his 1876 article, "Personal Relations between Librarians and Readers," Samuel Swett Green advocated for the addition of reference assistance to library services in the late 1800s. Green emphasized a user-centered approach to library services. He considered the librarian's role to extend beyond curating collections to ensure that user needs were met. He called for building rapport with users and asserted that the personal connection would help librarians understand users' research needs and help raise the reputation of the library in the community. Later, William Bishop, the Superintendent of the Library of Congress Reading Room, published an article in 1915 titled "The Theory of Reference Work," in which he asserted that reference work was not to do research for the patron, but to guide the patron in how to conduct research on his or her own.[40] Thus, the reference department grew as a specialized department within the library with its own reference desk, collections, and trained staff.[41]

Ohio University: A Case Study

The trajectory of growth of the American academic library is evident at Ohio University. Founded in 1804, Ohio University is a public university and is the oldest university in Ohio. Initially catering to only 14 students, the curriculum was similar to the lecture-and- recitation-based format used by the Colonial colleges with a focus on philosophy, history, languages, and rhetoric. By the 1920s, however, the curriculum had grown to include such subjects as education, music, stenography, bookkeeping, typing, electrical engineering, civil engineering, mining, agriculture, and domestic science. The diversity of the curriculum was due, in part, to the growing diversity of demand for a college education. Indeed, enrollment at Ohio University climbed to 1,065 in 1916. Such growth demanded that the library evolve to meet the growing requirements of the faculty

---

[39] Liya Deng, "The Evolution of Library Reference Services: From General to Special, 1876 1920s," *Libri* 64 no. 3 (2014): 255–56.
[40] Ibid., 254–62.
[41] Ibid., 254–62.

and students. The following sections track the expansion of the Ohio University libraries.[42]

Collections and Buildings

The first library purchases of Ohio University were funded by a $308 appropriation in 1811 followed by an additional $300 in 1812. The library received an official charter in 1814 and was originally housed in one room of the Academy, the first building on campus.[43] Noting that the growth of the university required a new building, the College Edifice, now Cutler Hall, was opened in 1818 and for nine decades housed the library in a room on the southwest corner of the third floor.[44] One room was sufficient at the time due to the small size of the collection.

Official inventory counts mapped the growth of the collection. Counts recorded 1,000 volumes in 1827, 7,000 volumes in 1885, 8,000 volumes in 1890, 12,000 volumes in 1893, 15,000 volumes in 1895, and reached 72,000 volumes by 1923. During the 1800s, books were primarily acquired by donation or on long trips required for other university work. However, a significant portion of the growth is attributed to merging the library with two literary society libraries on campus. The extensive growth of the collection is attributed to the goal of supporting the increasing fields of study of the undergraduate and graduate curriculum and the increased specialization of faculty research and publication. Noted to be an overcrowded fire hazard, the growing collection prompted the library to be moved from a single room to its first official stand-alone library building in 1905.[45]

The Carnegie Library of 1905 was, as its name implies, partially funded by Andrew Carnegie. Though academic libraries were not typically the focus of Carnegie's work, he was persuaded to contribute on the condition that the building was open to the public. The building was architecturally significant, containing a stained-glass dome. The growth of the collection, however, made Carnegie Library outdated even as it was being opened. After just 20 years, the collections had grown to 72,000 volumes, far beyond the capacity of the building. New libraries would be constructed in 1931 and 1965 to accommodate the growing collections. Though the library was relocated several times over the years, it has

---

[42] Ohio University Libraries, "200 Years of Shared Discovery: The Bicentennial of Ohio University Libraries." http://www.library.ohiou.edu/about/libraries-history/bicentennial-publication/.
[43] Ibid., 45.
[44] Ibid., 67.
[45] Ibid., 69.

always been located on the central college green, maintaining a prominent place on campus.[46]

Services and Access

The increasing accessibility of libraries was evident in the rules of Ohio University's library from its founding in 1814 to its first dedicated library building in 1905. In 1814, the library was only open one hour per week and students could only check out one book at a time, if it was wrapped with paper prior to checkout. If an item was damaged, the university president could assess a fine that ranged from six and a half cents to the full cost of the item. Other consequences for actions, such as a loss of a book, could carry a fine of fifty cents and loss of library privileges for three months.[47]

As Ohio University moved toward the twentieth century, it is evident that access improved. By 1878, any faculty, literary society member, or student could make use of the library. Reading hours were set to Monday through Saturday from 1 p.m. to 2 p.m. Patrons could check out two books at a time during the Saturday hour and they could keep the books for a loan period of two weeks. Overdue fines were fifteen cents per week. The complete 1878 rules and regulations are as follows:

1. The library shall be accessible – 1st, to members of the Faculty, – 2nd, to all members of the Literary Societies in actual attendance, who have paid their dues for the current term, – 3rd, to all other students and to honorary and non-attending members of said Societies on the payment of 50 cts. per term, in advance, to the Librarian.
2. The library shall be open for reading every day (except Sundays) from 1 to 2 o'clock P.M. and for drawing and returning books every Saturday from 9 to 10 o'clock A.M., and no book shall be drawn or returned except at the last named hour.
3. Books may be retained two weeks and only two; but on being presented to the Librarian may be redrawn for two weeks more. No book shall be issued to the same person a third time until one week after it has been returned a second time.
4. No person shall have more than two books from the library at the same time; except that any member of the Faculty shall have the privilege of selecting from the original college library such books as pertain to his own department and of retaining them for reference, provided a list of all such books be left with the Librarian.

---

[46] Ibid., 79.
[47] Ibid., 65.

5. Any person who shall injure, mutilate, or lose any book, shall pay to the Librarian the full amount of such injury or loss and shall be debarred from the privileges of the library until such payment is made.
6. Any person failing to return a book at the required time shall be fined 15 cents per week until said book is returned.
7. Conversation, except with the Librarian, smoking, making noise, spitting on the floor, and other conduct unbecoming the place are prohibited.
8. No person shall take from the shelves any book, except by express permission of the Librarian.
9. During vacation the library shall be under control of the Librarian, who may issue books on the same conditions as during college sessions.
10. Students may have the privilege of retaining books during vacation on depositing an equivalent with the Librarian.[48]

Early library pamphlets show increasingly lenient access during the early 1900s. At this time, the stacks were open from 8:00 a.m. to 8:30 p.m. during the week and open on the weekends for limited hours. Patrons were permitted to use books at will within the library, as opposed to the former rules that required the Librarian's permission to remove a book from the shelf. Free access was granted to anyone, though patrons could still only check out two books at a time. Fines were two cents per day, though an Ohio law existed that stated that a patron could be thrown in jail for up to 30 days if a book was torn or cut! The complete rules were published as follows:

1. The Library is open from 8:00 A. M. to 8:30 P. M. on Mondays, Tuesdays, Wednesdays, and Thursdays; and from 8:00 A. M. to 5:00 P. M. on Fridays and Saturdays. On Sundays, it is open from 2:00 P. M. for reference work only.
2. The Reference room is open from 9:00 A. M. to 12:00 P. M. and from 1:00 P. M. to 5:00 P. M.
3. The faculty, students and employees of the University and the residents of Athens are permitted to draw books from the library. If a resident borrows books for home use, he is requested to fill out a registration card. Non-residents may also draw books upon showing satisfactory references.
4. Free access to the stacks is given during all hours in which the Library is open. The books from the stacks may be used in the Library without making a charge. When a person wishes to take a

---

[48] Ohio University, "Rules and Regulations of the Joint Library of the Ohio University," Ohio University Alden Library Digital Collections. https://media.library.ohio.edu/digital/collection/archives/id/1791/rec/5/.

book from the building, he must under all circumstances have the book charged at the charging desk. Here the book card is stamped with the due date, and the borrower signs his name opposite the date. This card is then filed by the librarian. The due slip in the back of the book is then stamped with the date. A book may be kept for two weeks, provided the book is not in demand or not overdue.

5. When returning a book, the borrower presents it at the charging desk where the attendant cancels the charge.
6. Students using books in the stacks are requested not to return them to the stacks, but to leave them on the tables provided for the purpose.
7. All books in circulation are subject to recall at any time in case of need.
8. Two books at a time may be drawn, one only being fiction.
9. All books must be properly charged before they are taken from the library.
10. General reference books such as dictionaries, encyclopedias, atlases, etc., do not circulate.
11. Current periodicals may not be taken for home use. Back numbers not in demand may be borrowed for 24 hours. Bound periodicals may not be taken from the library, as they are needed for reference purposes at all times.
12. Books from the reserve desk may be drawn for home use until closing time. These books must be returned by 8:15 A. M. the following morning. A willful violation of this rule will result in the withdrawal of library privileges.
13. Whenever a borrower loses a book, he must forfeit the cost of the book.
14. A fine of two cents a day is charged on all overdue books. Notification of the fine will be sent when the books are one week overdue.
15. Hats, wraps and umbrellas should be left in the vestibule. Bags and satchels for carrying books are prohibited.
16. In order that the reading rooms may be kept quiet to afford the best opportunity for study, all persons should refrain from conversation.
17. There is a law of the State of Ohio which says, "Whoever intentionally defaces, obliterates, tears or destroys, in whole or in part, a newspaper, magazine, or periodical, or a file in a Reading Room, or cuts therefrom an article of advertisement, shall be fined not less than ten dollars nor more than one hundred dollars, or imprisoned not more than thirty days, or both."[49]

Reflected in the rules of the early 1900s is the use of more specialized library terminology, indicating the growth of the profession. The Ohio

---

[49] "Carnegie Library," Ohio University Alden Library Digital Collections. https://media.library.ohio.edu/digital/collection/archives/id/45648/rec/7/.

University pamphlet indicated the use of a reference room, reference desk, and "charging" books, giving a nod to modern circulation workflow. Several rules laid the foundation for current practice, including limited circulation of current periodicals and reference materials. With the growing collection, expansion of access, and specialized services, Ohio University's library is a model of the trajectory experienced throughout American higher education from 1860 to 1920.

Into the Future

As this chapter demonstrates, academic libraries responded to the major shifts in American higher education in the years between 1860 and 1920. From a small set of books limited to texts of the classic liberal arts to the vast collections that support diverse study and specialized faculty research, the library has adapted to the changing tides of higher education. Influenced by increased access and expansion of the curriculum to include practical studies, academic libraries adapted to support the changing needs of American higher education at the turn of the twentieth century. By professionalizing librarianship and increasing access, collections, and services, the academic library has remained the backbone and heart of the American higher education institution. This era of adaptation to the increasing scale and scope of American higher education certainly laid the foundation for the mega-libraries of the mid-twentieth century and the digital revolution of the turn of the twenty-first century. Through each era of change, the academic library remains a cherished and important partner in American higher education.

4

Decolonizing[1] Special Collections: Building the Native American Literature Collection at Amherst College

Mike Kelly

A central argument of anthropologist Patrick Wolfe's writings on settler colonialism and indigenous peoples is that settler colonialism, or "invasion" as he also puts it, is a structure, not an event.[2] Although we may prefer to imagine the era of frontier violence and dispossession of indigenous people is far removed from our current historical moment, Wolfe emphasizes that the same logic that justified frontier violence, "transmutes into different modalities, discourses and institutional formations as it undergirds the historical development and complexification of settler society."[3] Looking at the field of librarianship through Wolfe's lens helps us identify the ways that our institutional formations embed settler colonialism and White supremacy within our

---

[1] In the context of this chapter, I use *decolonizing* metaphorically. See Eve Tuck and K. Wayne Wang, "Decolonization Is Not a Metaphor," *Decolonization: Indigeneity, Education & Society* 1, no. 1 (2012): 1–40.

[2] For a brief summary of this argument, see Patrick Wolfe, "Settler Colonialism and the Elimination of the Native," *Journal of Genocide Research* 8, no. 4 (2006): 387–409; in *Traces of History: Elementary Structures of Race* (New York: Verso, 2016) Wolfe provides a deeper critique of settler colonialism and constructions of race.

[3] Wolfe. "Settler Colonialism and the Elimination of the Native," 402.

day-to-day work. As a profession that is dependent on structures and standards issued by a federal government agency—the Library of Congress (LC)—how do our tools embed the biases against people of color and marginalized groups that characterize other federal policies? How can we intervene to address those biases and begin to decolonize our profession?

E. Pauline Johnson (Tekahionwake) was a Mohawk author and performer born in Canada in 1861. She wrote extensively for magazines and published six books between 1895 and her death in 1913. *Flint and Feather*, a collection of her poetry, went through three editions between 1912 and 1914; *Legends of Vancouver* appeared in at least four editions between 1911 and 1922. Most of her books in the Amherst College Archives & Special Collections are shelved under the call number PR 9199.2 .J64—a subdivision of the LC class for "English Literature." Nearly all First Nations authors are shelved together in what amounts to a call-number classification ghetto —PR 9180 through PR 9199.4 is reserved for Canadian authors, regardless of racial identity. Johnson's tribal identity is erased and redefined by her relationship to Great Britain; all Colonial subjects are cordoned off into the subclass for "English literature outside of Great Britain." Maurice Kenny was also a Mohawk author, but he was born on the US side of the current US–Canada border in Watertown, NY. Unlike First Nations authors included in the PR (English Literature) subdivision, US Native American writers are found throughout the PS (American Literature) subclass. Amherst holds forty-four of Kenny's books, ranging from *Dead Letters Sent and Other Poems* (1958) to *Feeding Bears: New Poems* (2010). These books are shelved under PS 3561.E49, right between Susan Kenney and Arnold Kenseth. What better encapsulation of the ideals of rugged American individualism than reserving PS 700 through PS 3576 for "Individual authors." I doubt that any of the people involved in developing the PR and PS subclasses had the erasure of Indigenous presence as an explicit goal, but the effect of this system is precisely that. If we bear in mind that the Library of Congress is the government agency responsible for these classification decisions, it is less surprising that they echo US federal policies toward Indigenous peoples: the containment of the colonized other under the category "Canadian" and forced assimilation through termination of tribal identity in the PS class.

There is a growing body of criticism of the structural racism of library systems and information science that challenges many deeply held beliefs about the objective goodness of libraries. Todd Honma, in his essential essay from 2005, "Trippin' Over the Color Line: The Invisibility of Race in Library and Information Studies" writes about how these "idealized visions of a mythic benevolence" conceal the ways library structures support and perpetuate White privilege at the expense of others.[4] In the case of Kenny and Johnson, their shared Mohawk identity is overwritten by the division of Mohawk territory between two Colonial powers; Kenny is assimilated as simply an American writer, whereas Johnson is cordoned off in a special sub-sub-classification reserved for Canadian subjects of the British Empire.

Interventions intended to disrupt these Colonial structures within librarianship occasionally capture popular attention, as with recent efforts to petition the Library of Congress to drop *Illegal aliens* as a formal heading.[5] Librarians have often led efforts to critique and fix these structures of inequity, and we continue to do so as information technology changes and infiltrates every aspect of modern life. Laura Helton's exploration of Dorothy Porter's revision of the Dewey Decimal System to better represent the Black history collection she built at Howard University reminds us that librarians have a long history of such advocacy.[6] Meanwhile, the American Philosophical Society has launched a new Indigenous Subject Guide, which will undoubtedly be a major contribution to our own efforts to decolonize library taxonomies.[7] The deeper issue of racial bias and Colonial structures embedded within our search engines and computer algorithms is a far more complicated story, but one our profession needs to address. Safiya Noble sums it up neatly in *Algorithms of Oppression: How Search Engines Reinforce Racism*, referring to both historical and new systems: "Information organization is a matter of sociopolitical and historical processes that serve particular interests."[8] If we explore the past and the present of libraries through this particular lens—asking whose interests are served and whose are suppressed, and why—we can gain a clearer sense of the interventions our structures require if we are to remain viable cultural institutions for the future.

---

[4] Honma, Todd. "Trippin' Over the Color Line: The Invisibility of Race in Library and Information Studies," *InterActions: UCLA Journal of Education and Information Studies* 1, no. 2 (2005). https://escholarship.org/uc/item/4nj0w1mp/.

[5] For a brief summary, see Lisa Peet, "Library of Congress Drops Illegal Alien Subject Heading, Provokes Backlash Legislation," Library Journal June 14, 2016. https://www.libraryjournal.com/?detailStory=library-of-congress-drops-illegal-alien-subject-heading-provokes-backlash-legislation/.

[6] Helton, Laura, "Racial Imaginaries of the Catalog." Paper presented at the Past, Present, and Future of Libraries conference. American Philosophical Society, September 2018.

[7] Brian Carpenter, "Introducing the New Indigenous Subject Guide." Accessed January 27, 2019. https://www.amphilsoc.org/blog/introducing-new-indigenous-subject-guide/.

[8] Noble, Safiya Umoja, *Algorithms of Oppression: How Search Engines Reinforce Racism* (New York: New York University Press, 2018), 138.

The role of special collections in that future is an exciting one; our collection development practices and new efforts at outreach and community engagement, in particular. It is easy to critique the world of special collections as an elitist boys' club in which everyone chases the same high-value collectible books, generally written by English-speaking White men; the Gilded-Age collecting of the Folgers, the Morgans, the Huntingtons, and others has had a profound effect on what is deemed worthy of the special collections treasure room. It is equally true that special collections repositories have historically forged new collecting areas that have redefined literary history and scholarship. In the 1950s and 60s, Harry Ransom at the University of Texas at Austin aggressively collected twentieth-century literature in bulk—including Joyce, Beckett, and Pound manuscripts—shifting from a connoisseurship model that focused on unique treasures to a broader understanding of archival collecting. The Ransom Center continues to break new ground in collecting in bulk the papers of publishing companies and literary agents as well as those of individual authors, both living and dead. DeCoursey Fales donated his massive library of Victorian novels to New York University (NYU) in 1957 and spent the rest of his life working toward his goal of comprehensive documentation of the English novel at a time when academic interest in figures other than Charles Dickens and James Fennimore Cooper was very low. As scholars of the Victorian era became interested in recovering forgotten female authors, the Fales collection was ready and waiting for them. At the close of the last century, Marvin Taylor, Director of Fales, established the Downtown Collection at NYU with the acquisition of the papers of artist, activist, and writer David Wojnarowicz and the personal library of poet/pack rat Ron Kolm, among many others.[9] The Downtown Collection took an archival documentary approach to the literary, arts, music, performance, and theater scenes of lower Manhattan from the late 1960s through the mid-1990s and beyond; if it happened in Soho in the 1970s, it belongs in the Downtown Collection. Johan Kugelberg brought a similar vision to his efforts to document hip-hop music and culture; in 2007 his collection became the core of the Cornell Hip Hop Collection. Its stated goal is "to collect and make accessible the historical artifacts of Hip Hop culture and to ensure their preservation for future generations."[10] What distinguishes the efforts of

---

[9] Marvin Taylor's essay provides an excellent overview of the theoretical foundations of this collection, see "Playing the Field: The Downtown Scene and Cultural Production, An Introduction," in *The Downtown Book: The New York Art Scene 1974–1984*, ed. Marvin J. Taylor (Princeton, NJ: Princeton University Press, 2006).

[10] "The Cornell Hip Hop Collection." Accessed January 27, 2019. http://rmc.library.cornell.edu/hiphop/.

Harry Ransom and DeCoursey Fales from the Downtown Collection and the Hip Hop Collection is the level of community engagement. In both *The Downtown Book* and Kugelberg's *Born in the Bronx: A Visual Record of the Early Days of Hip Hop*,[11] the voices of the creators and communities behind these collections are published alongside those of the curators and academics. Both collections have also challenged and expanded the boundaries of what belongs in special collections: mixtapes, Xeroxed flyers, graffiti tag books, and 'zines, to name but a few examples. We looked at the models set by these two institutions and others as we began to build our Native American Literature collection at Amherst College.

In the fall of 2012, Amherst College hired professors Lisa Brooks and Kiara Vigil as new Native Studies faculty in the wake of Barry O'Connell's retirement.[12] Shortly after their arrival, antiquarian bookseller Ken Lopez advertised the sale of the collection of Pablo Eisenberg, a professor at Georgetown University who had amassed a personal library of nearly 1,500 books written by Native American authors. I immediately contacted Lisa and Kiara to alert them to this opportunity and to ask how this collection would support their work. Their enthusiastic responses convinced us that we needed to acquire this collection for Amherst; fortunately, we have very generous alumni. In the spring of 2013, Younghee Kim-Wait (class of 1982) stepped forward with funding that allowed us to purchase the entire Eisenberg collection. It was delivered to our reading room in Frost Library in August 2013 and was soon known as *The Younghee Kim-Wait (Class of 1982)/Pablo Eisenberg Native American Literature Collection*, or *The KWE* for short.

Throughout the unpacking and cataloging of this collection, librarians were in close communication with Lisa and Kiara, who connected us to the entire Five College Native studies community as well as local tribal community leaders. Finding ourselves in possession of a major new collection with two faculty members who were eager to dive in, we put all other cataloging work on hold to prioritize work on the KWE. Thanks to the efforts of Rebecca Henning, cataloger for special collections,

---

[11] Afrika, Bambaataa. *Born in the Bronx: A Visual Record of the Early Days of Hip Hop*, eds. Johan Kugelberg and Joe Conzo (New York: Rizzoli, 2007).

[12] Barry O'Connell began teaching at Amherst in 1972 and has published extensively on Native writing, especially the works of William Apess. Lisa Brooks recently published *Our Beloved Kin: A New History of King Philip's War* (New Haven, CT: Yale University Press, 2018); her book *The Common Pot: The Recovery of Native Space in the Northeast* (Minnesota, 2008) is essential reading. Kiara Vigil's *Indigenous Intellectuals: Sovereignty, Citizenship, and the American Imagination, 1880–1930* (Cambridge, UK: Cambridge University Press, 2015) complements Amherst alumnus Fred Hoxie's *This Indian Country: American Indian Activists and the Place They Made* (New York: Penguin, 2012) by focusing on the literary and intellectual activism and resistance of the past 200 years.

Figure 4.1 Samson Occom (Mohegan). *A Sermon, Preached at the Execution of Moses Paul …* (New London, 1772) is the earliest item acquired with the Younghee Kim-Wait/Pablo Eisenberg Collection at Amherst College.

Image courtesy of Amherst College Archives & Special Collections.

the entire collection was cataloged by May 2014. After eliminating duplicates within the collection and the few books already on our shelves, the Eisenberg collection stood at 1,395 items ranging in date from a copy of the fourth edition of Samson Occom's *A Sermon, Preached at the Execution of Moses Paul, An Indian* (New London, 1772) to Martin Cruz Smith's novel *Stalin's Ghost* from 2007 (Figure 4.1).

In addition to standard provenance notes, we added notes to identify authors' tribal affiliations whenever possible. We knew from working with local students and faculty that researchers will want to locate authors based on tribes; the question, "What Cherokee writers do you have?" is far more common than "Do you have the second printing of William Apess's *Eulogy on King Philip*?" (Answers: many; yes). Thus, adding the note "655 7 | a Mohawk Indian authors. | 2 local" both serves the immediate reference needs of our patrons and undoes the separation E.

Pauline Johnson and Maurice Kenny inflicted through the LC system. The subfield *2 local* reminds us that we are not altering the records for these books held elsewhere. For instance, a search for *Pueblo Indian authors* in the Five Colleges Library Catalog retrieves all of Martin Cruz Smith's novels, including *Gorky Park*; a search of Worldcat for the first edition of that novel retrieves a record that includes Amherst as a holding institution, but that record does not include our notes about his Pueblo and Yaqui ancestry. Our decolonizing intervention is a purely local one.

As we cataloged and researched the books in the collection, we had to consider what the scope and focus of the collection will be moving forward; we started receiving offers of items not owned by Pablo Eisenberg as soon as news of our acquisition reached the antiquarian bookselling community and those offers have not stopped. We drafted a formal collection-development policy for our Native American Literature Collection to make our collecting goals as transparent as possible. The full policy is available on our website, but this excerpt describes our current collecting focuses:

> The goal of our Native American collection is to represent, as comprehensively as possible, the full spectrum of Native American writing and intellectual life from the seventeenth century to the present. We focus on published works ranging from rare imprints and ephemera to mass-market books, rather than unique manuscripts and artifacts; our aim is to document the full range of *public expressions* and statements by Indigenous people. We collect books by Native writers comprehensively, regardless of genre, format, or audience. To a limited degree, we acquire related materials by non-Native writers.

Similar to Mr. Fales's pursuit of the English novel, if it is a book by a Native author, we want to have a copy regardless of that writer's literary reputation, sales figures, or other criteria. We emphasize "public expressions" in the policy to clarify that we are not an anthropological museum interested in acquiring arrowheads and similar objects, which we have already been offered and refused; Amherst's is primarily a rare book collection, so our focus is on the public/published aspect of Native writing.

Digitization was another area we began to consider as soon as we acquired the collection. We knew that we now held books known to exist in very few copies that were largely inaccessible to a nonspecialist audience. Toward that end, we have digitized 114 public domain books that are now freely available via Amherst College Digital Collections (acdc.amherst.edu). In addition to making those works available through digitization, our more ambitious idea is a data-visualization project that will locate the books and writers on a map and provide chronological browsing through a timeline. The working title for this project was initially the Digital Atlas of the Native American Book. In an effort to suggest a broader scope than merely printed books, that title was revised to The Digital Atlas of Native American Intellectual Traditions (DANAIT); that title is likely to change again as the project evolves.

We recognized that even works in the public domain under US copyright law could contain information that contemporary Indigenous communities might not want widely disseminated. Rather than attempting to tackle these issues in isolation, we sought a planning grant to bring together a wide range of librarians, Native studies scholars, tribal members, anthropologists, and technologists. The result of our efforts was a successful application for an Institute of Museum and Library Services (IMLS) National Leadership for Libraries Planning Grant under their National Digital Platform initiative awarded in 2015. Amherst College partnered with the Association of Tribal Archives, Libraries, and Museums (ATALM), the Digital Public Library of America (DPLA), and the Mukurtu project and was awarded $49,765. A steering committee was established to identify potential participants; the first half of 2016 was spent organizing a meeting hosted at Amherst College June 22–24. A total of 29 participants from as far away as Hawaii, Arizona, and the Pacific Northwest worked together to produce a statement of need, vision, and principles. Full documentation of that gathering is available online: danait.wordpress.amherst.edu/.

The single principle that emerged above all others in our wide-ranging discussions was relationality; a concept that is at the core of much Indigenous scholarship. If one of our problems is that current library metadata practices often obscure Indigenous identity and tribal sovereignty, the solution must involve building a relationship between librarians and Indigenous communities. Thus, our emphasis on networks—both human and technological—is central to this project. These networks will be built slowly, over time, and with broad consultation and collaboration; the value of building this as a network is that each node can contribute at its own pace, and partners can be added over time. Developing a network also builds in sustainability, as no single node is responsible for the entire network. The gathering at which these principles and goals were drafted was itself an example of this relationality and network building. At Amherst, we want to avoid recreating the Colonial project by claiming sole authority or ownership of whatever the Digital Atlas eventually becomes. Our role as responsible stewards of cultural heritage materials demands that we engage with these particular materials in an open, collaborative, and relational manner.

Building the human network around the Native Literature Collection began with our first exhibition and opening reception in the spring of 2014. Thanks to our connections to the local academic Native Studies community and the tribal communities beyond, we had a crowd of more than fifty visitors from around New England, most of whom had never before set foot in the Amherst College Archives & Special Collections. The Archives has hosted several open-house events and exhibitions in collaboration with the Five College Native American and Indigenous Studies program and we regularly mount small exhibitions to coincide with author visits and events. After participating in the IMLS-funded gathering, Patricia Marroquin Norby, then Director of the D'Arcy McNickle Center for American Indian and Indigenous Studies at the Newberry Library, asked whether Amherst would host the 2017 spring research methods workshop for the Newberry Consortium in American Indian Studies. This two-day workshop brought a new group of students and faculty working in Native American and Indigenous studies into close contact with our collections. In addition to access to rare materials, we also share our expertise in the fields of printing history and descriptive bibliography. Our aim is to bring tools and techniques of bibliography to the field of Native American and Indigenous Studies; we also feel compelled to share what we have learned from that field with the bibliography and special collections community. Toward that end, in June 2018, Amherst College hosted the first Rare Book School course on "A History of Native American Books & Indigenous Sovereignty," taught by Mike Kelly and Kiara Vigil. We intend to offer this course on a regular basis, revising our approach as the collection grows and changes.

Beyond merely raising awareness of our holdings, these efforts have brought new materials into the collection. A visit to the Archives is now a regular stop for the many Native authors brought to campus by our faculty and others working in the Five College Consortium. When Anishinaabe poet and scholar Gerald Vizenor came to visit, he commented that we did not appear to have all of his books; six months later Ken Lopez brokered the sale of 181 items from Vizenor's personal library to the Amherst College Archives to fill those gaps. Similarly, we purchased more than 500 books from the Greenfield Review Press operated by Abenaki author/editor/publisher Joseph Bruchac, along with 300 more books from his personal library. All of these books have provenance notes that clearly state where they came from and their relationships to donors and former owners. One of our copies of George Copway's *The Life, History, and Travels of Kah-ge-ga-gah-bowh, (George Copway): A Young Indian Chief of the Ojebwa Nation* (1847) has the note: "Vizenor, Gerald Robert, 1934–, former owner," a detail sure to be of interest to scholars of both Vizenor and Copway. Given the deeply destructive methods by which ethnographic and anthropological collections have been assembled and cataloged over the past 500 years, our goal is to make our sources and processes as transparent as possible.

We have also noted in the catalog record our efforts to engage with the current Native American literary marketplace. In the fall of 2016 Cassandra Hradil attended the first Indigenous Comic Con in Albuquerque, New Mexico, as part of her senior thesis under the guidance of Lisa Brooks.[13] The Indigenous Comic Con was created by Lee Francis, founder of Native Realities Press and the bookstore Red Planet; his efforts to foster a vibrant, future-oriented, Indigenous comic scene have earned him the nickname "The Stan Lee of Indian Country."[14] I met with Cassandra before her trip and asked her to purchase one copy of every Native-authored comic and 'zine available, for which she was reimbursed. This micronarrative of intervention is recorded in the notes for the copy of *The Poet: Pauline Johnson*, a comic-book biography of E. Pauline Johnson: "Amherst College Archives and Special Collections copy is in original color illustrated wrappers; purchased (at the 2016 Indigenous Comic Con in Albuquerque) to complement the Collection of Native American Literature." We continue to collect the output of Native Realities Press, including broadside prints, such as *Chief Cthulhu (Great Old One)* by Ryan Singer (Diné; Figure 4.2) and through Kickstarter-funded projects such as *Deer Woman* (2018; Figure 4.3). It is a testament to the vibrant and growing community of Native authors and artists working across analog and digital media today that there is simply too much material for a single institution to ever claim comprehensive coverage.

The Road Ahead

Another important aspect of relationality and networks that was highlighted at our June 2016 gathering was time. We collectively gave ourselves

---

[13] See Cassandra Hradil's online senior thesis: *Interactivity, Indigeneity, and the Digital Imaginary.* http://indigenousimaginary.com/.
[14] For a profile of Lee Francis, see "The Stan Lee of Indian Country: Comics Publisher Dr. Lee Francis," *Indian Country Today*. Accessed August 30, 2018. https://newsmaven.io/indiancountrytoday/archive/the-stan-lee-of-indian-country-comics-publisher-dr-lee-francis-yrRLiNq7HU-WtmA-ks5H-Q/.

Figure 4.2 Ryan Singer (Diné). *Chief Cthulhu (Great Old One)*. Broadside print (Albuquerque, NM: Native Realities Press, 2017).

Image courtesy of Amherst College Archives & Special Collections.

permission to move slowly; meaningful relationships take time to develop. Meanwhile, the Native American Literature Collection at Amherst has grown from just under 1,400 titles to 2,700 as of January 2019. We continue to purchase rarities through the antiquarian trade, such as an 1855 Cree-language catechism printed with a Cree typeface near Hudson Bay, the only copy now held in a library in the United States. We also added copies of recent works by living writers, such as Anton Treuer (Ojibwe) and Clyde Bellecourt (Ojibwe), both of whom inscribed their copies to the collection at Amherst while at a signing during the 2018 International Conference of Indigenous Archives, Libraries, and Muse-

Figure 4.3 Elizabeth LaPensée and Weshoyot Alvitre, editors. Cover of *Deer Woman: An Anthology* (Albuquerque, NM: Native Realities Press, 2018).

Image courtesy of Amherst College Archives & Special Collections.

ums. While the collection grows, we continue to build relationships and listen to the needs of Native authors and readers.

If we bear in mind Noble's caution to pay close attention to whose interests are served by our systems, it is incumbent upon us to better understand the interests of groups that have not been traditionally served by library information systems. Two participants in our Digital Atlas gathering are committed to understanding the specific history and structures of information systems in and across Native communities throughout North America. Marisa Duarte's *Network Sovereignty: Building the Internet Across Indian Country* is a deep exploration of information communication technologies and their significance for Native sovereignty.[15] While acutely aware of the physical and human challenges involved, she highlights the opportunities to intervene to shape these networks to best serve the community. "Through our uses of digital systems as Indigenous peoples, they become embedded with what we believe to be our Indigenous values" (142). By building and maintaining their own information networks, Native communities have the opportunity to undo some piece of Noble's algorithms of oppression and embed values specific to their own communities. Similarly, Sandra Littletree's study of tribal libraries explores the vital role these centers play as active sites of cultural and linguistic renewal. In her 2018 dissertation, *"Let Me Tell You About Indian Libraries": Self-Determination, Leadership, and Vision—The Basis of Tribal Library Development in the United States*, she describes tribal libraries as "important sites of decolonization, where sovereignty and self-determination are paramount" (University of Washington, 2018). The work that is happening within tribal communities around these issues is inspiring; our challenge is to build sustainable and meaningful partnerships that will connect these communities with the resources held by Colonial institutions.

Decolonizing our library and information systems requires far more than removing biased/Colonial labels and terminology; it must also make space for adding Indigenous intellectual and network sovereignty. Although this task feels daunting, many people are hard at work to engineer tools for our networked world that support and protect indigenous intellectual sovereignty. The Traditional Knowledge Labels developed by the Local Contexts project codirected by Jane Anderson and Kim Christen "offer an educative and informational strategy to help non-community

---

[15] Duarte, Marisa Elena. *Network Sovereignty: Building the Internet across Indian Country* (Seattle: University of Washington Press, 2017).

users of this cultural heritage understand its importance and significance to the communities from where it derives and continues to have meaning."[16] For example, a filmmaker in search of a piece of music in the public domain for a soundtrack might think twice about using a song tagged "Community Use Only" or "Culturally Sensitive," especially if others have been positively endorsed with the "Outreach" or "Community Voice" tags. Mukurtu takes community control over cultural heritage materials even further, providing an entire digital content management system designed to embed community values and protocols within item descriptions. Visitors to sites, such as "The Plateau People's Web Portal" and "Passamaquoddy People: At Home on the Ocean and Lakes," will see only those materials and descriptions that community members have formally reviewed and approved.[17]

While we continue to make our local interventions in Machine-Readable Cataloging (MARC) records, we are laying a sound foundation for the next generation of library discovery engines and myriad digital humanities projects. Linked Open Data and the digital humanities in general offer many new tools that can make a Digital Atlas possible, and many Indigenous interventions in cyberspace are well underway. The Five Colleges is a partner in the development of the FOLIO (Future of Libraries Is Open) system, a community collaboration of libraries, vendors, and developers coming together to build an open-source library services platform that may offer opportunities to incorporate some of the principles identified through the DANAIT gathering and elsewhere.

The future is certainly promising, but the primary role for the special collections library remains rooted in the physical volumes standing on shelves—our collections are the fuel for the engine room of the humanities, digital or analog. The growth of this collection, from the acquisition of Eisenberg's library until today, is a literal act of decolonization. Prior to 2013, the presence of Indigenous authors in the Archives was minimal; today there are 2,700 books on those same shelves. We will continue to add books to this collection as long as we can find Native-authored works not already held at Amherst while constantly asking ourselves what interventions are necessary to better serve the interests of those

---

[16] "Traditional Knowledge (TK) Labels." Accessed January 27, 2019. http://localcontexts.org/tk-labels/.
[17] "The Plateau People's Web Portal." Accessed January 27, 2019. https://plateauportal.libraries.wsu.edu. "Passamaquoddy People: At Home on the Ocean and Lakes." Accessed January 27, 2019. http://passamaquoddypeople.com/.

traditionally excluded from special collections work. As our library systems evolve and change, we hope to build on the lessons learned at our IMLS gathering and in the years since to engage with Indigenous communities to undo the damage our systems have done.

III

Access and Accessibility

5

Take Me into the Library and Show Me Myself: Toward Authentic Accessibility in Digital Libraries

Dorothy Berry

Historian Edward Porter Alexander once described poet and activist June Jordan as a "militant minority" based on the following quote from a museum seminar:

> Take me into the museum and show me myself, show me my people, show me soul America. If you cannot show me myself, if you cannot teach my people what they need to know—and they need to know the truth, and they need to know that nothing is more important than human life—if you cannot show and teach these things then why shouldn't I attack the temples of America and blow them up? The people who hold the power, and the people who count pennies, and the people who hold the keys better start thinking it all over again.[1]

Jordan's call-to-arms against underrepresentation sounded a clarion call to museum curators across the United States. The desire expressed in that line calls equally to those working toward more diversely represen-

---

[1] Edward Porter Alexander, *Museums in Motion: An Introduction to the History and Functions of Museums* (Walnut Creek, CA: Altamira Press, 1979), 7. Though this quote has been reused/reclaimed with great frequency, the details of when and where Jordan spoke these words are opaque.

tative collections in archives and special collections libraries. Museums, archives, and libraries face many of the same barriers inching toward inclusion, and the same solution is often presented: a complete reworking of collection practices moving forward.[2] Newfound dedication to actively collecting and preserving materials related to African American history and culture is certainly laudable, but the complex nature of acquisitions and collection development presents an opportunity to rectify representational issues by looking within existing collections. Discovering African American materials within currently inventoried and described collections, and then making those materials accessible through both digitization and redescription, was the goal of a two-year Council on Library and Information Research Cataloging and Digitizing Hidden Special Collections and Archives grant-funded project, "Digitizing African American Archival Materials Across University of Minnesota Collections" (DAAAUMN). This project provides an example of how rediscovering what's in our own stacks can bring an immediacy to increasing patron discoverability of marginalized peoples' histories, all the while opening the eyes of archivists and librarians to the wealth of materials they may already possess.

DAAAUMN was conceived within the context of Umbra Search African American History, a widget and search tool developed at the University of Minnesota to aggregate African American-related materials from digital collections nationally. DAAAUMN took the now common practice of surfacing hidden histories through collection surveys a step further by not just publishing a list of African American materials in a single collection or repository, but by gathering together those materials through digitization and aggregation. By identifying, describing, and digitizing African American materials across the University of Minnesota Archives and Special Collections, DAAAUMN troubled the common definition of *hidden collections*, as unique and rare materials deserving of highlight (but already known to collectors and scholars), and instead investigated how and why certain historical and cultural threads remain hidden within larger archival collections. The project was framed as part of the larger Umbra Search program, which began with the design and launch of the web tool years earlier.

---

[2] See Brian Keough, "Documenting Diversity: Developing Special Collections of Underdocumented Groups," *Library Collections, Acquisitions, & Technical Services* 26, no. 3 (2002): 241–51; Ian Johnston, "Whose History Is It Anyway?," *Journal of the Society of Archivists* 22, no. 2 (2001): 213–29; and Kären M. Mason, "Fostering Diversity in Archival Collections," *Collection Management* 40, no. 2 (2005): 123–45 for examples of proactive diversity-centering collecting policies.

Umbra Search, the brain-child of curator Cecily Marcus, the principal investigator for the project grant, seeks to smooth out a complex web of digitized archival records through the focused aggregation of African American materials from across hundreds of repositories. The site harvests from major institutions, including the Schomburg Center for Research in Black Culture and the Library of Congress, as well as from smaller but potent collections held by regional historical societies and county libraries. The aggregation of more than 900,000 digitized records has created a new corpus of African American material, located not in a physical space but rather in the *ur*-archive of the human mind. Records in digital space are encoded with provenance/ownership metadata, but through focused aggregation, when pulled together by the common thread of Black life, for example, photos of rural life from several different repositories are no longer presented primarily as institutional research capital, but rather as the associated records, photos, and ephemera that make up African American history.

This focused pulling together is at the heart of *authentic* accessibility. There is a popular idea in contemporary librarianship that creation of digital collections leads to increased accessibility, that removing materials from the intimidating and prohibitive physical spaces of archives and special collections removes the primary barrier to access. Although the physical spaces housing our collections undeniably place physical and cultural barriers around materials, digitization as panacea assumes both that complicated and sometimes idiosyncratic catalogs and findings contain all the information that users need for digital discovery, and furthermore that the institutional digital access points, often behind university logins and paywalls, are somehow less intimidating and prohibitive. We hoped the latter issue was addressed through the user-focused design of the Umbra Search web application, but the accessible interface depends on a foundation of harvestable records. Descriptions that serve effectively to help researchers decide whether to visit a certain library and view materials in person, however, become utterly inefficient when used to provide a complete illustration of a digital record's content and context.[3]

Challenges surrounding descriptive metadata emerged as some of the most significant facing the growth of a multiinstitutional, African

---

[3] John Overholt, "Five Theses on the Future of Special Collections," *RBM a Journal of Rare Books, Manuscripts and Cultural Heritage* 14, no. 1 (2013): 15 provides a challenge to digital access at the single institutional level under the thesis "The future of special collections is distribution," whereas Giordana Mecagni problematized the commercial barriers set up by the majority of nonpublic-funded archival databases in her 2017 presentation "'Why Don't People Just Get Over It?' Bringing the Archives to Boston's Conversation on Resilience and Race Equity" (Annual Meeting of the Society of American Archivists, Portland, OR, July 28, 2017).

American-focused digital collection. Over the course of this project three broadly construed obstacles became apparent: limited resources for archival processing, conventions around archival arrangement and description, and a lack of transferable documentation.[4] In exploring each obstacle individually, there is an awareness of the extreme fluidity between one issue and the next. The problematics that follow don't illustrate discrete issues so much as a collections worldview that is in a state of flux, grappling with the preservation of historical methods in the face of emerging technologies and users who've come to expect them.

Limited resources for description, particularly archival processing, have necessitated an overhaul of traditional, item-by-item methodologies. Most archives have years-long backlogs of unprocessed collections, compounded by the continuous acquisition of new materials. Growing collection backlogs have been addressed in recent years by doing what is known as *minimal processing*, inspired by Mark A. Greene and Dennis Meissner's incredibly influential 2005 article "More Product, Less Process: Revamping Traditional Archival Processing."[5] Greene and Meissner argue that archives have awarded "a higher priority to serving the perceived needs of our collections than to serving the demonstrated needs of our constituents" by allowing large amounts of materials to sit unprocessed until such a time that resources allowed for complete, item-level inventorying and finding aid creation. Their article championed methods to expedite physical access, including, most relevant to digital archives aggregation, description of materials "*sufficient* [emphasis added] to promote use."

"Description sufficient to promote use" in a physical setting, where human mediation is possible, is entirely different from "description sufficient to promote use" by both computer systems looking for records to aggregate, and by users searching for individual files among hundreds of thousands of digital records. Although the methodology promoted in "More Product, Less Process," known colloquially as *MPLP*, has led to huge strides in physical accessibility for researchers, it has also led to workflows around describing digital objects that build up barriers around

---

[4] Although these three, often overlapping, obstacles provided stumbling blocks to creating a better aggregation of African American materials, they are representative of the difficult transitions in the field toward what Kate Theimer describes as "Archives 2.0," that is a more open, facilitation-centered, technologically savvy archive. Kate Theimer, "What is the Meaning of Archives 2.0?" *The American Archivist* 74, no. 1 (2011): 61–64.

[5] Mark A. Greene, and Dennis Meissner. "More Product, Less Process: Revamping Traditional Archival Processing," *The American Archivist* 68, no. 2 (2005): 212–13. See also "Guidelines for Efficient Archival Processing in the University of California Libraries" (University of California, 2012). https://libraries.universityofcalifornia.edu/groups/files/hosc/docs/_Efficient_Archival_Processing_Guidelines_v3-1.pdf, based largely on Greene and Meissner's work.

access.[6] Where previously boxes of manuscripts would lie in wait for an archivist to remove every staple before providing access to researchers, the new minimal methods have served to make materials available to researchers at a notably faster rate, cutting down backlogs and encouraging a well-planned action plan for each unique collection. A hypothetical example: An archive has an unprocessed collection of twenty boxes from a local African American social worker, titled "Jane Doe Collection." In a pre-minimal processing world, an individual archivist might spend hours and hours, if not days and months, researching Jane Doe, arranging and describing the materials, removing paperclips and replacing folders, and then writing up a finding aid describing the foldered contents of each box, with time spent on detailing the condition of each individual record. All of this work would be done before any researchers had access to materials. With minimal processing principles in mind, that collection might be processed into a finding aid quickly, either at collection, box ("Jane Doe Collection. Photographs, 12 Folders"), or folder level ("Photographs; November 1942–January 1943"). This has the effect of greatly speeding up accessibility for researchers on site, who can look at the finding aid and request the box "Photographs" from the Jane Doe collection. Even if a collection is only processed at its highest level, researchers would still have an idea of the types of materials an institution holds.

However, when that same repository decides to digitize those records, there are now either 250 item-level records all with the title, "Photographs; November 1942–January 1943," or 12 unwieldy, complex digital objects representing those folders, requiring the user to scroll through hundreds of images in hopes of finding something relevant. In the case of researchers looking specifically for marginalized histories, that search is even more onerous, as there is no telling whether a specific folder contains relevant materials. Since keywords would have been applied to the totality of the folder-level record, researchers searching for Christmas 1942 photographs must sift through all the photos, each of which shares only the broad keywords *Jane Doe, Social Workers, Photographic Negatives*. This research obstacle is not an issue with minimal process on a basic level, but rather an emerging division between physical accessibility and digital discoverability. "Guidelines for Efficient Archival Processing in the University of California Libraries," asks processing archivists to "Resist

---

[6] "Guidelines for Efficient Archival Processing in the University of California," 50. "To digitize archival collections efficiently, provide an equivalent level of access online as you might provide in the reading room."

the impulse to handle material at the item level,"[7] a key element in disrupting processing backlogs that comes into direct conflict with digital accessibility, where researchers are conditioned to search for individual items. The propensity for aggregate description is not strictly a result of MLPL processing, as archival practice has often avoided item-level processing for large collections, but the widespread implementation of minimal processing standards has increased the disconnect between description that is useful for reading room discovery versus digital discovery.

Minimal processing is dependent on a common description practice used across the field. Conventions around archival description are standardized in the United States in the form of *Describing Archives: A Content Standard (DACS)*.[8] DACS is designed to work with a variety of information formats, including "manual and electronic catalogs, databases, and other finding aid formats," while acknowledging that "DACS will be used principally with the two most commonly employed forms of access tools, catalogs and inventories." The structures that make up archival description are built on iterative levels of organization (collections, series, boxes, folders, etc.) that, although still physically in place, become less obvious in a digital collection, and practically invisible in a digital aggregate. Although *DACS* is the definitive guidebook to archival description, a digital archive composed of individual image files, for example, requires a descriptive level completely outside the best practices for archival access. If a researcher were to physically visit an archive with a reference request for photographs of 1930s' jazz performances in Harlem, staff would most likely bring out a box from the Cab Calloway Collection, from which the researcher would pull a folder titled something like "Photographs; Cotton Club, 1931." In the digital archives setting, on the other hand, you simply type "1930s jazz," limit your results to images, and hope for the best. Digital collections continue to be created in a world where digital objects are perceived primarily as physical surrogates, ignoring the inevitable differences in experience between a facilitated experience in a controlled, professional, physical setting and logging into a catalog search from one's favorite coffee shop.

Aggregation by its nature contradicts what has been referred to as the guiding principle of archival theory: *respects des fonds*. Michel Duchien provided the following definition of *respects des fonds*: "to group, without mixing them with others, the archives (documents of every kind) created

---

[7] "Guidelines for Efficient Archival Processing in the University of California Libraries," 5.
[8] *Describing Archives; A Content Standard*. (Chicago: Society of American Archivists, 2013), xxi. I am referencing the second edition of *DACS*, which is currently under revision.

by or coming from an administration, establishment, person, or corporate body."⁹ The *entire* appeal, however, of an aggregation platform like Umbra Search or the Digital Public Library of America is to group by mixing archives of selected establishments, persons, and corporate bodies with others. In a physical archive, a single photo is not handed out, removed from the context of its folder and box, whereas in a digital setting having to go through a box's worth of photos to get the one you want is experienced as a design failure.

This reordering of principle is made even more clear in the use of keywords and/or subject headings. Grouping information by linked keywords is a given in a digital setting, but the use of keywords in the archival setting is one of the most idiosyncratic elements of description. Library of Congress Subject Headings are a common standard but lack many signifying headings that would assist in pulling together relevant data, as illustrated by a search for the subject "African American culture," which leads to the options "African American men in popular culture" and "African American women in popular culture," or a search for the seemingly logical subject heading "United States–History–African American," which produces zero results. This is compounded by complex shifts in self-identification by African Americans over time and across communities. Users who are used to organic language hashtags resist the use of subject headings that assume a collegiate level of research methods training. These descriptive issues come together to create digital records that are difficult for computers to parse for relevancy, and difficult for users to explore thematically.

A lack of digitally transferable documentation is the crux of the first two obstacles: minimal processing and the translation of traditional archival practice into a digital ecosystem. Though minimal processing may lead to digital records with overly broad titles, and the difficulties around description for digitized records may lead to those same records being decontextualized and lacking in efficient keywords, it is not because detailed information does not exist. Archivists and librarians are astounding in their ability to quickly amass subject knowledge in their collection's holdings, but the funding and time to retrofit descriptive practice for the digital age simply isn't there. The mental metadata about finding aids and collections held within archives staff and faculty is overwhelming and outstanding, but most digitization efforts constantly juggle time

---

⁹ Michel Duchein, "Theoretical Principles and Practical Problems of *Respect des fonds* in Archival Science," *Archivaria, the Journal of the Association of Canadian Archivists* no. 16 (Summer 1983): 64.

management and financial issues, leaving few resources for creating extensive subject authorities or spending hours writing folder-level descriptions. Researchers with physical and financial capabilities can visit archives and benefit from the archivists' subject knowledge, but those using digital records miss out. This disparity becomes much more severe with materials by/about marginalized peoples. A single archivist may be a champion for African American records in their collection and hold a wealth of knowledge about its holdings, but if there is no transferable documentation, when that standard bearer quits, retires, or passes away, a huge hole appears in the understanding of some of the most underrepresented communities' histories.

With the aforementioned obstacles in mind, DAAAUMN had to consider how the process of identifying and describing materials would need to move beyond looking at the future digital records as completely analogous to their physical antecedents. At end count, DAAAUMN led to the creation of over 350,000 Tag Image File Formats (TIFFs) tied together as thousands of complex digital objects at the folder-record level, located in seventy-four different archival and rare book collections. Creating the new digital objects required the unique, enhanced descriptive metadata. The transition to digital objects from boxes and folders can feel opaque: a folder titled "African American Social Group: Minneapolis" might contain fifty sheets of paper, which when scanned front and back create one hundred digital files, that is, one new record, one complex digital object made up of one hundred new files. The digitization workflow was envisioned as holistic, including assessing and confirming the rights required to put documents online, enhancing the existing folder-level description to make clear the relevance to African American history, digitizing each folder in full, and uploading the materials to UMedia, the University of Minnesota's institutional repository, to then be harvested by the Digital Public Library of America and then Umbra Search in turn.

DAAAUMN provides a case study for digital accessibility, a project designed to identify, digitize, and redescribe materials, within the greater context of cross-institutional aggregation. In seeking digital solutions for digital problems, attempts were made to automate the discovery process. Before moving toward a more human-driven solution, an effort to create computing systems that would bypass these descriptive and organizational obstacles hit roadblocks not only because of the relatively small sample size of digitized African American materials, but also because of the metadata accompanying those records: descriptions, subject headings, keywords, tags. A 2017 experiment at a University of Minnesota campus coding event illuminated the problem's complexity. A set of 1,500 records pulled from the Digital Public Library of America, one of the largest sources for records on Umbra Search, was used as a test sample and marked for relevancy/irrelevancy by members of the Umbra Search team. University of Minnesota research system engineer David Olsen was able to design an algorithm that, using frequency of keywords, was able to match the relevancy markings of the human-defined set far above 50 percent. The discrepancies in those minority mismatches, however, reified the major complicating factor of aggregating archival records in a cross-institutional, digital setting: archival descriptive practices that assume access to an in-person, human arbiter of information.

The materials that were identified correctly tended to have clear keywords in their descriptions, "African American," "Civil Rights Movement." Materials that were described outside of those obvious categories provided some of the best examples of the sort of material a project like this is designed to reveal. Two examples of flawed exclusion/inclusion that showed the limits of designing a simple computerized selection process were found in a record titled "Justice Department Report on the Shooting of Michael Brown by Ferguson, Missouri Police Officer Darren Wilson," and in a variety of records for eighteenth-century broadside ballads.[10] During the coding experiment, the set defined by humans marked the Michael Brown record as relevant, but the computing system did not, with the opposite outcome for the ballads. When outcome of the Michael Brown record was shared, people reacted with shock—obviously this record is relevant to African American history! The metadata for the file, however, included only the keywords "Civil Unrest," "Justice Department," "Michael Brown," "Darren Wilson," "Ferguson, Missouri." Those keywords meld together in the zeitgeist, creating a shared mental set of extended keywords like "Police Violence," and "Black Lives Matter," but the computer systems work only with the technical metadata tied to a record, not the intellectual metadata tied to contemporary understandings. The issue becomes even more pressing when viewed in relation to today's quickly moving half-life for news. Archives are supposedly designed to preserve information ad infinitum, but without essential context, future generations of emerging Black scholars looking for themselves in the archive may have access to that record but would have no description inviting them to examine it further.

---

[10] This is not to claim that the design of such a system is impossible, rather that it was beyond the scope and funding of the project.

The inclusion of the ballads was less evocative but presented an equally notable problem. The texts were all originally published in the United Kingdom and were included by the algorithm because they used the word *nigger*. In reading the words of the ballads, however, the word was used as a comparative—"I'd work as hard as a nigger to win your fair heart," to paraphrase. Although this clearly provided information about conceptions of Black people in the minds of some British people in the late eighteenth century, is this relevant enough as "African American material" to be included in an aggregation such as this? A similar example was found in an earlier search when a field recording of the Child Ballad "The House Carpenter" or "The Daemon Lover" turned up within the Umbra Search corpus. This variant performance read, "I have three ships with seven slaves upon them" instead of the traditional "I have seven ships upon the seas. ... And seventeen mariners to wait on thee." Again, this has some deep ethnomusicological research interest, but doesn't necessarily belong in a collection of African American materials. When designing a system to recognize relevant words, clearly, the assumed simplest approach—look for *slave, nigger,* and so on, excludes important works while including a great many with minor relevancy.

Before description and digitization came the foundational work of finding these hidden materials in the first place. Some preparatory work to identify relevant collections was completed as part of the grant application process, leading to an initial estimate of 500,000 files, but upon initiating the project, it became clear that large portions of the identified materials would have to be excluded from digitization due to irreconcilable rights issues. The issues around rights were less connected to the materials being related to African American history, and more connected to the transition into digital collections. When most of these materials were originally acquired, the concern was having physical access to the materials. Deeds of gift and chains of custody are often nebulous when it comes to intellectual rights and were often conceived before digital collections were even imaginable. Physical ownership assuages rights concerns for researchers who can come to the archives themselves, but creating online access means having signed off intellectual rights. If permissions are received from the estate of the ethnographic photographer who took images of African Americans, are we assuming he received permissions from his subjects? By putting those materials online with his permission, are we tacitly confirming the collector's authority? On the other hand, by not putting those materials online, are we denying stakeholder communities their only access points to their own histories? Overlapping legal, ethical, and practical issues accompany any large digitization, but are perhaps particularly salient when working with the records of already marginalized peoples.

The subtraction of materials with intractable rights concerns led to a much smaller group of useable files, from 500,000 to around 180,000. A new search methodology was established with the knowledge that hidden collections sometimes take more digging to uncover than expected, along with the strong belief that with effort, African American materials can be revealed in any large survey representing American history. A list of relevant terms used across time to refer to African Americans and their history was devised along with a comprehensive and systematic search strategy, going through every available finding aid for each collection, numbering in the hundreds, slowly revealed more and more content. The list of terms included historical synonyms for *African American*: *Colored, Coloured, Negro, Nigger, Afro-American, Black,* as well as historical terms related to race in the United States: *Intergroup Relations, Human Relations, Race Relations, Mixed-Race, Integrated, Segregated, Miscegenation, Racial Mixing*. The purpose of the search strategy was twofold: to discover the more opaquely relevant materials, and practically, to give boundaries to a two-year funded project. This systematic approach, individually searching each finding aid, unearthed around 300 previously unidentified folders in seventy-six additional collections. Although the project's final file numbers fell well below original estimates, in the mid-300,000s, we expanded the amount of represented collections by more than twice over.

"Metadata enhancement" had been written into the DAAAUMN grant, though perhaps a better term for the process of guiding the project toward authentic accessibility would be *descriptive equity*. Equity came to the forefront of the project's orientation as the search for African American materials revealed itself to be more and more complicated. By the project's end, the goal was that each digitized record would, bare minimum, have some sort of keyword that would ping the aggregation coding to recognize the materials as "African American history/culture related," but also provide the user with a detailed-enough description to know that this stand-alone folder titled "Outdoor Activities" was in fact full of photographs of Harlem youth enjoying a Fresh Air Fund camping trip. Detailed descriptive work provides more equitable search results for researchers looking specifically for African American history and culture resources, although the practice flies in the face of important work cutting down collections' backlogs. It is easy to find materials organized by their relation to historic White men of a certain class, but developing an effective search strategy to dig up materials related to African Americans was involved for a professional with a master of library science degree. Most materials identified for this project were not from collections identified with "African American History." Some of the largest and richest groups of digital objects came from collections that had never been considered relevant, because although the preponderance of their content had no direct relation to African American people or culture, when removed from their original order and proactively highlighted, the proportionally small amount of relevant material created a notable collection in its own right. The most emotionally resonant example of which came from the YMCA armed services scrapbooks and photographs collection of the Kautz Family YMCA Archives.[11]

The YMCA armed services scrapbooks and photographs collection contains 151 boxes of imagery, dating from 1863–1981. The boxes were loaded with photos described at the folder level with titles like "Girls Service Organization (GSO), undated," "Informal Groups, undated," or "Religious Activities, undated." The collection came to the project's attention thanks to the "Race Relations, undated" folder, but in pulling that folder it became clear that while the folders around it might not be labeled as having African American materials, they were full of both posed and candid photos of African American servicepeople and their families throughout the 1940s, 50s, 60s, and 70s. In an effort that would be completely unworkable in a processing workflow, a week of labor was spent going through all the boxes in the collection's photographs series searching for photos of African Americans. Though these photos still lack the detailed context of individual history, researchers of war history looking for African American involvement now have a new access point, as do casual users who just want a look into the past.

Once the collections search was completed, with final record list in hand and the long list of obstacles to accessibility in mind, the descriptive equity review began in full force. This project provided the rare opportunity to experiment with description and arrangement, acknowledging that processing archivists don't have the time or ability to add folder- or item-level subjects, or to go through individual folders looking for hidden histories, an economic reality that inadvertently privileges majority representation. The project presented the opportunity to redress those

---

[11] YMCA armed services scrapbooks and photographs. Y.USA 4-5. Kautz Family YMCA Archives, University of Minnesota Libraries.

more efficiently described materials, for example, to go through a similar collection of college and university memorabilia and give the appropriate subject heading to each historically Black college or university (HBCU), as well as a geographic subject, for example, "African Americans–Georgia–Atlanta." This sort of detailed work is not financially viable or time-efficient enough to fit into the workflow of generally already overtaxed processing departments, but in a project-funded situation can greatly further accessibility, while providing examples that could potentially be applied using a more streamlined approach to conventional processing workflows in the future.

New descriptions were created to forefront hidden materials' relevance to African American history and culture, while naming protocols were used to maintain the context of the physical archival organizational hierarchy. Although digital objects are not solely surrogates for physical materials, they also cannot be presented as if created from whole cloth. A descriptive format was standardized across the project, beginning with a collection-level sentence description and then a specific description of the folder's content. For example: "This folder contains materials created/collected by Organization X. Organization X was a Civil Rights group founded in 1947. This folder specifically contains promotional materials from Organization X's 1962 National Conference on Race Relations." The newly described digital objects were given titles that highlighted archival organizational structure, formatted "Series. Subseries. Folder Title. (Folder Number, Box Number)."

This format was designed to be effectively descriptive and platform agnostic, whether objects are accessed on the Umbra Search web application, where each folder would be viewed, initially, out of collection-level context, by users looking specifically for materials relating to African American history and culture, or when viewed through other access points like ArchivesSpace, UMedia, and DPLA, each with its own distinct display and search functions. If a digital object is found through ArchivesSpace, the user would, by design, be aware of the finding aid's hierarchy. In that context, it would be clear that a folder within the "Organization X records, 1950–1970" was created/collected by Organization X. There would also, most likely, be collection-level description telling the history of that organization.

Digital collections aggregators like Umbra Search and DPL unmoor these folders from their collections, removing the prerequisite knowledge of archival organization but adding a further wrinkle in description. A folder titled "Outdoor Activities, 1967–1968" has descriptive context when discovered via the Harlem YMCA Photographs collection finding aid. The title by itself, however, gives very little context as to relevancy to African American history or to the broader organizational structure. The choice to detail collection context in folder-level description and to detail organizational information in the record titles was made to give as much necessary information as possible to researchers reaching the materials through a variety of access points.

Newly selected subject headings were designed with similar goals of increasing accessibility within interoperating systems. We chose to source primarily from Library of Congress Subject Headings (LCSH) and Library of Congress Name Authority Files (LCNAF) because those descriptors' wide usage would make them most convenient in a cross-collections aggregation context, although using only newly created localized headings would have provided more freedom in exploring radical descriptive frameworks.[12] Some local subject headings were created to bring attention to African American individuals and organizations that previously may have been difficult to discover, but when there was an applicable LCSH term, it was used. Most of the newly created local subjects were for discrete organizations and individuals that may not have LCNAF or LCSH but were coming up repeatedly within our own collections, especially with collections in the Social Welfare History Archives, where numerous mentions of obscure African American social and political organizations began to form a subject-worthy corpus.

Due to the nature of LCSH terms, the new additions often took the form of what I've come to think of as African American Mad Libs: African American + [occupation], African American + [gender], African American + [city, state], and so on. Although there is a lack of nuance in this format, the decision was made to move forward with these subjects, as the popularity of LCSH increases the probability of cross-referencing in an aggregation context. A great deal of research has taken place and continues around the nature of taxonomies versus folksonomies in libraries, especially those dealing with marginalized peoples' histories. *Folksonomy*, a term credited to information architect Thomas Vander Wal refers to user-generated and defined taxonomies, often created through

---

[12] The limitations of using LCSH to describe marginalized peoples' materials has been raised since at least the 1970s, polemically described in Sanford Berman, *Prejudices and Antipathies: A Tract on the LC Subject Heads Concerning People* (Metuchen, NJ: Scarecrow Press, 1971). For a retrospective of Berman's influence, see Steven A. Knowlton, "Three Decades Since *Prejudices and Antipathies*: A Study of Changes in the Library of Congress Subject Headings," *Cataloging & Classification Quarterly* 40, no. 2 (2005): 123–145.

social tagging.[13] Although folksonomies can have a liberatory effect, allowing individuals to define for themselves and their communities how they should be described,[14] the very nature of that idiosyncratic process competes with this project's desire to aggregate and pull materials together. This decision was one of the most difficult parts of project planning, and sheds light on the inherent issues surrounding normalization for aggregative purposes.

DAAAUMN provides an example of how dedicating time in pursuit of authentic accessibility to materials related to marginalized people can lead to huge increases in available records, as well as force staff to forefront those materials in the course of their daily labor. Identifying these records as related to African American history and digitizing them with a note referencing the project provides a sort of accessibility, and often is the end stage of a mass digitization project. Accessibility is assumed in the sharing of thousands of newly digitized records. As has been reiterated throughout this chapter, however, the act of putting something online does not make it de facto discoverable. The key feature in providing authentic accessibility in this case was in providing descriptive equity across records. Not every institution can be awarded a Hidden Collections Grant to fund full-time work on a similar mass-digitization project; this work can be executed on a smaller scale over a longer period. The digital landscape provides an opportunity to look at materials outside of the context of their collections without having to physically reorder them, disrupting concepts and principles that historically favor the discoverability of histories of privilege and power by working to provide authentic accessibility to histories that take more work on the back end to surface.

Bibliography

Adler, Melissa. "Transcending Library Catalogs: A Comparative Study of Controlled Terms in Library of Congress Subject Headings and User-Generated Tags in LibraryThing for Transgender Books." *Journal of Web Librarianship* 3, no. 4 (2009): 309–31.

---

[13] Thomas Vander Wal, "Folksonomy" (presentation, Online Information, London, UK, 2005).
[14] See Melissa Adler, (2009) "Transcending Library Catalogs: A Comparative Study of Controlled Terms in Library of Congress Subject Headings and User-Generated Tags in LibraryThing for Transgender Books," *Journal of Web Librarianship* 3, no. 4 (2009): 309–31. Though descriptive issues for LGBTQ+ collections can differ from African American collections, both the intersectionality of identity and the nature of cultural marginalization make this a relevant reading.

Alexander, Edward Porter. *Museums in Motion: An Introduction to the History and Functions of Museums.* Walnut Creek: Altamira Press, 1979.

Berman, Sanford. *Prejudices and Antipathies: A Tract on the LC Subject Heads Concerning People.* Metuchen, NJ: Scarecrow Press, 1971.

Describing Archives; A Content Standard. Chicago: Society of American Archivists, 2013.

Duchein, Michel. "Theoretical Principles and Practical Problems of Respect des fonds in Archival Science." *Archivaria, the Journal of the Association of Canadian Archivists,* no. 16 (Summer 1983): 64–82.

"Guidelines for Efficient Archival Processing in the University of California Libraries," University of California, 2012. https://libraries.universityofcalifornia.edu/groups/files/hosc/docs/_Efficient_Archival_Processing_Guidelines_v3-1.pdf.

Greene, Mark A., and Dennis Meissner. "More Product, Less Process: Revamping Traditional Archival Processing." *The American Archivist* 68, no. 2 (2005): 208–63.

Johnston, Ian. "Whose History is it Anyway?" *Journal of the Society of Archivists* 22, no. 2 (2001): 213–29.

Keough, Brian. "Documenting Diversity: Developing Special Collections of Underdocumented Groups." *Library Collections, Acquisitions, & Technical Services* 26, no. 3 (2002): 241–51.

Knowlton, Steven A. "Three Decades Since *Prejudices and Antipathies*: A Study of Changes in the Library of Congress Subject Headings." *Cataloging & Classification Quarterly* 40, no. 2 (2005): 123–45.

Mason, Kären M. "Fostering Diversity in Archival Collections." *Collection Management* 27, no. 2 (2002): 23–31.

Mecagni, Giordana. "'Why Don't People Just Get Over It?' Bringing the Archives to Boston's Conversation on Resilience and Race Equity." Presentation at the Annual Meeting of the Society of American Archivists, Portland, OR, July 28, 2017.

Overholt, John H. "Five Theses on the Future of Special Collections." *RBM: A Journal of Rare Books, Manuscripts, and Cultural Heritage* 14, no. 1 (2013): 15–20.

Theimer, Kate. "What is the meaning of Archives 2.0?" *The American Archivist* 74, no.1 (2011): 58–68.

Vander Wal, Thomas. "Folksonomy." Vanderwal.net. February 2, 2007. https://vanderwal.net/folksonomy.html.

6

Changing Attitudes Toward Access to Special Collections

Jae Jennifer Rossman

Ideas about access to special collections have changed significantly since the inception of rare book and manuscript collections as separate departments within an academic library in the early twentieth century. As these departments came into existence, so, too, did the idea of "rare book librarianship." This exploration of literature and professional standards focuses on the idea of access to materials in special collections departments in academic libraries, and, in particular, the changing attitudes of rare book librarians. Although the term *access* has many connotations, the primary focus here is on researcher access to physical collections in a secure reading room or classroom. Practitioners in the field of rare books/special collections are aware of changes in attitudes toward access, yet the trajectory of these changes appears not to have been investigated in a systematic way in the critical literature. This chapter provides evidence of a development in the library profession that is commonly accepted as true and explores other ideas connected to the dominant narrative.

Background and Context

Although the length of this essay precludes in-depth exploration of larger societal trends, acknowledging them, even in broad strokes, enables fuller understanding of the factors that contributed to changing ideas over the course of the twentieth century about access to special collections materials. Four trends are particularly important: changes to American higher education starting in the late nineteenth century, changes in academic library collections, the development of librarianship as a profession, and libraries' embrace of technology.

American higher education started its move from solely classical traditions to include practical education in the late nineteenth century, in response to industrialization and the Morrill Acts of 1862 and 1890 to support land grant institutions (Hamlin 1981, 46–47). In addition, universities began moving beyond the classical curriculum by embracing the idea that independent research was a core element of education (Hamlin 1981, 47). Industrial magnates supported higher education with an influx of funding that allowed the building of facilities and library collections (Hamlin 1981, 47–48). After World War I, an increasing percentage of American students attended some form of college, including junior colleges and technical schools, and the post-World War II GI Bill increased that number further (Kenny et al. 1998, 5; Westmeyer 1985, 107). After the postwar boom of the 1950s and 1960s, the economic troubles of the 1970s caused many higher education institutions to make cutbacks at the same time that students demanded more effective teaching and more attention to cultural studies (Westmeyer 1985, 144–45). The civil rights movement and the allied movements of the 1970s changed the American societal dialog about access to more than just library materials. The 1980s featured a strong focus on support for faculty and their cutting-edge research in major universities, often at the expense of the undergraduate population (Kenny et al. 1998, 5). The 1998 publication *Reinventing Undergraduate Education: A Blueprint for America's Research Universities* (aka the "Boyer Report") marks a shift in higher education pedagogy at large research-intensive universities—which often have large special collections—to focus on the quality of undergraduate education. Libraries reflected all of these points of significance in higher education and the country at large.

The period from 1876 to about 1920 featured exponential growth of library collections at universities in response to the changes in curriculum discussed previously (Hamlin 1981, 48). In the early twentieth century, American academic libraries experienced a dramatic transformation from predominantly haphazard, donated collections of a few thousand items to the current multimillion-volume collections found in R1 institutions. By about 1920, these libraries had become so large that they were often broken into smaller, subject-specific sections (M. Harris 1999, 253). This specialization coincided with the professionalization of scholarship in the United States in the late nineteenth and early twentieth centuries, and with the donation to a number of universities of large, private collections that were to be administered separately from the main collection (Bidwell 1983, 103; M. Harris 1999, 249–53; N. Harris 1990, 66–70; Silver 1961, 447). In response to the growing number of students on campus, a trend to permit student access to the stacks started in the 1930s; this contributed to the creation of rare book collections as separate administrative entities (Bishop 1942, 375; Byrd 1957, 441).

Library education professionalized in the late nineteenth and early twentieth centuries, starting with Melvil Dewey in 1887. As Dewey's program became the model for librarian education, the profession became known as more administrative than scholarly and rapidly changed from a male- to female-dominated profession. This "feminization of librarianship" that started in the 1920s overlapped with the rise in administratively separate rare book collections (M. Harris 1999, 291). In the early days of rare book libraries, the caretaker of the collection was a scholar/curator and not a professionally trained librarian (T. Adams 1957, 428–29). In fact, a rivalry between librarians and the "bookmen" of the rare book profession developed, with the literature containing both neutral and spiteful comments about the transition from scholars to library administrators running rare book rooms.[1]

For example, Powell (1949) commented that "If the library wishes to emphasize *acquisition* of rare materials rather than the *service* they will be put to," do not hire a "library school graduate" (11). Randolph Adams, in a now notorious essay from 1937, portrayed librarians as enemies of books (325). Wyllie (1957) disparaged the approach of library school education when he termed his librarian colleagues in the rare book field as "so-called trained librarians" (4). These comments on the professional capabilities of librarians provide insight into attitudes toward access in addition to direct professional discussions of how and by whom rare book rooms should be used.

Most recently, technological innovation has worked alongside a growing pedagogical emphasis on undergraduate exposure to primary sources to further the library profession's goal of access. Technology has created advances in description, preservation, and digital surrogates that

---

[1] For examples, see R. Adams (1965), T. Adams (1957), Cave (1976), Joyce (1988), Luft (2015), Peckham (1957), Silver (1961), or Wyllie (1949).

have expanded physical and virtual access to both general and special collections. In particular, the Internet has changed the way libraries connect with their readers. Technology that supports improved access is a vital part of special collections, yet special collections discovery systems have often lagged behind or been separated from those of general collections. Creating methods for federated searching across special and general collections facilitates access and also supports the movement in academic libraries to foreground their "distinctive" collections (Hickerson 2011, 5–6).

The Idea of "Access" and Official Statements

Access to information is the cornerstone of librarianship. The value, fragility, or scarcity of an object should not interfere with this primary goal, though this challenge of access is inherent to special collections librarianship (Berger 2014, 10). The evolving language of professional standards and guidelines offers evidence of changing attitudes toward access in special collections. A review of language in the earliest official statements raises the questions: Why did professional organizations feel the need to specify that access should not be restricted (except for legal reasons)? Does the creation of these statements imply that access was previously not egalitarian? As context, consider that the Society of American Archivists (SAA) was founded in 1936 and the Rare Book and Manuscript Section (RBMS) of the Association of College and Research Libraries /American Library Association was started as a committee in 1955 and became a section in 1958, while the first access statements were not unveiled until 1974 and the release of codes of ethics followed in the 1980s. Although the underlying impetus to write the statements is not revealed in the official documents, the changes in language over time are reflective of changes in the profession.

The term *access* can apply to many components of librarianship. *Public services* covers a broad range of patron access issues, including reference, instruction, and physical access to materials. This idea of "service" has varied with time; initially scorned as the driving force behind professionalized librarians who were not scholars, it became less controversial, but still somewhat restrictive, in the mid-twentieth century, and today includes audiences of all ages and education levels, including off-site readers (R. Adams [1941] 1965, 145; T. Adams 1957, 428–29; Bahde 2011, 75–6; Dekydtspotter and Williams 2013, 67; Peckham 1957,

420; Visser 2003, 29–30; Wright 1957, 434). Public service also overlaps with technical services, which provide the infrastructure necessary to provide access, such as digitization and description. In fact, providing catalog cards, finding aids, and inventories is called a *responsibility* in the earliest professional statements on access and is still included in the most recent version (RBMS 1974, 114; SAA 1974, 153; RBMS and SAA 2009, sec. 2).

In addition, preservation is an important component of access in special collections. Yet, access and preservation have long been considered conflicting components of librarians' responsibilities (Cave 1982, 100; Haugh 1957, 467; Traister 1987, 145). Preservation is addressed in professional statements and guidelines as a core component of a librarian's or an archivist's responsibilities. Antonetti (1987) cautions "'to preserve' should never be construed to mean 'to keep out of the hands of'"; instead "custodian" should become "facilitator" (177–78). Note that contemporary conversations about providing access are centered on physicality of the object, not on who has access.

Official Statements Regarding Access

The earliest official statements found in the literature were issued in 1974 separately by SAA and RBMS. The statements are similar in tone and content, including exact duplication of some sentences, which suggests collaboration between the professional organizations. Of particular interest are the qualifications on access terms in the first section of the 1974 RBMS document: "It is the responsibility of a library, archives, or manuscript repository to make available to *qualified* researchers, *as defined by the respective institutions*, on equal terms of access, research materials in its possession" (114; emphasis added). The issue of who qualifies as a researcher has been and continues to be debated (R. Adams [1941] 1965, 146–51; Peckham 1957, 418; Traister 2000, 67–68; Visser 2003, 31). Letters of recommendation and/or an interview by a staff member to determine a researcher's qualifications were a prerequisite for granting access to many special collections (Cave 1976, 108; Haugh 1957, 468–69). Today, a more commonly accepted means of prequalification is presentation of designated forms of identification as recommended by the *ACRL/RBMS Guidelines Regarding Security and Theft in Special Collections* (RBMS 2008, sec 6).

In 1993, the joint statement was further revised to include two additions: definitions of terminology and a reference to code of ethics documents created in the 1980s. The most recent version of the RBMS/SAA joint statement on access is from 2009, and includes a new idea: Not only should repositories provide access freely, they should have "a clearly defined and publicized institutional access policy" (sec. 1). This move from professional courtesy to official policy signals a change in professional practice. Now expectations of equal access are codified in writing at each institution—in theory—and not solely by the professional organizations.

Attitudes Prior to Official Statements by Professional Organizations

Since the inception of special collections, ideas of access have fluctuated, and conflicting attitudes can be found as early as the 1930s. Powell (1939) offers an attitude on access that seems in line with today's expansive opinions. He felt that "too often rare books are allowed to live a sort of hallowed, touch-me-not, existence. If we should not circulate them carelessly, neither should we hoard them from sight and touch" (Powell 1939, 100). Furthermore, Powell quotes from the McGregor Plan, which supplied funding from the American Historical Association to academic libraries for the purchase of rare books on Americana and was run by men important in the rare-book-world network. Powell quotes that libraries must "plan for careful and appreciative use of the books by undergraduates as well as graduate students" (Powell 1939, 101). Advocating for use of rare books by undergraduates in the late 1930s was unusual, and the same men later changed their minds.

A contrasting view is put forth by Randolph Adams: "The librarian who allows rare books to be used without proper restrictions is an enemy of books" (R. Adams 1937, 325). He goes on to say rare books must be "kept away from all unfit persons" and those who are "unqualified" (R. Adams 1937, 325–26). In a footnote, R. Adams (1937) further explains: "The librarian must distinguish carefully between the reader who is adding to human knowledge and the reader who is merely training himself so that later he may add to human knowledge" (326). Most undergraduates and perhaps even graduate students would likely fall in the latter category. Randolph Adams has become representative of early twentieth-century views on rare book access because his articles have been referenced repeatedly.[2] Sydney Berger (1987), a noted scholar of

---

[2] For examples, see T. Adams (1957), Archer (1965), Cave (1976), French (1965), Goff (1957), and Tree (1957).

the rare book profession, cited R. Adams as the beginning of the critical literature of the rare book profession (9).

In the aftermath of World War II, however, a consensus seems to emerge. In a 1949 Association of College and Research Libraries (ACRL) conference report, *Rare Books in the University Library*, Powell reverses his previous stance to advocate that "rare books have small place in the undergraduate program" and that "Use of the collections should be regarded as a privilege" (Powell 1949, 7, 10–11). Another conference participant is even more dismissive of underclassmen: "early editions ... must be protected from the all-devouring maw of the undergraduate" (Wyllie 1957, 5). Powell attributes his earlier comments to "the optimism of youth" and confesses that they were an "idealistic outburst" (Powell 1949, 7). When he was advocating their use by undergraduates in 1939, he was a junior librarian working in the "accessions" department of the University of California, Los Angeles (UCLA), and was not yet an insider to the rare book world (Wiegand 1983, 266). A decade later, he had completely reversed his position and even renounced his earlier work. Powell had also become part of the inner circle of bookmen by this time, adopting the opinions of a small network of rare book curators and scholars. His position as the University Librarian and the head of the Clark Library at UCLA also confirmed his insider status (Wiegand 1983, 268). This tight network of bookmen can be seen through visualization of their citation network (see Appendix A). Whether through citation of published works by their rare book colleagues or through mentioning the names of colleagues—and their impressive acquisitions or credentials—in the text, the interconnectedness of a relatively small group of primarily men is evident in the print history of the profession.

Perhaps these harsher attitudes toward access were influenced by the cumulative effect of the newly open stacks as well as the increase in college attendance after World War II. Wyllie's (1957) remarks support this idea:

> One of the chief reasons for the need of rare book rooms in our university libraries today is the locust-like descent of great swarms of people on our collections. The locusts fall into two general categories: the student and the so-called trained librarian. (4)

The derogatory attitude toward trained librarians as caretakers of rare books is a recurrent theme in the early literature, especially when these librarians aim to provide equal access to all.

In 1957, shortly after the founding of RBMS as a committee in 1955, *Library Trends* devoted an issue to rare book librarianship. Although there is continued justification for the practices of vetted and controlled access—the preservation argument—there is also a reticent widening of access, albeit for qualified readers. For instance, in an article on the "utility" of the rare book library, Wright (1957) implores accessibility, noting "It should be a platitude by now that the privately endowed library of rare books has no justification for existence unless it serves in the advancement of learning by making its literary resources available to qualified scholars" (434). In addition, Wright (1957) says that rare book libraries are effective because they are "making their materials available to the individuals who can best use them" (434). These statements leave many unanswered questions. Who is a "qualified scholar" who can "best use" the materials? And more important, who determines these unpublished qualifications and who arbitrates each patron's potential?

The issue's editor, Peckham (1957), makes it clear that the patrons bear the responsibility of proving their worth to use the collections:

> Readers have to identify themselves and sometimes prove their competence by deposing that they have exhausted the secondary materials on their subject. Since most of the patrons are doing research, a very high percentage of them are scholars, as distinguished from the lay public and children. (418)

Wroth (1957) widens the pool to include mature readers, scholars, bookmen, and advanced students (425). The most inclusive attitudes toward access come from the two female contributors to the issue. One article discusses special collections in public libraries and advocates for the entertainment value of the collection to all ages and educational levels (Shaffer 1957, 455–56). The other surveyed institutions about their reader policies; Haugh (1957) concludes:

> If a trend may be discerned, it is toward effort to encourage greater use of the materials, especially in those collections which are part of an academic institution. Necessity to justify existence in competition with other library service units may be partially responsible, as well as the genuine desire of the librarian to stimulate students to become acquainted with fine books. Hence, for them, there is no barring of the inexperienced student for lack of credentials or purpose, and a welcoming atmosphere free of obvious restrictions is sought. (474)

Yet, at the same time, most collections reported tightening their rules because of increased usage (Haugh 1957, 474). It is noteworthy that

Haugh (1957) indicates that the person encouraging use of the rare book collection is a librarian—not a scholar, curator, or bookman—when her own title was *curator*.

The tension between bookmen and librarians and the transition of rare book administration from bookmen to librarians contributed to the changing attitudes toward access over time. As rare book collections were created, largely from the 1910s through the 1940s, the administrative head of these collections was typically a male scholar, often called a *bookman*. As seen previously, these bookmen were minimally interested in ideas of access from the library profession. In addition, these bookmen were a relatively close-knit group of scholars who respected and reinforced the others' ideas. A visualization of the citation network of the 1957 *Library Trends* issue devoted to rare books shows that four contributors were most active in citing and had overlaps in their citation choices (see Appendix). Also, the data visualization shows that these primary actors in the network frequently mentioned in the text or cited other scholars, collectors, and bookmen, thus linking themselves to a host of worthy allies. The authors connected themselves not only to contemporaneous colleagues, but to those considered foundational to the idea of the collector as one whose forethought and perseverance in collecting materials paved the way for great scholarship, such as Thomas Jefferson, James Lenox, and John Carter Brown. Adding additional literature from the 1930s to the 1960s to the citation network map shows the continuation of a closely linked network through the interconnectedness of the visualization. The tendency to give extensive examples of respected figures is seen in the visualization as many rays emanate from a singular point. For example, Edwin Wolf in his essay on the development of American rare book collections cited or mentioned over 200 names in an article of only 15 pages!

In the 1960s, the literature shows evidence of new attitudes toward access; a good example is *Rare Book Collections* published by ACRL in 1965. Despite a backward-looking introduction that reminds the reader of Randolph Adams's belief that books should be kept away from the "average barbarian" (Archer 1965, 3), the contributors make statements about access that, although guarded, appear to be the beginning of a more equitable approach. Wynne wants to combat the idea "that everything therein is to be gazed upon but not touched" (Wynne 1965, 4). The idea that preservation trumps access is still present throughout the publication (French 1965, 92; Harlow 1965, 86). French argues that security is also a form of preservation, especially knowing each reader in detail, thus reinforcing the requirements of reader vetting before collection use. However, she also states that "reference service ... is the signpost to use" and "The idea of service seizes the imagination as the older, purely custodial concept never could" (French 1965, 97). The use of rare books in the classroom is mentioned only briefly (French 1965, 100), but presages what would develop into today's strong focus on the importance of primary source materials in graduate and undergraduate learning.

Women's contributions to the field in its early days are sparsely documented in the literature. The 1957 *Library Trends* issue had two women out of eleven contributors. *Rare Book Collections* (1965) made only a minor improvement with three out of eleven contributions penned by women. Although the role of women in the early and mid-twentieth-century rare book world is not extensively apparent in the literature, they were involved. Beyond the few early prominent female rare book specialists, such as Belle DaCosta Greene of the Morgan Library, women were working in rare book rooms, even if not in the lead role. Further investigation into the role of women in the formative days of the rare book field in the academic library would provide valuable insight into the opinions of bookmen preserved in the literature.

Attitudes after Official Statements by Professional Organizations

The special collections/rare books literature of the 1970s through the early 2000s engendered a more frequent discussion of access-related issues, particularly about technology, audience and outreach, and pedagogy. The 1980s saw growth in the number of articles on special collections access in response to rising automation, preservation, and book history trends (Berger 1987, 10–11; Cloonan 1987, 4–5). Also, the economic hardship of the 1980s provoked librarians to view access through the lens of use. From the 1990s to the present, a change in higher education pedagogical practices to favor inclusivity, active learning, and object-based learning elicited many articles on outreach efforts and how to better integrate special collections into the curriculum. Also notable is that because the number of staff supporting special collections units had grown over time, typically, the scholar/bookman took on the full-time curator role while a professional librarian became the administrative head of the unit, with a different set of professional priorities becoming the foundation of service.

Access and Use

Cave's *Rare Book Librarianship* represents the profession's views in the early 1970s. Of particular note is how he addresses the conflict between preservation and use, advocating that collections should be "restricted to those who really need them" (Cave 1976, 108). When this work was updated in 1982, several years after the publication of the RBMS and SAA statements, the term *access* was included in the index to cover the section previously indexed as *admission*. The conflict between preservation and use is highlighted more strongly by Cave in the 1982 edition, calling it "a sort of professional schizophrenia," (100) whereas in 1976 it was merely a "dichotomy" (107).

The justification of the expense of special collections by use statistics is a reflection of the difficult economic times in the United States, and therefore in academic institutions, prevalent during the 1970s and early 1980s. Matheson (1984) surveyed academic rare book collections and although the topic of justification was not on his original survey, it was mentioned in the comments so frequently he felt compelled to address it (50–51). This documents a reason other than broadening attitudes toward who could use special collections that drove increased access and use. By the late 1980s, the role of special collections in academic libraries was clear enough that justification arguments were no longer needed (Berger 1987, 12). However, the theme returned in the 1990s because of new economic hardships in that decade (W. Jones 1993, 80–81). In the 2000s, efforts to increase collection use through instruction were common.[3]

Technology

In *Rare Books and Manuscripts Librarianship*, the journal of the RBMS started in 1986, many articles from the 1980s and 1990s centered on technological advances of the core functions of description and conservation. In 1987, *Library Trends* again devoted an issue to special collections, in which most of the articles concerned technical advances in description and preservation. Concerns about use of deteriorating collections also became important to the research library as a whole in the 1980s (Ferguson 1987, 158). A major issue was the perceived inaccessibility of archival collections due to processing backlogs, which was addressed in the early 2000s. Of particular note are the articles "Hidden Collections, Scholarly

---

[3] For examples, see Alvarez (2006), Bahde (2011), Dekydtspotter & Williams (2013), Gardner & Pavelich (2008), Robb (2009), Smith (2006), Taraba (2003), and Vong (2016).

Barriers: Creating Access to Unprocessed Special Collections Materials in America's Research Libraries" (2004) and "More Product, Less Product: Pragmatically Revamping Traditional Processing Approaches to Deal with late 20th Century Collections" (2005), as well as the results of the Association of Research Libraries' survey of special collections authored by Panitch (2001). Although many articles focused on details of the technology, improved access was typically the desired outcome.

Audience and Outreach

The literature of the early 1980s discussed which audiences to target to increase collection use. For example, Traister (1983) argued for outreach methods to reach potential audiences, but focused on the expected faculty and donors (115–16). Mortimer (1983) made an argument for allowing undergraduates to use rare books, an idea that became a significant trend. Cave (1982) calls outreach "salesmanship," which may be a reflection of the larger discussion about use justifying the existence of rare book collections (100). Even while touting the expanded access and use of collections, a strong emphasis that preservation of the physical artifact should always trump access in special collections remained (Traister 1987). It is noteworthy that the conversation about access begun in the 1980s still centers on who is a qualified reader, even if that definition has broadened.

Articles in the 1990s that discussed engaging new audiences were often about a wider disciplinary approach, while continuing to focus on faculty and graduate students. The same "scholarly" audience of the earliest rare book rooms is still present in articles from the 1970s until Allen's (1999) survey on undergraduate instruction and Henderson's (1999) article on purposeful outreach initiatives. Allen's article is now frequently cited as the beginning of this important twenty-first-century trend. Henderson cites multiple examples of private special collections doing outreach to the public through exhibitions and event programming, and of public academic institutions reaching out to K–12 students and teachers, who are now seen as important audiences. Focus on the general public and K–12 students as a "typical" audience did not become more widely accepted until the twenty-first century, which may be driven by the rise of the Internet as a method of access (Visser 2003, 30).

In 2000, the RBMS journal changed names, dropping *librarianship* in favor of *cultural heritage*. The inaugural issue contained a polemical essay intended to ask hard questions about who has access to special collections. Traister (2000) questions not only the qualifications, but who has the right to determine who is qualified. He proclaims that withholding of access from those deemed not qualified is "simply idiotic ... mean-spirited, judgmental, exclusionary, hierarchical, and otiose" (61). This essay records an important moment in a shift in attitudes toward access, but is also surprisingly late. Like the first official statements on access, the fact that Traister felt the need to write this in the year 2000 implies that it was still an issue. By 2017 the profession seems to have caught up, with the ACRL *Competencies for Special Collections Professionals* stating that librarians must work with "the institution's full range of audiences and communities" (sec. III.D.).

Pedagogical Changes

Pedagogical changes in the academy after the "Boyer Report" are evidenced in special collections through an increased focus on instruction as a form of outreach and an increased discussion of teaching for an undergraduate audience; Allen's (1999) survey showed that this was happening in Oberlin Group institutions in the late 1990s. In the 2000s, multiple publications explore undergraduates as an audience for instruction with special collections materials.[4] The most contemporary of these articles no longer formally argue for why undergraduates are an appropriate audience, but merely document innovative pedagogy for this now-accepted audience. The topic is important enough to warrant at least two major publications related to instruction in special collections in the last seven years: *Using Primary Sources: Hands-On Instructional Exercises* (2014) and *Past or Portal? Enhancing Undergraduate Learning through Special Collections and Archives* (2012), as well as a section dedicated to instruction in *Collaborating for Impact: Special Collections and Liaison Librarian Partnerships* (2016). Also in the last decade, special collections' increasing importance in the academy has been covered in journals not solely dedicated to special collections such as *The Journal of Academic Librarianship* and *portal: Libraries and the Academy*.

Conclusions

This chapter traced changing attitudes toward special collections access within the profession, with a focus on the difference in attitudes expressed

---

[4] For examples, see Berenbak et al. (2010), Krause (2010), Thomas & Whittaker (2017), and Visser (2003).

in the literature before and after official statements on access were made by the professional groups RBMS and SAA. Although here we focused on the rare books part of special collections, it is important to acknowledge the significant contribution archivists made and are still making to ideas of access in academic libraries. As higher education and cultural institutions broadened their base of users, special collections followed, by necessity and desire. Attitudes about access began to expand as professional librarians, who were trained to focus on service, became a larger part of rare book/special collections. Although the transition from "bookmen" to professionally trained librarians as the main administrators of rare book/special collections appears to roughly parallel changes in attitude toward special collection use, further detailed research is needed to prove a true cause-and-effect relationship. Through this brief examination of the literature and professional standards, it appears that a combination of the importance of access as a core element of librarianship and larger societal trends toward equal access to institutional resources, as well as economic pressures and pedagogical changes in academia, drove the change in special collections from a "gentleman's club of English or history professors" (Visser 2003, 30) to the service- and education-oriented departments and institutions of today.

As Jacquelyn Dowd Hall (2005) warned that historians must be careful not to portray the civil rights movement as "a natural progression of American values," I advocate a similar caution for the increased openness to the use of special collections by a wider audience (1235). Attitudes about wider access and the promotion of special collections to the public and others who are not "scholars" can be found in early writings on the twentieth-century administrative phenomenon of the rare book room, so it is not a new idea. Although there is certainly evidence that significant change has occurred, access to special collections remains more restrictive than to general collections. This is not only because of the necessary preservation aspect of being responsible stewards of rare and unique materials, but because a certain level of cultural knowledge is necessary to understand their purpose and even know of their existence. As the importance of primary source research and object-based learning to successful undergraduate pedagogy grows, it is hoped that this will further integrate the use of special collections into college students' understanding of the range of library resources and aspires to become part of the precollege students' education as well.

Bibliography

* = Publication surveyed for the data set used for the citation networks visualized in the Appendix.

*Adams, Randolph G. "Librarians as Enemies of Books." *The Library Quarterly: Information, Community, Policy* 7, no. 3 (1937): 317–31.

*———. "Who Uses a Library of Rare Books?" In *English Institute Annual 1940*. New York: AMS Press, 1965.

*Adams, Thomas R. "Rare Books: Their Influence on the Library World." *Library Trends* 5 (1957): 426–33.

AHA Committee on Americana for College Libraries. *The McGregor Plan for the Encouragement of Book Collecting by American College Libraries*. Ann Arbor, MI: American Historical Society, 1937.

*Alden, John E. "Cataloging and Classification." In *Rare Book Collections: Some Theoretical and Practical Suggestions for Use by Librarians and Students*, edited by H. Richard Archer, 65–73. Chicago: American Library Association, 1965.

Allen, Susan M. "Rare Books and the College Library: Current Practices in Marrying Undergraduates to Special Collections." *Rare Books & Manuscripts Librarianship* 13, no. 2 (1999): 110–19.

Alvarez, Pablo. "Introducing Rare Books into the Undergraduate Curriculum." *RBM: A Journal of Rare Books, Manuscripts & Cultural Heritage* 7, no. 2 (2006): 94–104.

Antonetti, Martin. "The Subtle Symbiosis: Rare Books and Manuscripts at Mills College." *Library Trends* 36, no. 1 (1987): 171–78.

*Archer, H. Richard. "Introduction." In *Rare Book Collections: Some Theoretical and Practical Suggestions for Use by Librarians and Students*, edited by H. Richard Archer, 1–3. Chicago: American Library Association, 1965.

Bahde, Anne. "Taking the Show on the Road: Special Collections Instruction in the Campus Classroom." *RBM: A Journal of Rare Books, Manuscripts & Cultural Heritage* 12, no. 2 (2011): 75–88.

Berenbak, Adam, Cate Putirskis, Genya O'Gara, Claire Ruswick, Danica Cullinan, Judy Allen Dodson, Emily Walters, and Kathy Brown. *Special Collections Engagement: SPEC kit 317*. Washington, DC: Association of Research Libraries, 2010.

Berger, Sydney E. "What Is So Rare … : Issues in Rare Book Librarianship." *Library Trends* 36, no. 1 (1987): 9–22.

———. *Rare Books and Special Collections*. Chicago: Neal-Schuman, 2014.

Bidwell, John. "Rare Books for Research: Separately Housed Collections." *Wilson Library Bulletin* 58, no. 2 (1983): 102–06.

*Bishop, William W. "Rare Book Rooms in Libraries." *The Library Quarterly: Information, Community, Policy* 12, no. 3 (1942): 375–85.

Brown, Amanda H., Barbara Losoff, and Deborah R. Hollis. "Science Instruction through the Visual Arts in Special Collections." *portal: Libraries and the Academy* 14, no. 2 (2014): 197–216.

*Byrd, Cecil K. "Rare Books in University Libraries." *Library Trends* 5 (1957): 441–50.

Cave, Roderick. *Rare Book Librarianship.* London: Clive Bingley and Hamden, CT: Linnet Books, 1976.

———. *Rare Book Librarianship.* London: Clive Bingley, 1982.

Cloonan, Michèle V. "Introduction." *Library Trends* 36, no. 1(1987): 3–8.

Dekydtspotter, Lori Lynn, and Cherry Dunham Williams. "Alchemy and Innovation: Cultivating an Appreciation for Primary Sources in Younger Students." *RBM: A Journal of Rare Books, Manuscripts & Cultural Heritage* 14, no. 2 (2013): 67–81.

Ferguson, Stephen. "Rare Books in University Libraries." *Library Trends* 36, no. 1 (1987): 157–70.

*French, Hannah D. "Access, Service, and Publications." In *Rare Book Collections: Some Theoretical and Practical Suggestions for Use by Librarians and Students*, edited by H. Richard Archer, 92–107. Chicago: American Library Association, 1965.

Gardner, Julia, and David Pavelich. "Teaching with Ephemera." *RBM: A Journal of Rare Books, Manuscripts & Cultural Heritage* 9, no. 1(2008): 86–92.

*Goff, Frederick R. "Who Uses Rare Books and What For?" *Library Trends* 5 (1957): 459–66.

Greene, Mark A., and Dennis Meissner. "More Product, Less Process: Pragmatically Revamping Traditional Processing Approaches to Deal with Late 20th Century Collections." *American Archivist* 68, no. 2 (2005): 208–63.

Hall, Jacquelyn Dowd. "The Long Civil Rights Movement and the Political Uses of the Past." *The Journal of American History* 91, no. 4 (2005): 1233–63.

Hamlin, Arthur T. *The University Library in the United States: Its Origins and Development.* Philadelphia; University of Pennsylvania Press, 1981.

*Harlow, Neal R. "Physical Housing and Equipment." In *Rare Book Collections: Some Theoretical and Practical Suggestions for Use by Li-*

brarians and Students, edited by H. Richard Archer, 86–91. Chicago: American Library Association, 1965.

Harris, Michael H. *History of Libraries in the Western World*. Lanham, MD: The Scarecrow Press, 1999.

Harris, Neil. "Special Collections and Academic Scholarship: A Tangled Relationship." In *Libraries and Scholarly Communication in the United States: The Historical Dimension*, edited by Phyllis Dain and John Young Cole, 63–70. New York: Greenwood Press, 1990.

*Haugh, Georgia C. "Reader Policies in Rare Book Libraries." *Library Trends* 5, no. 4 (1957): 467–75.

Henderson, Cathy. "Negotiating New Borders for Special Collections." *Rare Book & Manuscript Librarianship* 14, no. 1 (1999): 9–17.

Hickerson, Thomas. "Rebalancing the Investment in Collections." *Research Libraries Issues* 277 (2011): 1–8.

Jones, Barbara M. "Hidden Collections, Scholarly Barriers: Creating Access to Unprocessed Special Collections Materials in America's Research Libraries." *RBM: A Journal of Rare Book, Manuscript, and Cultural Heritage* 5, no. 2 (2004): 88–105.

Jones, William Goodrich. "Leaner and Meaner: Special Collections, Librarians, and Humanists at the End of the Century." *RBML: Rare Book & Manuscript Librarianship* 8, no. 2 (1993): 80–91.

Joyce, William. "The Evolution of the Concept of Special Collections in American Research Libraries." *RBML: Rare Book & Manuscript Librarianship* 3, no. 1 (1988): 19–29.

Kenny, Shirley Strum, Bruce Alberts, Wayne C. Booth, Milton Glaser, Charles E. Glassick, Stanley O. Ikenberry, Kathleen Hall Jamieson, Robert M. O'Neil, Carolynn Reid-Wallace, Chang-Lin Tien, and Chen Ning Yang. *Reinventing Undergraduate Education: A Blueprint for America's Research Universities*. Stoney Brook, NY: Boyer Commission on Educating Undergraduates in the Research University, 1998.

Krause, Magia G. "'It Makes History Alive for Them': The Role of Archivists and Special Collections Librarians in Instructing Undergraduates." *The Journal of Academic Librarianship* 36, no. 5 (2010): 401–11.

Luft, Eric v.d. "Between Tradition and Automation in Special Collections: A Memoir." *RBM: A Journal of Rare Books, Manuscripts & Cultural Heritage* 16, no. 2 (2015): 93–100.

Matheson, W. "Institutional Collections in the United States." In *Rare Books 1983–84: Trends, Collections, Sources*, edited by Alice D. Schreyer, 33–52. New York: R. R. Bowker., 1984.

Mitchell, Eleanor, Peggy Seiden, and Suzy Taraba, eds. *Past or Portal?: Enhancing Undergraduate Learning through Special Collections and Archives.* Chicago: Association of College & Research Libraries, 2012.

Mortimer, Ruth. "Manuscripts and Rare Books in an Undergraduate Library." *Wilson Library Bulletin* 58, no. 2 (1983): 107–10.

Panitch, Judy M. *Special Collections in ARL Libraries: Results of the 1998 Survey Sponsored by the ARL Research Collections Committee.* Washington, DC: Association of Research Libraries, 2001.

*Peckham, Howard H. "Introduction." *Library Trends* 5 (1957): 417–21.

*Powell, Lawrence Clark. "The Functions of Rare Books." *College & Research Libraries* 1(1939): 97–103.

*———. "Policy and Administration." In *Rare Books in the University Library*, 7–11. [Chicago?]: Association of College and Research Libraries, 1949.

Rare Books in the University Library. [Chicago?]: Association of College and Research Libraries, 1949.

RBMS. "ACRL Code of Ethics for Special Collections Librarians." Rare Book and Manuscript Section website. Last modified 2003. https://rbms.info/standards/code_of_ethics/.

RBMS Committee on Manuscripts Collections. (1974). "Statement on Access to Original Research Materials in Libraries, Archives, and Manuscript Repositories."*College & Research Libraries* 35: 114.

RBMS Committee on Manuscripts Collections. (1976). "Statement on Access to Original Research Materials in Libraries, Archives, and Manuscript Repositories. *College & Research Libraries* 37: 272–73.

RBMS Committee on Professional Ethics. (1984). "Standards for Ethical Conduct for Rare Book, Manuscript, and Special Collections Librarians." *College & Research Libraries News* 45: 357–58.

RBMS & SAA. "ACRL/SAA Joint Statement on Access to Research Materials in Archives and Special Collections Libraries." Rare Book and Manuscript Section website. Last modified 2009. http://www.ala.org/acrl/standards/jointstatement.

RBMS Security Committee. "ACRL/RBMS Guidelines Regarding Security and Theft in Special Collections." Rare Book and Manuscript Section website. Last modified 2008. http://www.ala.org/acrl/standards/security_theft.

RBMS Task Force on Core Competencies for Special Collections Professionals. "Competencies for Special Collections Professionals." Rare Book and Manuscript Section website. Last modified 2017. http://www.ala.org/acrl/standards/comp4specollect.

Robb, Jenny. "The Opper Project: Collaborating with Educators to Promote the Use of Editorial Cartoons in the Social Studies Classroom." *RBM: A Journal of Rare Books, Manuscripts & Cultural Heritage* 10, no. 2 (2009): 70–94.

Society of American Archivists. "Standards for Access to Research Materials in Archival and Manuscript Repositories." *The American Archivist* 37, no. 1 (1974): 153–54.

———. "Code of Ethics and Commentary." *The American Archivist* 43, no. 3 (1980): 414–18.

———. "Code of Ethics for Archivists and Commentary." Illinois Institute of Technology Ethics Codes Collection. Last modified 1992. http://ethics.iit.edu/ecodes/node/4559.

———. "Code of Ethics for Archivists." Illinois Institute of Technology Ethics Codes Collection. Last modified 2005. http://ethics.iit.edu/ecodes/node/4560.

———. "SAA Core Values Statement and Code of Ethics." Last modified 2011. http://www2.archivists.org/statements/saa-core-values-statement-and-code-of-ethics.

*Shaffer, Ellen. "The Place of Rare Books in the Public Library." *Library Trends* 5, no. 4 (1957): 451–58.

Silver, Rollo. "The Training of Rare Book Librarians." *Library Trends* 8 (1961): 446–52.

Smith, Steven Escar. "From 'Treasure Room' to 'School Room': Special Collections and Education." *RBM: A Journal of Rare Books, Manuscripts & Cultural Heritage* 7, no. 1 (2006): 31–39.

Taraba, Suzy. "Now What Should We Do with Them?: Artists' Books in the Curriculum." *RBM: A Journal of Rare Books, Manuscripts & Cultural Heritage* 4, no. 2 (2003): 109–20.

Thomas, Lynne M., and Beth M. Whittaker, eds. *New Directions for Special Collections: An Anthology of Practice*. Santa Barbara: Libraries Unlimited, 2017.

Traister, Daniel. "Rare Book Collections: The Need for Interpretation." *Wilson Library Bulletin* 58, no. 2 (1983): 115–19.

———. "A Caucus-Race and a Long Tale: The Profession of Rare Books Librarianship in the 1980s." *Library Trends* 36, no. 1 (1987): 141–56.

———. "Is There a Future for Special Collections? And Should There Be? A Polemical Essay." *RBM: A Journal of Rare Books, Manuscripts & Cultural Heritage* 1, no. 1 (2000): 54–76.

*Tree, Roland A. L. "Fashions in Collecting and Changing Prices." *Library Trends* 5, no. 4 (1957): 476–82.

Visser, Michelle. "Inviting in the Rabble: Changing Approaches to Public Service and Access in Special Collections." *Public Services Quarterly* 1, no. 4 (2003): 29–41.

Vong, Silvia. "A Constructivist Approach for Introducing Undergraduate Students to Special Collections and Archival Research." *RBM: A Journal of Rare Books, Manuscripts & Cultural Heritage* 17, no. 2 (2016): 148–71.

Westermeyer, Paul. *A History of American Higher Education*. Springfield, IL: Charles C. Thomas, 1985.

Wiegand, Wayne A. "Lawrence Clark Powell." In *Leaders in American Academic Librarianship: 1925–1975*, edited by Wayne A. Wiegand, 262–287. Pittsburgh: Beta Phi Mu, 1983.

*Wright, Louis B. "Utility of the Special Research Library." *Library Trends* 5, no. 4 (1957): 434–40.

*Wroth, Lawrence C. "A Negotiation and Some Affirmations." *Library Trends* 5, no. 4 (1957): 422–25.

*Wyllie, J. C. "The Need." In *Rare Books in the University Library*, 3–6. [Chicago?]: Association of College and Research Libraries, 1949.

*Wynne, Marjorie. G. "The Nature and Importance of Rare Books. In *Rare Book Collections: Some Theoretical and Practical Suggestions for Use by Librarians and Students*, edited by H. Richard Archer, 4–10. Chicago: American Library Association, 1965.

Appendix
Data Visualization of Citation Networks of Selected Special Collections Literature from 1937 to 1965

Each citation network is shown twice: (1) without name labels to better depict the connections and (2) with name labels to identify the actors in the network. Colors indicate the type of institution or profession of the person making the citation. Arrows indicate the direction of citation. Color of arrow is determined by the source of citation.

Changing Attitudes Toward Access to Special Collections

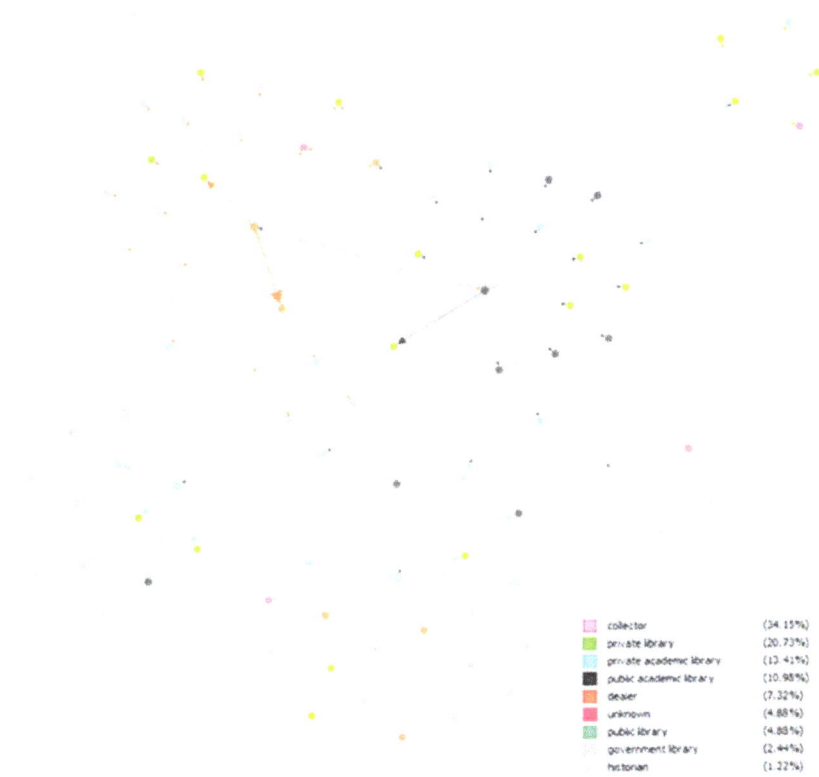

Library Trends, vol. 5, 1957—without name labels.

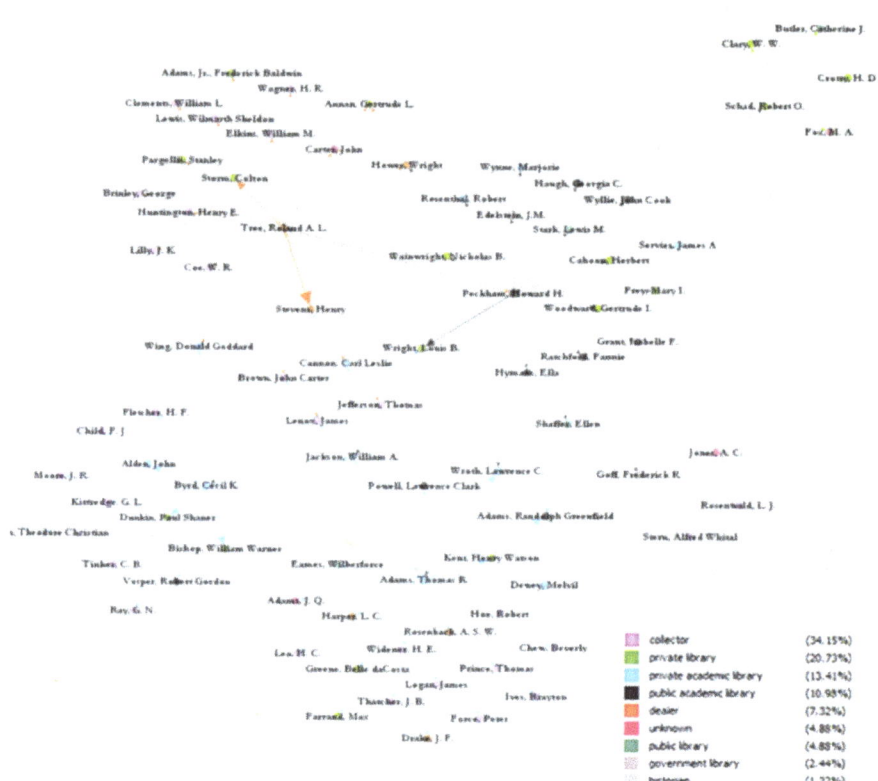

Library Trends, vol. 5, 1957—with name labels.

Changing Attitudes Toward Access to Special Collections 149

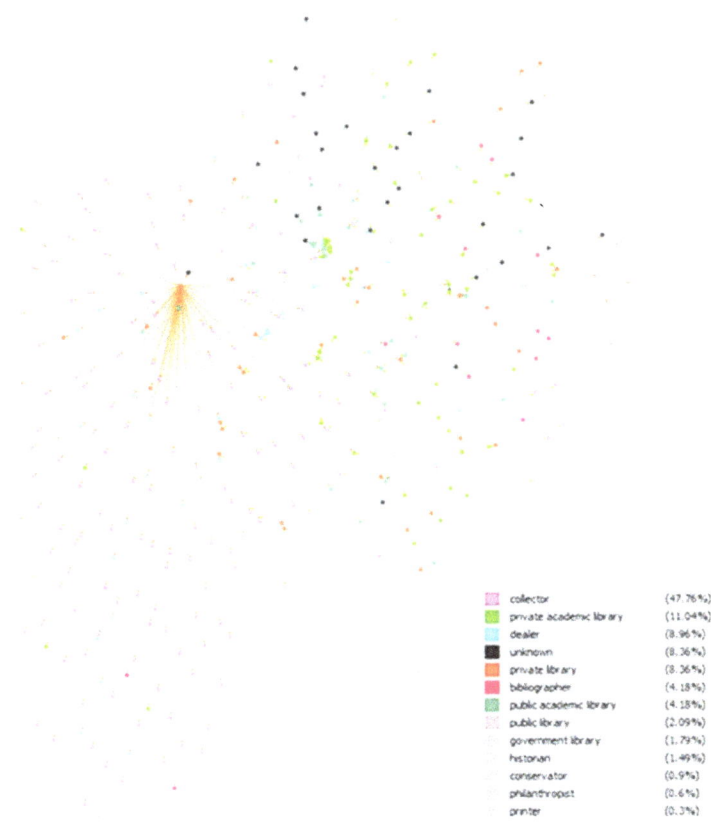

Larger data set with selected literature from 1937 to 1965 (including *Library Trends*, vol. 5, 1957)—without name labels.

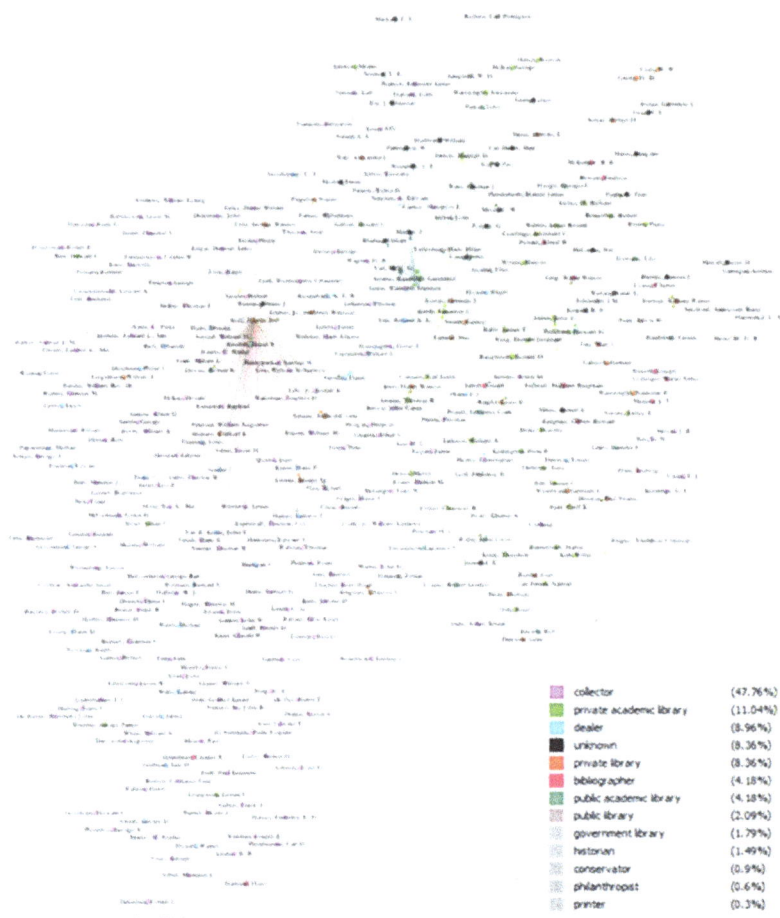

Larger data set with selected literature from 1937 to 1965 (including *Library Trends*, vol. 5, 1957)—with name labels.

7

Preservation of Electronic Government Information: An Urgent National Priority

Scott Matheson*

Many of the richest collections in American libraries have been built in part through the physical deposit of government-produced information. From the earliest days of the Republic[1] though the end of the last century, government policy favored publication and wide dissemination of government information at the federal[2] and state[3] levels. This resulted in relatively easy access to public information by citizens, which served the government's need for an engaged citizenry and the complementary desire of citizens to be informed about their government. The system of geographically dispersing deposits also served the need of research collections for information in all disciplines and the complementary need for preservation of that information.[4] The publica-

---

* Funding note: The Preserving Electronic Government Information project is made possible in part by the Institute of Museum and Library Services grant #LG-88-17-0129-17. Additional funding is from the University of North Texas Libraries and the Center for Research Libraries.

[1] Act for the more general promulgation of the law of the United States, Ch. 50, 1 Stat. 443 (1795).

[2] Depository Library Act of 1962, Pub. L. No. 87-579, 76 Stat. 352 (1962); Public Printing and Documents, Pub. L. No. 90-620, 82 Stat. 1238 (1968) (recodifying Title 44 U.S.C.).

[3] Many states have both open records laws, e.g., Fla. Stat. Ch. 119, and systems for deposit of publications, e.g., 15 Ill. Comp. Stat. 320. A summary list is available at State Depository Library Systems, https://wikis.ala.org/godort/index.php/State_Depository_Library_Systems/. Accessed August 31, 2018.

[4] James A. Jacobs, *Born-Digital U.S. Federal Government Information: Preservation and Access*, March 17, 2014, https://www.crl.edu/node/10225/.

tion and deposit system served the parallel goals of civic engagement[5] and dissemination of knowledge produced or cataloged by government agencies.[6] The first part of this chapter outlines the imperfect history of government information distribution and its collection by research libraries.

As government publications transitioned to electronic distribution,[7] the existing system of dissemination to and incorporation into library collections largely continued in parallel for many years.[8] More recently, government publishers have changed the nature of their information dissemination, in many cases foregoing traditional publication patterns in favor of direct digital dissemination.[9] It is this change from disseminating finished publications to providing more raw information, not the earlier change from paper to electronic format, which presents the biggest threat to the twin goals of civic engagement and knowledge dissemination—and likely a larger threat to the latter. Because this threat to access has the potential to affect our research collections, government and academic librarians are working to maintain continuity in local collections and prevent the loss of access to this information. The second part of this chapter details efforts to manage this transition and explain how information professionals are using existing expertise to ensure researchers maintain access to the corpus of government-produced information.

The transition in dissemination method affects governments at all levels and libraries and archives of all sizes. Here we focus on US federal government electronic (or "born-digital") information and academic research libraries. Archival treatment of scheduled records is only addressed in passing. International, state, and local governments have similar problems with the transitions discussed and archivists and archives have both similar and differently complicated challenges. What librarians, archivists, and records managers have in common are the awareness of these issues and the skills to manage information in new ways while

---

[5] Through wide distribution of, e.g., the *Federal Register* and the *Congressional Record*.

[6] For example, the reports of the Fremont expedition, the *Statistical Abstract of the United States*, and the *Patent and Trademark Gazette*.

[7] US Government Printing Office Electronic Information Enhancement Act, Pub. L. 103-40, 107 Stat 112 (1993).

[8] Gil Baldwin, "Fugitive Documents—On the Loose or On the Run." *Administrative Notes* 24, no. 10, (2003): 4. https://www.govinfo.gov/content/pkg/GOVPUB-GP3-849c445ba7debf10b1c116284b6aa82b/pdf/GOVPUB-GP3-849c445ba7debf10b1c116284b6aa82b.pdf/.

[9] Federal Research Division, Library of Congress, *Disseminating and Preserving Digital Public Information Products Created by the U.S. Federal Government: A Case Study Report*, August 2018. https://www.fdlp.gov/news-and-events/3630-agency-digital-products-case-study-report-now-available/.

ensuring that it remains accessible for researchers.[10] The conclusion of this chapter describes a useful model for organizations concerned with these challenges to use to address them collectively[11] and calls for engagement with efforts to define a national agenda to meet the challenge of ensuring continued access to government information.

History of Access to Government Information

The Constitution sets out the first requirement of public access to government information by requiring that Congress keep journals and publish them.[12] The American Enlightenment ideals that influenced the Founders are reflected in the founding documents, but also more directly in their writings. James Madison wrote that

> A popular Government, without popular information, or the means of acquiring it, is but a Prologue to a Farce or a Tragedy; or, perhaps both. Knowledge will forever govern ignorance: And a people who mean to be their own Governors, must arm themselves with the power which knowledge gives.[13]

Madison was referring directly to the funding of public education, but the animating ideas of the early requirements for publication of government records are clearly on display.[14]

Among the first laws passed related to printing. The third Congress required printing of all laws passed though that session[15] and their distribution among the states and territories. The law required that the printed set of laws be "deposited in such fixed and convenient place" in each county deemed "most conducive to the general information of the

---

[10] "Preservation at GPO," accessed August 31, 2018. https://www.fdlp.gov/preservation/preservation-at-gpo; "Position Statements & Resolutions," accessed August 31, 2018, https://www2.archivists.org/statements/.

[11] John Kania and Mark Kramer, "Collective Impact," *Stanford Social Innovation Review* 9, no. 1 (Winter 2011): 36–41.

[12] Art. 1, §5. Note that the Articles of Confederation before it also required journals be kept and distributed to the several states' legislatures upon request. Art. 9 and the Declaration of Independence include in its bill of complaints against the king that he called meetings of legislatures at places "distant from the depository of their public Records."

[13] James Madison to W. T. Barry, August 4, 1822, *Writings* 9:103. Available at *Founders' Constitution*, accessed August 31, 2018. http://press-pubs.uchicago.edu/founders/documents/v1ch18s35.html/.

[14] See William Seavey, "Musings on the Past and Future of Government Information," *American Libraries* 36, no. 7 (2005): 42–44.

[15] Act for the more general promulgation of the law of the United States, 1.

people." In 1814, Congress, by joint resolution, added the American Antiquarian Society to the list of recipients of congressional journals, laws, and documents.[16] Through the nineteenth century, Congress continued to adjust where and how government information was deposited for the pubic to consume. In 1860, Congress created the Government Printing Office (GPO)[17] in an effort to improve fiscal control and to standardize the quality of printing. In 1895, depository operations were consolidated with the GPO, including the mandate that the agency develop a national bibliography. The landmark Depository Library Act of 1962[18] is significant for its explicit mandate of public access and creation of regional depository libraries as distinct from other depositories with more selective collections. Although there were legislative and political changes that affected the volume of material printed and distributed, the system remained largely unchanged from 1895 through the twentieth century.[19] The 1993 GPO Access Act[20] set the stage for the transition from print to electronic document dissemination but did not account for the transition from traditional documents to more advanced information dissemination products (IDPs)[21]—complicated web services largely unimaginable in 1993.

From the founding through the 1993 Act, both the amount of and public access to government information had increased consistently. Policies led to greater access through increases in production, better distribution, adoption of new technologies, and guarantees of public access. The constant since 1861 has been GPO's ability to capture the information produced by government agencies as those documents move through the GPO-managed printing process.

Librarians tell ourselves a nice story about this print-based system: that it was a good system to use to get every collection all the right

---

[16] Joint Res 13-7, December 1, 1814, 3 Stat. 248.

[17] *GPO* was the Government Printing Office until 2014, when the name was changed to *Government Publishing Office*. Consolidated and Further Continuing Appropriations Act, Pub. L. 113-483 §1301, 128 Stat. 2130, 2537 (2014).

[18] Depository Library Act of 1962, 2.

[19] See, e.g., Aimée C. Quinn, "Keeping the Citizenry Informed: Early Congressional Printing and 21st Century Information Policy," *Government Information Quarterly* 20, no. 3 (2003): 281–93; Cassandra J. Hartnett, Andrea L. Stevenson, and Eric J. Forte, *Fundamentals of Government Information*, 2nd ed. (Chicago: ALA Neal-Schuman, an imprint of the American Library Association 2016), 12; *Keeping America Informed*, rev. ed. (Washington, DC: US Government Printing Office 2016). Available at https://www.govinfo.gov/content/pkg/GPO-KEEPINGAMERICAINFORMED-2016/pdf/GPO-KEEPING AMERICAINFORMED-2016.pdf/.

[20] U.S. Government Printing Office Electronic Information Enhancement Act, 7.

[21] An unwieldy term from a reform proposal introduced in the 115th Congress, *The FDLP Modernization Act of 2018*, H.R. 5305 (115th Congress, introduced March 14, 2018).

documents to serve the patrons of that library. With the rise of desktop publishing in the 1990s, librarians saw an increase in so-called "fugitive documents"—those produced outside of the GPO workflow and not captured in the national bibliography or the depository distribution system.[22] We know that in reality there were fugitive documents that never made it into the system. Those who work with depository collections know that print materials are subject to loss, damage, and theft— like any other library material. We know that depository libraries were sometimes "shorted"—not sent publications they should have received—due to printing or shipping errors, or even a burned-out lightbulb.[23] In theory the regional depository libraries were supposed to receive and retain all distributed documents, but "regionals" did not exist until the 1962 Act, and many were designated much later than that. In reality, the print system was not perfect, but it was a system with more than 1,200 participating libraries, so chances were good that at least a few collections ended up with the information and researchers could get access to it.

After the implementation of the GPO Access Act in 1994, electronic versions of print documents were collected in the GPO Access system, which was designed for public access. In the 2000s, GPO developed a more comprehensive workflow management and access system dubbed *FDSys* although this was still a document-focused system. GPO began experimenting with web harvesting of agency and web sites to capture information within the scope of the depository library program, but that was not being printed. Experiments in distribution of electronic files— later to be dubbed *digital deposit* by advocates[24]—also began but remained document focused due to both GPO's enabling legislation and the nature of federal web publishing. In recent years, GPO has developed a modern user interface to FDSys called *Govinfo.gov*, which became the sole public user interface in 2019, although the underlying repository remains FDSys. With the advent of an international standard for "Trusted Digital Reposi-

---

[22] Baldwin, "Fugitive Documents," 8.
[23] See photo of the "lighted bin" shipping system in US Government Publishing Office, *Picturing the Big Shop: Photos of the U.S. Government Publishing Office, 1900–1980* (Washington, DC: US Government Publishing Office, 2017), at 208. When the system lit up the light over a library's shipping box, it meant a document was to be placed in that box. When a bulb burned out, that box would not get the selected document.
[24] See, e.g., Freegovinfo.info archives of digital deposit posts, accessed August 31, 2018. https://freegovinfo.info/node/tag/digital_deposit; "Recommendations & Commendations of the Depository Library Council to the GPO Director," Dec. 2018, https://www.fdlp.gov/file-repository/about-the-fdlp/federal-depository-library-council/council-recommendations/3806-recommendations-commendations-of-the-depository-library-council-to-the-gpo-director-fall-2018 (recommendation #3 is the creation of a working group on digital deposit).

tory" certification (ISO-16363), GPO pursued certification of FDSys/Govinfo.[25] The certification was granted in January of 2019 and included evaluation of GPO's infrastructure and policies in addition to technical evaluations of the system.[26] As government information in document form moved to online distribution, the existing system has managed to continue capturing, describing, and preserving many documents, even providing catalog records pointing to the electronic documents to libraries so that their catalogs will reflect the new material.

The Current Environment and New Threats to Access

Government information is a broad term that encompasses formal published documents, officially scheduled records of government agencies, data produced by agencies carrying out their statutory mandates, and broader still, all information or data created by the government. Traditionally, libraries and GPO provided access to documents published by the government, whereas archives (chiefly the National Archives and Records Administration [NARA] and its predecessor agencies) provided access to records of the government. As the line between publication and record has become less clear, at least to those creating the information, access has been threatened because agencies do not always clearly define publications and records. This results in some types of valuable information falling into a gap because it is neither a scheduled record nor a formal publication. Because records schedules vary by agency[27] and because it is difficult to know what records future researchers may find valuable, the scope of the potential preservation problem also varies. In either case, access can be lost due to differences between library and archive access policies and procedures. Although publications in a library generally stay available to researchers unless they are stolen or damaged, archival materials may be preserved but not be open to research due to embargos, because they are classified, or simply because they have not been processed. NARA works to reduce these barriers to access, but it

---

[25] "Trusted Digital Repository ISO 16363:2012 Audit and Certification," accessed August 31, 2018. https://www.fdlp.gov/preservation/trusted-digital-repository-iso-16363-2012-audit-and-certification/.

[26] "GPO's Govinfo Makes History by Earning Global Certification for Trustworthiness," accessed January 28, 2019. https://www.gpo.gov/who-we-are/news-media/news-and-press-releases/gpos-govinfo-makes-history-by-earning-global-certification-for-trustworthiness/.

[27] Schedules are available at https://www.archives.gov/records-mgmt/rcs (accessed August 31, 2018) and agency Records Management Self-Assessments are summarized annually by NARA, accessed August 31, 2018. https://www.archives.gov/records-mgmt/resources/self-assessment.html/.

is possible that information once freely available on an agency website may be removed from public access and not be available for research again until NARA is able to process the records of that agency.

In the 1990s, the advent of desktop publishing and a reduction in GPO printing for agencies foreshadowed the current transition from the creation of discrete publications to a broader array of IDPs. These interactive, dynamic, data-driven communications are more complicated to produce, distribute, and preserve than traditional documents. More troubling for library collections, there are policy gaps that result in these IDPs escaping the notice of GPO and librarians.

Executive policy under the Clinton administration set the stage for agencies to communicate more directly with the public on websites.[28] The move to wider use of direct communication continued in the next decade with the rise of social media and adoption of these platforms by agencies. In addition to new types of information products, research shows that they are often created in agency communication, IT, or public relations departments, not in a traditional publication workflow.[29] Because they are not produced by the same people or in the same way as traditional documents, they escape the built-in compliance methods that GPO has developed to ensure they are captured, described, and distributed to library collections. Moreover, the more complicated and feature-rich these IDPs are, the more difficult they are for libraries to independently capture and add to the library collection at the request of a researcher.[30]

Even when digital documents are discovered and described by GPO and added to local catalogs in depository libraries, long-term access problems can remain. For many digital documents, GPO captures a copy of the files and stores them in a digital collection it maintains. For other documents for which the GPO has an agreement with the publishing agency, the agency commits to maintain the document and provide access to the public. In either case, GPO creates a permanent link (a persistent uniform resource locator [PURL], similar to a handle or digital object identifier) and uses this in the catalog record. This allows users to access

---

[28] See, e.g., United States Office of Management and Budget, "Circular A130: Management of Federal Information Resources" (Transmittal 2, 1994), accessed August 31, 2018. https://clintonwhitehouse1.archives.gov/White_House/EOP/OMB/html/omb-a130.html/.

[29] See Federal Research Division, *Disseminating and Preserving*, 9; Roberta Sittel, "Report of Marine Mammal Commission interview" (July 12, 2017; on file with author).

[30] For example, patrons have requested that a library capture a robust web-based data-mapping application from an agency site. Although it was possible to capture the underlying data, capturing and maintaining the mapping application would have been much more difficult and resource intensive.

the document on the agency site or in GPO's archive should it disappear from the agency site. This system relies on a single point of failure—a single harvest of the document and storage in one system. Even in a technically robust system, this approach leaves access vulnerable to political or policy risk. A system that more closely mirrors the distribution system of print deposits, a digital deposit system in which copies of files are held in the custody of individual libraries could insulate the documents from some of this risk. This difference has been described as the difference between "pointing" at a digital document and "holding" the document in your own collection.[31] A network of libraries, the LOCKSS (Lots of Copies Keeps Stuff Safe)–USDOCS program, does this with information in FDSys/Govinfo. Legislation proposed in the 115th Congress would have specifically empowered GPO to implement more broadly a voluntary digital deposit system with its depository library partners.[32]

One important issue that has been described in discussions between librarians and archivists is the difference in access policies between libraries and archives. Although librarians who lose access to a document on an agency website might worry that the document is "gone," archivists may know that the document is in fact preserved according to a record schedule. This may result in a document being available on a site for several years, then being transferred to the custody of NARA, according to the agency's published record schedule. The document will seem to a librarian to have disappeared although NARA has custody of the document and is preserving it. NARA can only make it available as dictated by the agency's record schedule and NARA's ability to describe and review it. If librarians or researchers are able to navigate the various silos of federal information they may discover that the document is at the archive and ask for its release under the Freedom of Information Act. Although the document is not lost or in danger of being lost, this scenario presents a significant barrier to access compared with the historic system of printed document deposit.

It is worth noting that the conversion of the existing corpus of government information from print (or microform or other tangible format) to digital format is a separate and ongoing issue, though the way it is proceeding can be instructive. Some conversion is done by

---

[31] James A. Jacobs, "When We Depend on Pointing Instead of Collecting," (March 23, 2013). https://freegovinfo.info/node/3900/.
[32] FDLP Modernization Act of 2018, H.R. 5305, 21.

government agencies,[33] some is done by research libraries or consortia,[34] and some by commercial interests in collaboration with libraries or archives.[35] Experience with these models, and in managing the converted digital objects the projects generate[36] can inform efforts to capture born-digital information generated in the past several decades.

Current Efforts to Capture, Describe, and Provide Access[37]

Just as the print distribution and access system grew over time, electronic, or "born-digital" government information distribution and access is evolving quickly both within government and in the private sector. The National Archives and GPO have both developed systems for collecting and preserving digital information, though systems thus far have adapted workflows developed for tangible information products to electronic information.[38] In 2000, the Library of Congress launched major work on digital preservation generally through its National Digital Information Infrastructure Preservation Program, which continues through the National Digital Stewardship Alliance (NDSA), now a part of the Digital Library Federation.[39]

In addition to the agencies with central preservation and access mandates like NARA and GPO, other agencies, including the Smithsonian and the FedLink network of federal libraries, participate in preservation of digital government information through partnerships with organizations like the NDSA.[40] Other agencies (and depository programs[41]) have

---

[33] See, e.g., "GPO & Library of Congress Begin Digital Release of Historical Congressional Record," accessed August 31, 2018. https://www.gpo.gov/who-we-are/news-media/news-and-press-releases/gpo-library-of-congress-begin-digital-release-of-historical-congressional-record/.

[34] See "UC Libraries Mass Digitization Projects" (summarizing projects with the Internet Archive and with Google), accessed August 31, 2018. https://www.cdlib.org/services/collections/massdig/faq.html/.

[35] See "Digitization Partnerships," (outlining NARA's many non-profit and for-profit partnerships), accessed August 31, 2018. https://www.archives.gov/digitization/partnerships.html/.

[36] Notably, the large-scale projects undertaken by HathiTrust, Library of Congress, and the Digital Public Library of America.

[37] For more detailed discussion, see PEGI (Preserving Electronic Government Information) environmental scan (Sarah K. Lippincott, *Environmental Scan of Government Information and Data Preservation Efforts and Challenges* [Atlanta, GA: Educopia Institute, 2018]). https://educopia.org/pegi-environmental-scan/; Federal Research Division, Disseminating and Preserving, 9.

[38] "National Archives Electronic Records Archives (ERA)," accessed August 31, 2018. https://www.archives.gov/era/; "About FDsys," accessed August 31, 2018. 1https://www.gpo.gov/fdsysgpopages/fdsysinfo/aboutfdsys.htm/.

[39] "About" [digitalpreservation.gov], accessed August 31, 2018. http://www.digitalpreservation.gov/about/.

[40] "NDSA Members," accessed August 31, 2018. https://ndsa.org/members-list/.

[41] To some extent the United Nations Depository Library Programme, to a larger extent the Canadian Depository Services program.

focused on building services around their digital information products like the US Patent and Trademark Office, which transitioned its Patent and Trademark Depository Library program to a service model, renaming partner libraries *Patent and Trademark Resource Centers*.[42]

Official efforts to make government data—not published documents—systematically available to the public grew during the 2010s. Chief among these was Data.gov, operated by the General Services Administration.[43] Under the terms of the 2013 Open Data Policy, many agencies were required to treat their data collections as assets and make lists of the data assets available in a way that allowed them to be centralized into the Data.gov portal.[44] This executive policy was reinforced in the Foundations for Evidence-Based Policymaking Act of 2018,[45] which extends the data-management requirements and supports public access, but does not mention preservation of the data assets or continuous public access. The new law does instruct agency heads to "use existing procedures" to carry out the requirements of the law, so data assets should be scheduled as agency records for preservation by NARA.

Private organizations work to collect and provide access to electronic government information individually and in partnerships with government agencies. A long-standing example of this is the collaboration among many partners, including the California Digital Library, the University of North Texas, GPO, Library of Congress, and the Internet Archive, to conduct the End of Term harvest. Since 2008,[46] this effort has archived government websites at the end of each presidential term. The 2016–17 effort captured over 250 terabytes of information from federal websites and government File Transfer Protocol (FTP) sites.[47] The project worked with the Data Refuge project at the University of Pennsylvania to capture some sites identified in the work done at the various Data Rescue events coordinated by Data Refuge.

Grassroots efforts by researchers and others who care about the government information they need for their work have led to the forma-

---

[42] "Support Centers," accessed August 31, 2018. https://www.uspto.gov/learning-and-resources/support-centers/patent-and-trademark-resource-centers-ptrcs/.

[43] "About Data.gov," accessed January 28, 2019. https://www.data.gov/about/.

[44] "M-13-13 Memorandum for the Heads of Executive Departments and Agencies," accessed January 28, 2019. https://project-open-data.cio.gov/policy-memo/.

[45] Foundations for Evidence-Based Policymaking Act of 2018, Pub. L. No. 115-435, 132 Stat. 5529. (2019).

[46] NARA conducted web harvests in 2001 and 2004 but announced that it would no longer conduct wholesale harvests. Accessed August 31, 2018. https://www.archives.gov/records-mgmt/memos/nwm13-2008.html/.

[47] For a fuller list of partners and history of the project over time, see http://eotarchive.cdlib.org/background.htm (accessed August 31, 2018).

tion of groups focused on the information of specific disciplines and on different parts of the information lifecycle. Data Refuge focused on capturing environmental data and preserving it in an independent repository and is now collecting stories of how researchers use government data.[48] The Environmental Data and Governance Initiative (EDGI) was a key partner for the Data Rescue events organized by Data Refuge. One of the things EDGI focuses on is use of data governance policies as a way to ensure continued access to environmental data.[49] EDGI also systematically monitors government websites in an attempt to identify trends in changes and information that may be made less accessible to the public.

Other efforts started in a more focused way, like the CyberCemetary at the University of North Texas. This project began as a way to capture the websites of agencies and commissions that were being eliminated through sunset provisions or reorganizations. The project is one that has fully developed policies and partnerships. UNT has formal agreements with GPO and NARA (as an affiliate archive) to preserve the content of the project.[50]

The Legal Information Preservation Alliance's (LIPA) Chesapeake Project brought together the Georgetown Law Library with the Maryland and Virginia State Law Libraries to pilot digital preservation of important legal information created in digital format. The pilot has expanded to the Legal Information Archive.[51] LIPA and the Center for Research Libraries exemplify library collaborations initially concerned with preservation of print materials that are now converted to digital formats, but that are increasingly working with born-digital materials.

Other organizations focus on providing access to government information that is not generally available in existing programs. Organizations like Transactional Records Access Clearinghouse (TRAC)[52] or the National Security Archive[53] use freedom-of-information requests to gather

---

[48] "DATA REFUGE," accessed August 31, 2018. http://www.ppehlab.org/datarefuge/.
[49] "Capacity and Governance," accessed August 31, 2018. https://envirodatagov.org/capacity-and-governance/.
[50] "CyberCemetery," accessed August 31, 2018. http://govinfo.library.unt.edu/default.htm; The University of North Texas: First Federal Information Preservation Network (FIPNet) Partner, https://www.fdlp.gov/all-newsletters/partnership-showcase/2343-the-university-of-north-texas-first-federal-information-preservation-network-fipnet-partner/.
[51] "The Chesapeake Project," accessed August 31, 2018. https://lipalliance.org/related-projects/the-chesapeake-project/.
[52] "TRACFED—A Unique Source of Authoritative Information about the Federal Government's Enforcement Activities" accessed August 31, 2018. http://tracfed.syr.edu/.
[53] "About the National Security Archive," accessed August 31, 2018. https://nsarchive.gwu.edu/about/.

information not otherwise published. Because of TRAC's focus on current transactional data, it deals in particular with born-digital information. These organizations and related journalism organizations like MuckRock[54] and ProPublica[55] perform the important function of providing access to existing government information not otherwise available. What remains unclear is whether the detail available in current records received from agencies in response to contemporary freedom-of-information requests will be similarly available from government archives for future researchers—or even whether it should be, given the real costs of effectively preserving digital information. Depending on how agencies schedule their records, questions journalists can get answers to today may be unanswerable to future historians.

Conclusions: Preserving Electronic Government Information Project

After the Leviathan work at the Center for Research Libraries (CRL),[56] a GPO-sponsored national meeting at the American Library Association (ALA) in San Francisco[57], the Libraries+ meeting in 2017,[58] and two further stakeholder meetings held in conjunction with meetings of the Coalition for Networked Information, a group of government information advocates committed to developing a national agenda for action on preserving access to electronic government information. After securing support from the Institute of Museum and Library Services, the Preservation of Electronic Government Information (PEGI) Project steering committee has worked to determine key stakeholders, the most important information needed for research, the information most likely to be at risk, the nature of those risks, and the current state of existing efforts to preserve access to the information. In December of 2018, the PEGI Project convened a national forum to produce a whitepaper that included a common vocabulary, a draft set of goals, and metrics to assess progress on preservation of electronic government information.[59]

---

[54] "About MuckRock," accessed August 31, 2018. https://www.muckrock.com/about/.
[55] "ProPublica: About Us," accessed August 31, 2018. https://www.propublica.org/about/.
[56] "Leviathan: Libraries and Government Information in the Age of Big Data," accessed September 24, 2018. https://www.crl.edu/events/leviathan-libraries-and-government-information-age-big-data/.
[57] US Government Publishing Office, "Federal Information Preservation Network (FIPNet): A National Dialogue." (University of California Hastings College of Law Library, San Francisco, June 25, 2015).
[58] "Libraries+Network," accessed August 31, 2018. https://libraries.network/.
[59] "PEGI Project: Raising Awareness for the Preservation of Government Information," accessed August 31, 2018. https://pegiproject.org/.

Using the collective impact model[60] to highlight existing projects, encourage new efforts, and facilitate communication among stakeholders, the project hopes to engage all interested libraries, archives, agencies, and researchers in this important work. During 2017 and 2018, the steering committee learned that many researchers are eager to identify the information they consider both valuable and at risk. Similarly, many organizations are willing to undertake limited projects to serve needs identified by their patrons. Other large, well-funded programs are working on parts of the problem. By providing a consistent vocabulary and framework for projects large and small, each interested organization should be able to leverage the work of others, whether national in scope like GPO's depository program and HathiTrust, or more locally focused like a local historical society or public library preserving and making local electronic government information available. The collective impact model also calls for a "backbone organization" that serves a coordinating, communication, and clearinghouse function. Initial investigations suggest there are several existing organizations that might be positioned to serve this ongoing coordination function.

The scope of the issues related to preserving access to electronic government information at all levels of government is too large for one organization or project to address. However, by engaging as a community, libraries, archives, scholars, and government can ensure that this vital part of our collective collection is both preserved and remains accessible to future researchers.

---

[60] Kania and Kramer, "Collective Impact," 11.

IV

Tools and Technologies

8

The Schoenberg Database of Manuscripts: A Special Collections Research Tool for the Twenty-First Century

Emma Cawlfield Thomson

The Schoenberg Database of Manuscripts (SDBM) is redefining the relationship between a scholarly information resource and its users. What began as a flat-file database compiled by a private manuscript collector has, over the last twenty years, grown into a powerful online finding aid and metadata aggregator for the world's pre-modern manuscripts. In 2017, the database relaunched as an open-access, community-driven tool, allowing its users to contribute their own knowledge as standardized, searchable metadata. Not simply a repository, the SDBM (www.sdbm.library.upenn.edu) offers avenues for researchers to collaborate with each other via user groups and comment threads. These in-app workspaces nurture a burgeoning community of manuscript enthusiasts who gather to share their research, ask questions, and develop projects. The SDBM recently began publishing its data set as linked data in order to forge new partnerships with related projects and foster further advances in scholarship. This chapter provides an overview of these collaborative initiatives, paying special attention to the contributions of the SDBM's user community over the past year. Framed by an understanding of the database's history as well as its new forays into linked data and the Semantic Web, this appraisal demonstrates how the SDBM has thrived by embracing its users as active partners in its creation and maintenance.

Project History

The SDBM began in 1997 as the personal project of Larry Schoenberg, an avid manuscript collector who was especially interested in tracking the provenance and price changes of manuscripts over time. Using an earlier data set created by the historian John Feldman as his starting point, Larry began manually building the SDBM, first in Excel and later in an Access relational database. Larry and his wife, Barbara Brizdle, dedicated their time to scouring the world for sources of manuscript data and entering the information into the SDBM. Initially they focused on data from auction and sale catalogs, later expanding the scope to any source containing manuscript data. Their devotion to the project resulted in a quickly expanding data set that soon began to attract the attention of other scholars and manuscript enthusiasts. It became clear that the SDBM would benefit from a more public interface, and from the expertise of trained information professionals to manage it. In 2005, the database moved to Larry's alma mater, the University of Pennsylvania, where it was migrated to an Oracle relational database, adopting new content standards and policies in the process. In 2011, the SDBM became a cornerstone project at the newly created Schoenberg Institute for Manuscript Studies, yet another initiative founded by Larry and Barbara to support manuscript scholarship at the University of Pennsylvania and beyond. Throughout these iterations, Larry and Barbara remained involved in every aspect of the database's production and management. Larry passed away in 2014, just as the SDBM prepared to embark on its greatest initiative yet, the redevelopment into the collaborative resource used today.

The Present Database:
SDBM Redevelopment via National Endowment for the Humanities Grant 2014–17[1]

In 2014, the SDBM received a three-year grant from the National Endowment for the Humanities to redevelop the database into an open-access, user-driven, community-built research tool. The desire for an interactive application capable of crowdsourcing data curation stemmed both from the recent explosion of manuscript data readily accessible via the Internet, as well as the untapped expertise of the SDBM user community. Rather than relying on a few staff members to add and edit data, the database would be open to anyone who desired to contribute.

These goals mandated a revision of the SDBM data model, a task not possible without first clearly articulating the mission of this new application.

SDBM Mission

The SDBM is not actually a database of manuscripts, but rather a database of observations about manuscripts. The database aggregates information as it appears in other sources: auction and sale catalogs, bookseller websites, institutional and private collection catalogs, inventories, handlists, blogs, Facebook, or any other citable resource. The resulting data tracks the movement of manuscripts across time and place, as well as changes in manuscript scholarship over time. Because of the nature of its sources, the SDBM makes no claims for the objectivity or truth of its data. A person should not consult the SDBM looking for the "correct" description of a manuscript, or even its current location. Instead, one should come to compare prior descriptions of a manuscript, or search for its last recorded location. In the simplest terms, the SDBM stores what others have said about manuscripts: It is up to the user to interpret that data.

New SDBM Data Model

The SDBM data model consists of core entities that form the building blocks for the structure of the database. The scope of this chapter revolves around three of these entities: Entry, Source, and Manuscript Record.

---

[1] For a summary report of the SDBM's redevelopment and data model, see Lynn Ransom et al., "The New Schoenberg Database of Manuscripts: Creating an Open-Source Tool for Manuscript Research and Discovery," in *Care and Conservation of Manuscripts 16: Proceedings from the Sixteenth International Seminar Held at the University of Copenhagen 13th–15th April 2016*, ed. M. J. Driscoll (Copenhagen: Museum Tusculanum Press), 91–105.

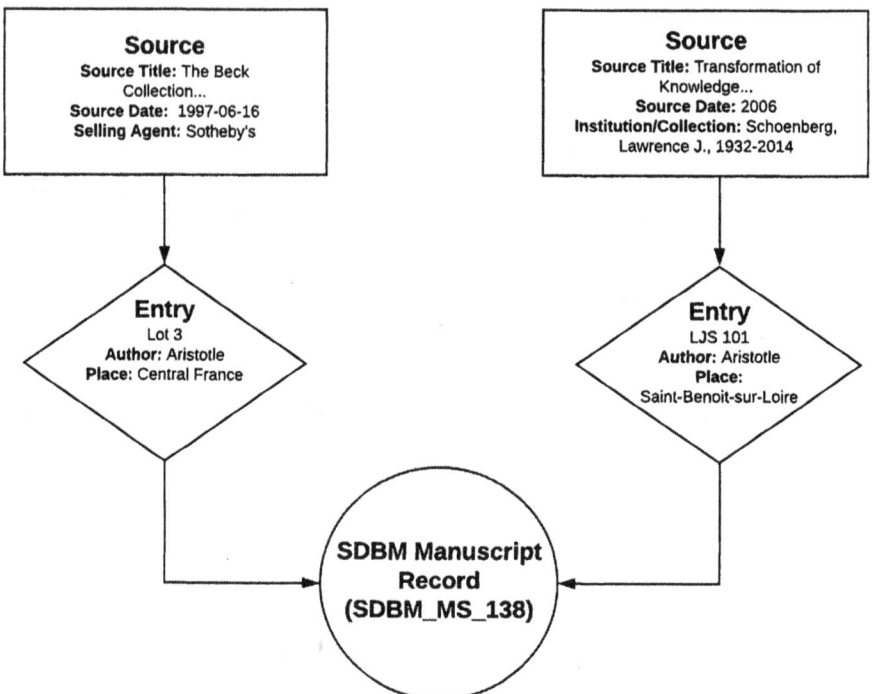

Figure 8.1 Three core entities of the SDBM data model.

Each entity has a separate function within the database and includes different sets of data fields. The Entry is the core of these concepts: It stores data related to a single observation of a manuscript. This could be a single lot in an auction catalog, an item in a library catalog, and so on. The Source is just that, the source of the information about the manuscript. This could be an auction or sale catalog, a bookseller website, a catalog of an institutional or private collection, a blog post, or any other citable resource that describes manuscripts. Every Entry links to the Source from which it derives its data, providing users with clear documentation for each piece of information in the SDBM. The Manuscript Record, though it contains no unique data itself, serves as a linking node whereby Entries that describe the same manuscript are linked together, aggregating the data from all the Entries for easy comparison and study. At the time of this writing, the SDBM consists of over 240,000 Entries derived from over 13,500 Sources, with over 24,500 of those Entries linked to form Manuscript Records. Figure 8.1 illustrates the relationships among these three core entities.

The Historical Integrity of SDBM Sources

The SDBM recognizes its data sources as historical evidence in their own right. As people study and catalog manuscripts over time, the understanding of that manuscript changes. A monastic inventory from the fifteenth century will contain far less descriptive information than an auction catalog of the twenty-first century. Besides changes in description, these resources also indicate the knowledge and motivations of the people who wrote them. Scholarship appears outdated or incorrect in older catalogs. Information in a dealer catalog demonstrates the interests and sales tactics of the seller. To preserve these variations, the SDBM now records the data contained in each source as close to verbatim as possible. This is an attempt to respect the integrity of the original sources and preserve their information for future scholars. No type of source receives precedence over another. When a user examines an SDBM Manuscript Record, he or she can compare the information of each Source against each other, taking note of the variations in description among the Entries. The differences in manuscript description preserved by the SDBM indicate broader changes in intellectual history over time.

Legacy Data

The 2014–17 redevelopment process resulted in a host of new policies and content standards to support the new data model. *Legacy data* refers to all content added prior to these changes. Due to the database's long history, the vast majority of its content is now legacy data. Records in this category display a label cautioning users to consult the information sources directly, if possible, because prior policies often dictated different or less stringent data standards. Manually updating these legacy data records will be an ongoing task for many years to come. The SDBM's new collaborative features permit the entire user community to assist in this process, and as will be demonstrated in the following text, this work has already begun in earnest.

The Power of Collaboration

The SDBM is a scholarly information resource designed for individuals with some degree of specialized manuscript knowledge: scholars, librarians, booksellers, collectors, students, and other enthusiasts. As of December 2018, 330 individuals have created SDBM user accounts, representing the entire range of these perspectives. This group provides a large and trustworthy pool of contributors whom the database can harness to crowdsource additions and improvements. Several tools and strategies were devised to cultivate user contributions in the new SDBM, the most important being the Personal Observation record, comments, and user groups.

Personal Observations

SDBM users often possess knowledge that does not yet appear in traditional manuscript sources. These users are the people studying manuscripts in reading rooms, buying and selling manuscripts at auctions and bookshops, and cataloging manuscripts in their institutions. As discussed previously, the SDBM preserves the integrity of its source material, reproducing any errors or inconsistencies contained within them. Often these variations are of minimal importance, such as typos or slight differences in descriptive characteristics. However, in some instances errors in sources have significant ramifications: A typo in a shelf mark can result in confusion at best and misidentification of the object at worst. Besides errors in the source information, the rate at which manuscripts change owners often outpaces the publication of that information. Sales and bequests occur constantly, and acquisition information can take years to appear in printed catalogs. In the case of private buyers, provenance information may never be publicized. The Personal Observation provides an outlet for SDBM users to contribute their own knowledge about specific manuscripts into the database, without needing to cite a secondary resource. This is a particularly useful activity for experts who study these manuscripts directly.

The Personal Observation, a special type of Entry, cites the knowledge of an individual as the Source of its data. It contains exactly the same transaction, descriptive, and provenance data fields as a typical Entry. The Personal Observation then links to all other Entries that describe the same manuscript, forming a Manuscript Record that aggregates the user's knowledge alongside information found in historical resources. This generates new information published only in the SDBM. Since this capability officially launched in 2017, users have contributed 209 Personal Observations to the database. Figure 8.2 shows an example of a Personal Observation that provides updated provenance information, noting the manuscript's new shelf mark (KW 1900 A 007) and location (Koninklijke Bibliotheek, Netherlands). This Personal Observation links to the Manuscript Record (SDBM_MS_24378) that aggregates the other

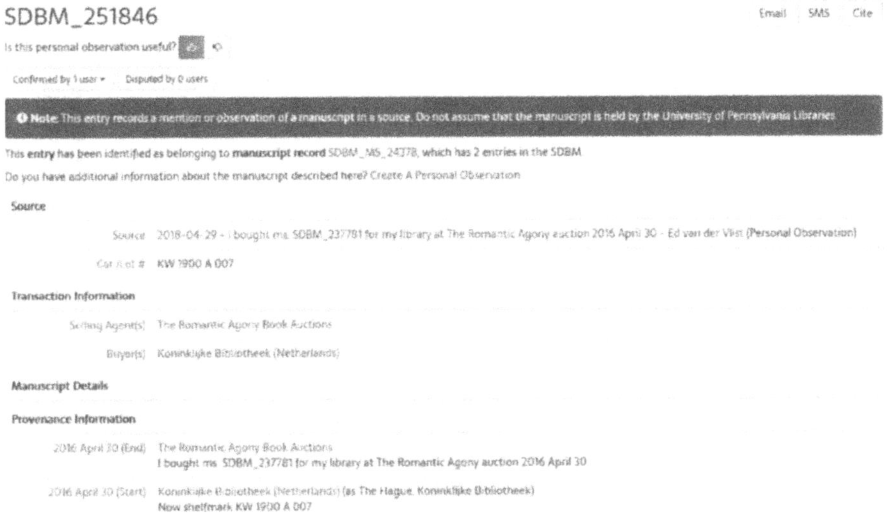

The Schoenberg Database of Manuscripts 173

Figure 8.2 View of a Personal Observation.

Entries that also describe this manuscript, based on Sources previously added to the database. A user who encounters any one of these earlier Entries will be able to access the latest shelf mark and location of the manuscript via the link to the Manuscript Record.

Personal Observations allow users to contribute data about single manuscripts on a case-by-case basis. As users peruse the database, they can quickly contribute their own knowledge of the manuscripts as they come upon them, in a computationally useful format. In previous iterations of the SDBM, the data model depended on data additions from entire collections at once. To capture this new shelf mark information from Figure 8.2 in the old SDBM, the institutional catalog for the Koninklijke Bibliotheek's manuscript collection would have been added as a Source to the database, and then Entries created individually for each of the nearly 400 manuscripts in their collection. Entering data on entire collections like this takes a significant amount of time, especially when done manually. Rather than waiting for SDBM staff to create Entries for entire collection catalogs, users can simply create a Personal Observation when they notice that the SDBM does not contain the latest provenance information.

Comments

Every record in the SDBM contains a discussion area for users to post comments. As users search the database and come upon ambiguous,

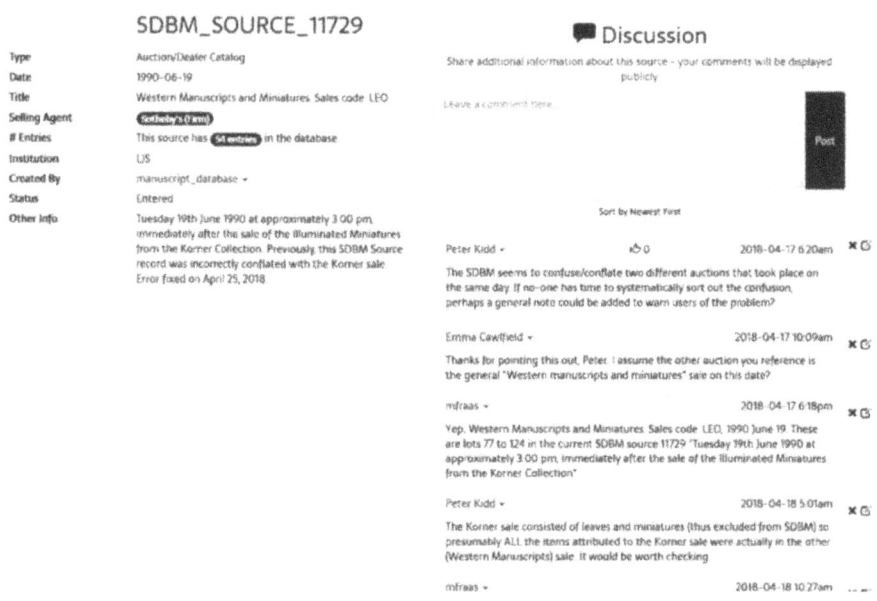

Figure 8.3 View of a Source record, showing user comments in the Discussion area on the right.

incorrect, or misleading data, they can quickly leave comments to alert other users about the issues and suggest emendations. Over the past year, users have left 430 comments in the database. Figure 8.3 shows a comment thread that led to improved data in the SDBM. A user noticed that a Source record confused one Sotheby's auction with another, and left a comment explaining the problem. Two other users joined the discussion, and through their conversation, they untangled the data. An SDBM administrator then edited the Source record to reflect the correct information. This comment thread will be permanently displayed along with the rest of the Source data, documenting the history of the Source record itself.

These comments, though incredibly useful, can only be stored as plain text. They are not searchable or standardized in any way. In some cases, users leave comments whose information would be more useful as a Personal Observation, which can be linked to other records and indexed properly. Many new users, however, prefer the ease and speed of commenting to the more involved process of constructing a Personal Observation. SDBM administrators monitor all user comments and, when necessary, contact users directly to offer guidance on how to create better data.

Groups

The SDBM's Group tool provides dedicated workspaces within the database where users can gather related Entries to better analyze and edit data. One Group in particular has already made great progress, demonstrating the powerful functionality of this tool. In early 2018, Frank Treschel, Emeritus Professor of Language and Linguistics at Ball State University, contacted the project with a desire to update and improve our existing data on a collection of Mexican manuscripts once owned by Agustin Fischer, confessor to Maximilian I of Mexico. These particular manuscripts initially appeared in an 1869 sale catalog titled "Bibliotheca Mejicana." Dr. Treschel is interested in tracking the past and current whereabouts of these books. The SDBM already contained some data on these manuscripts, derived from a few sale catalogs, but this content contained many legacy-data issues. The data needed updates to become useful for research purposes, but as a new user, Dr. Treschel did not possess the skills necessary to accomplish this task by himself. This was the perfect opportunity for a crowdsourced project.

The Bibliotheca Mejicana group began its work by creating a Group page, which contained links to the original 1869 catalog along with all associated Entries from that catalog already within the database. A call for participants was publicized within the SDBM and on social media, with six users signing up to contribute. The initial task involved verifying the old SDBM data and editing it as necessary to bring the information up to current standards.

Participants used the discussion area within the Group page to divide the work, ask questions, and cheer each other on. The group quickly finished updating the initial catalog data and has since moved on to revising data from other catalogs in which these manuscripts later appeared. Many of the manuscripts have now been tracked into the twentieth century. Figure 8.4 shows the initial Bibliotheca Mejicana Group page, which describes the goals of the Group and links to the original sale catalog, the associated Entries, and the user profiles of all participants.

The Role of Administrators in a Collaborative Environment

Within the framework of this interactive community, the SDBM administrators adopted a new role. In the earlier versions of the database, staff members alone created and edited data.

Figure 8.4 View of a Group, with associated Entries linked on the right.

Now, SDBM staff are still active contributors and editors, but they also monitor all activity and model good behavior within the database for other users. Staff can and do submit Personal Observations, just as any community member can. They comment on records and create Groups about content that is important to them. In cases for which a user creates data that needs modification, the SDBM administrators will contact the user directly instead of editing the data for them. Multiple avenues for communication between users exist, including in-app messaging, public forums, comments, and private emails. This policy of direct and consistent communication helps to build relationships between administrators and other users, which strengthens the community as a whole.

If You Build It, Will They Come?

The new collaborative tools available within the SDBM allow its user community to participate in the production and maintenance of their own information resource. As an accessible, interactive, and useful application, the SDBM has positioned itself to continue to grow both its data set and its user community in the years to come. Simply building a useful tool, however, does not ensure that people will actually use it. In order to continue to attract new and active users, the SDBM administrators seek to build a data set and a user community that accommodates the widest possible range of geographic and cultural traditions. As discussed in the text that follows, broadening the scope of the data set and collaborating with other related projects remains paramount to the SDBM's relevance.

The Future: Global Pre-Modern Manuscript Data

Broadening the Scope of the SDBM's Data Set

The SDBM's mission to gather metadata about pre-modern manuscripts limits the data set to material produced roughly before the year 1600 CE, but not to a specific geographic region or cultural tradition. Despite this broad mission, the actual data in the SDBM shows a clear focus on Western Europe. The vast majority of the sources that comprise the SDBM were written in English, and consequently the majority of the manuscripts it documents were either produced in Western Europe or owned by someone in Europe or North America. This narrow focus came about both from the original purpose of the SDBM (a research project to track manuscript price changes over time, mainly in the Western art market) as well as the limitations of a small staff, nearly all of whom possess little to no knowledge of non-Western languages. However, the SDBM's new community-driven capabilities allow anyone to add data about manuscripts that are important to him or her. These capabilities mitigate the limitations of the SDBM staff and provide the framework to build a data set that includes diverse geographies and cultures that serve the research needs of a wider audience.

By absorbing data from other related projects, the SDBM can now rapidly expand its data set. In 2017, the SDBM ingested data from an inventory of manuscripts produced by Dr. Benjamin Fleming at the Rāmamālā Library in Comilla, Bangladesh.[2] These Sanskrit and Bangla manuscripts were catalogued as a part of the British Library's Endangered Archive Programme, with additional support from the Schoenberg Institute for Manuscript Studies. As a result of this ingest, 8,570 new Entries

---

[2] For more information on this important project, see the Endangered Archives Program website: "Rāmamālā Library manuscript project (EAP683)," *Endangered Archives Program*. British Library, accessed November 18, 2018, https://doi.org/10.15130/EAP683/.

Figure 8.5 A portion of the Rāmamālā ingest, created via a .csv file import.

now exist in the SDBM, increasing the database's Sanskrit manuscripts by nearly a hundredfold. Figure 8.5 shows a tabular view of a small portion of the Rāmamālā data. All of this data would have been typed into the database by hand prior to the redevelopment. Importing these 8,570 Entries saved countless hours of human labor.

SDBM administrators spearheaded the Rāmamālā ingest, but non-staff users are also expanding the scope of the SDBM through their own data contributions. Thanks to a user's contributions, several SDBM Entries containing a particular work, titled in English the *Iqbal-namah'i Jahangiri*, now also contain the title in its original Persian script. Users can now search for the work using either the Roman or Persian alphabet. Figure 8.6 shows the search results for this query using the title in the Persian alphabet.

These efforts to expand the regional scope of the SDBM are already attracting new users to the project. Figure 8.7 displays an Entry from the Rāmamālā ingest. SDBM user Neelbrata Roy added a comment at the bottom of the Entry describing additional information about the work contained in the manuscript. Roy writes, "There are generally 5 books of Nigam namely nigamlata, nigamtatwa, nigam kapadrum, nigamanada and nigamkalplata [sic] ... " The Entry in question references only "nigama kalpadruma," so this comment could help other users who are expecting more data or references to other texts.

At the time of this writing, the SDBM contains data on manuscripts written in 234 different languages and dialects. Arabic, Persian, and Hebrew are among the top ten most frequently cited languages, and these three languages comprise 19 percent of the entries in the SDBM.

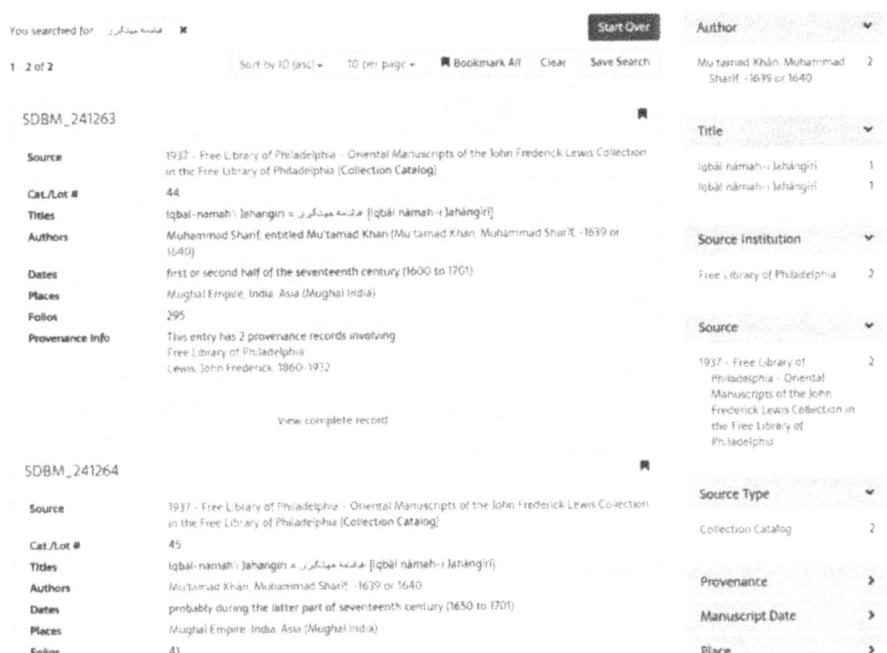

Figure 8.6 Search results on the Title field using a Persian-language title.

Despite these positive developments in the expanding scope of the database, a clear challenge remains in expanding the accessibility of the SDBM. The application uses English alone as its language of instruction and communication. The user manual, video tutorials, in-app instructions, and tooltips are only available in this single language. Anyone without strong reading knowledge of English then has the additional burden of producing a translation of this content before they can actively participate in the project. If the SDBM hopes to attract users from outside of the English-speaking world, it must take the initiative in offering instructional content in other languages.

Mapping Manuscript Migrations with Linked Data

In 2017, the SDBM began participating in a grant-funded initiative as a part of the Trans-Atlantic Platform (T-AP) Digging into Data Challenge: The Mapping Manuscript Migrations (MMM) project. This international venture, funded in part by the Institute of Museum and Library Services, aims to unite disparate manuscript data sets from three institutions: the SDBM; the Bodleian Library at Oxford University; and the Institut de

Figure 8.7 SDBM user comments on new data from the Rāmamālā ingest.

la recherche et d'histoires des textes, part of the Centre national de la recherche scientifique.[3] These separate institutions each generate unique but related information about pre-modern manuscripts: where they were produced, who owned them, and where they are now. Unfortunately, the various standards, interfaces, and project goals unique to each data set make it difficult to analyze the information across the collections. The SDBM gathers metadata on manuscripts from all over the world, whereas the Bibale database[4] at the IRHT focuses on provenance data from manuscripts in French collections and the Bodleian Library manu-

---

[3] Toby Burrows, "Mapping Manuscript Migrations," accessed August 11, 2018, http://mapping manuscriptmigrations.org/.

[4] Hanno Wijsman, (2017) "The Bibale Database at the IRHT: A Digital Tool for Researching Manuscript Provenance," *Manuscript Studies* 1, no. 2 (2017): Article 10. https://repository.upenn.edu/mss_sims/vol1/iss2/10/.

scripts catalog describes manuscripts that are owned by that library alone.[5] Each project has its own particular data model and format that prevents easy interoperability with data from other institutions. The MMM project aims to change that by producing a single interface for searching across all three collections, powered by a unified Resource Description Framework (RDF) data set that harmonizes each project's unique data. The final product will reveal new connections between the data in these three collections and expand the possibilities for large-scale analyses.

As a direct result of the MMM project, the entire SDBM data set itself is now published in an RDF triplestore, in addition to the original MySQL relational database. RDF triplestores permit vastly superior queries and analyses compared to relational databases. In the relational version of the SDBM, a user can search for manuscripts previously owned by Sir Thomas Phillipps. Users cannot easily search for manuscripts once owned by Sir Thomas Phillipps that were subsequently owned by institutions located in Germany in the twentieth century. This latter query is impossible in the relational database due to its inherently hierarchical data structure. In RDF, this query is no trouble at all.

To encourage the use of this new data, the SDBM now hosts a SPARQL Protocol and RDF Query Language (SPARQL) endpoint on its website. This interface can be used to search the RDF data using the SPARQL query language, permitting complex and novel queries such as the one mentioned earlier. Over the next year, the SDBM administrators intend to develop instructional content to help both themselves and other users take full advantage of this new data format. The SDBM's RDF triplestore, along with .csv (comma-separated value) files of the original SQL database, are available for download under a Creative Commons Attribution-ShareAlike 4.0 International License. This license gives people the freedom to download, transform, and share the data however they like, provided they publish this adapted data according to the same license.[6] Although data entry and management still occur in the SQL database, the RDF triplestore updates in real time as changes occur.

Conclusions

Rather than only passively searching and referencing the SDBM, users can now interact with the data and contribute to it. The first year of the

---

[5] "Medieval Manuscripts in Oxford Libraries," accessed October 5, 2018, http://medieval.bodleian.ox.ac.uk/.
[6] "Attribution-ShareAlike 4.0 International (CC BY-SA 4.0)," accessed August 5, 2018, https://creativecommons.org/licenses/by-sa/4.0/.

fully operational, redesigned SDBM, 2018, marked the beginning of its transition from a siloed information resource into an interactive and interoperable application. Users added new Entries, updated legacy data, alerted other users about questionable data, and developed projects to collaborate with each other over shared research interests. The SDBM's clearly defined mission and data model support a resource that is both refined in its structure and flexible in its scope. As new technologies continue to emerge—especially new avenues for sharing data across institutional and linguistic boundaries—the SDBM can utilize its adaptability to take advantage of every new opportunity to share its data with the world.

The growth of the database's user community is paramount to its continued relevance as an information resource. By empowering its users to become active participants in its development and maintenance, the SDBM cultivates the community it needs to survive. The database continues the work begun by Larry Schoenberg over twenty years ago: to track the movements of pre-modern manuscripts across time and place. Its new methods for data curation and user engagement generate an enhanced understanding of the world's shared cultural heritage.

Bibliography

"Attribution-ShareAlike 4.0 International (CC BY-SA 4.0)." Accessed August 5, 2018. https://creativecommons.org/licenses/by-sa/4.0/.

Burrows, Toby. "Mapping Manuscript Migrations." Accessed August 11, 2018. http://mappingmanuscriptmigrations.org.

"Medieval Manuscripts in Oxford Libraries." Accessed October 5, 2018. http://medieval.bodleian.ox.ac.uk.

Ransom, Lynn, Doug Emery, Emma Cawlfield, Benjamin Heller, and Matija Budisin. "The New Schoenberg Database of Manuscripts: Creating an Open-Source Tool for Manuscript Research and Discovery." In *Care and Conservation of Manuscripts 16: Proceedings of the Sixteenth International Seminar Held at the University of Copenhagen 13th–15th April 2016*, edited by M. J. Driscoll, 91–105. Copenhagen: Museum Tusculanum Press, 2018.

"Rāmamālā Library manuscript project (EAP683)." *Endangered Archives Program*. British Library. Accessed November 18, 2018. https://doi.org/10.15130/EAP683.

Wijsman, Hanno. "The Bibale Database at the IRHT: A Digital Tool for Researching Manuscript Provenance." *Manuscript Studies* 1, no. 2 (2017): article 10. https://repository.upenn.edu/mss_sims/vol1/iss2/10.

9

Virtual Reality and the Academic Library of the Future

*Zack Lischer-Katz
and Matt Cook*

Virtual reality (VR) and 3D-scanning technologies are poised to expand the academic library's mission by enhancing access to information resources and providing new analytic tools that enhance understanding of spatial information (e.g., artifacts, spaces, molecular structures, architectural designs, etc.; Cook and Lischer-Katz 2019; Lischer-Katz et al. 2019). Using interfaces that engage the user's body more fully than typical mouse and keyboard configurations, these technologies promote "embodied understanding," a type of engagement with information resources that can promote learning and research in new ways (Cook 2018). These emerging tools enable researchers and students alike to engage with digital surrogates of physical artifacts in a way that is analogous to how ebooks and journal databases expanded access to collections of texts and other traditional two-dimensional materials.

Recent VR prototypes and related 3D data types, deployed at academic libraries and in laboratories around the world, have shown the potential for these new technologies to function as research and instructional tools beyond the uncritical promotional hype of technocratic discourse (e.g., Lischer-Katz, Cook, and Boulden 2018; Pober and Cook 2016, 2019). In this chapter, we first contextualize 3D/VR within the intellectual history of immersive media technologies, describe cases of technological innovation using 3D/VR technologies in academic library contexts, and finally, drawing on the previous sections, offer predictions about the role played by 3D/VR in the library of the future, in particular, describing areas in which libraries can serve as global leaders.

Briefly, VR technologies combine immersive and interactive interfaces with stereoscopic sound and image to produce the impression of being physically present in virtual environments among simulated phenomena (Bowman and McMahan 2007). In its most idealized form, VR would provide stimuli for all of the human senses, recreating all sensory aspects of human experience, including smell, taste, and the range of embodied sensations, fully transporting users to simulated worlds. Contemporary head-mounted displays (HMDs), which comprise the VR hardware that most end users today are familiar with, are defined by their ability to track head and body movement while recreating a sense of depth perception via stereoscopic displays (two mini-video screens arranged in the headset direct slightly different images to the user's left and right eyes). Examples of these popular, affordable HMDs include the Oculus Rift, the HTC Vive, and the various Windows Mixed Reality headsets offered by manufacturers, including Samsung, Acer, and HP.

The other side of VR technology is the content, which may take the form of 3D models, 360 videos, or other forms of data captured from the world or created in the design studio (see Lischer-Katz 2020 for a discussion of 3D/VR formats). 3D content includes scans of archaeological objects and cultural heritage sites, as well as computer-generated 3D visualizations, such as complex protein structures and weather simulations, and hand-modeled 3D designs. 3D models of all sorts are becoming widely accessible through online hosting platforms, including commercial platforms, such as Sketchfab,[1] and academic platforms, such as Morphosource,[2] and increasingly they are being incorporated into teaching and research in K–12 and higher education. As 3D and VR become more widely used in educational and research contexts, libraries are taking the lead in providing access for a diverse range of users and for curating and preserving these complex new information resources for a variety of present and future uses and users (Hall et al. 2019; Lischer-Katz 2020; Lischer-Katz et al. 2019).

In light of these trends to increase adoption of 3D/VR in libraries, it is important to understand the emergence of VR technologies within

---

[1] http://www.sketchfab.com/.
[2] https://www.morphosource.org/.

the history of other immersive media technologies in order to ensure that they are incorporated into library services and resources in ways that support fundamental library values. This requires developing a critical discourse around technologies at the time of their adoption that considers the historical context of VR so that librarians can avoid uncritically importing the epistemological assumptions and cultural biases of the technologists who designed them. The field of media studies has widely understood that media technologies are never neutral conduits of perception. For instance, film and media historian Brian Winston (1996) has pointed out how early Kodak color film systems privileged Caucasian skin tones in their design.

Moreover, as information professionals committed to the American Library Association (ALA) Code of Ethics, librarians must ensure that these new technologies serve all library patrons and do not directly or indirectly erect new barriers to accessing the most current information resources. Article 1 of the ALA Code of Ethics specifies that librarians should "provide the highest level of service to all library users through appropriate and usefully organized resources; equitable service policies; equitable access; and accurate, unbiased, and courteous responses to all requests."[3] The following brief genealogy of immersive media provides the grounding for a critical engagement with emerging library technologies that is in dialogue with these library values.

A Brief Genealogy of Immersive Media Technologies

The human desire to inhabit imaginary worlds predates the current interest in VR technologies. If we stretch the definition of *immersive media*, we could even trace the birth of VR to early fireside storytelling, in which flames and tales presented orally were the first multimedia experience for humans. We can follow the development of techniques for producing immersive experiences through the elaborate history of storytelling and theatre, as humans have long desired to inhabit imaginary lands and virtual worlds fashioned through the various arts and sciences available at the time. In the modern era, two intellectual trends have been particularly instrumental in the conceptual development of what we today call *VR*: the rationalization of physical space through geometric projections and measurement, and perceptual research and the quest for verisimilitude.

---

[3] http://www.ala.org/tools/ethics/.

The Rationalization of Space

The development of three-dimensional digital technologies is based on the rationalization of physical space. 3D data is derived from measuring the world (typically using optical or radiation-based devices, although sounds waves have also been used) and this process depends on breaking space down into standardized units that can be precisely measured with reliable instruments.[4] The rationalizing of space has historically been used to support bureaucratic state administration and imperialist action (Damerow 2016).[5] It is telling that the first applications of 3D data-collection techniques served surveying, mapmaking, and military purposes. A popular technique used today to construct 3D models, *photogrammetry*, was developed in the mid-nineteenth century to survey and measure large geological and architectural features (Luhmann et al. 2014). Photogrammetry uses a set of photographs (today these can number in the hundreds or thousands) produced by cameras that are systematically positioned and calibrated to produce accurate measurements of things in the world.[6] See Figure 9.1 for an example of a nineteenth-century patent for an airborne photogrammetry technique using hot air balloons. These techniques of measurement emerged within discourses that framed the physical properties of the world as calculable and knowable via geometric functions (Schemmel 2016) and optical technologies (Crary 1990).

The movement toward scientific abstraction and measurement had early analogs in conceptions of vision, as promoted by Renaissance painters, such as Leonardo da Vinci, who broke the visual world up into geometric abstractions in order to make them more amenable to painterly

---

[4] The epistemological foundations for these techniques can be linked to broader trends in Western society, including the rise of quantification as a dominant mode of thinking emerging in the early modern period, or in the words of Alfred W. Crosby (1997), "a new way, more purely visual and quantitative than the old, of perceiving time, space, and material environment" (p. 227). To emerge, the rationalizing of space relied upon a system of equally spaced intervals (e.g., the Cartesian coordinate grid), precise means of measurement and a science of metrology that could cross cultures and geographic boundaries (Wise 1997), standardized units of measurement (Alder 1998), and conventions of trust, i.e., belief in the veridical and objective status of the numeric representations that scientists produced (Porter 1996).

[5] Effective bureaucratic administration relied on a constellation of techniques and technologies, including "the creation of permanent last names, the standardization of weights and measures, the establishment of cadastral surveys and population registers, [and] the standardization of language and legal discourse" (Scott 1998, p. 2).

[6] It became clear early in the development of photographic technologies that photographs could be used as measuring tools if the scaling ratio of the photographic image to the profilmic space was calculated. This enabled the calculation of accurate x,y coordinates (well suited for measuring architectural façades, along horizontal and vertical axes). Laussedat, an officer in the French military, began experiments with photogrammetry as early as 1849 (Luhmann et al. 2014).

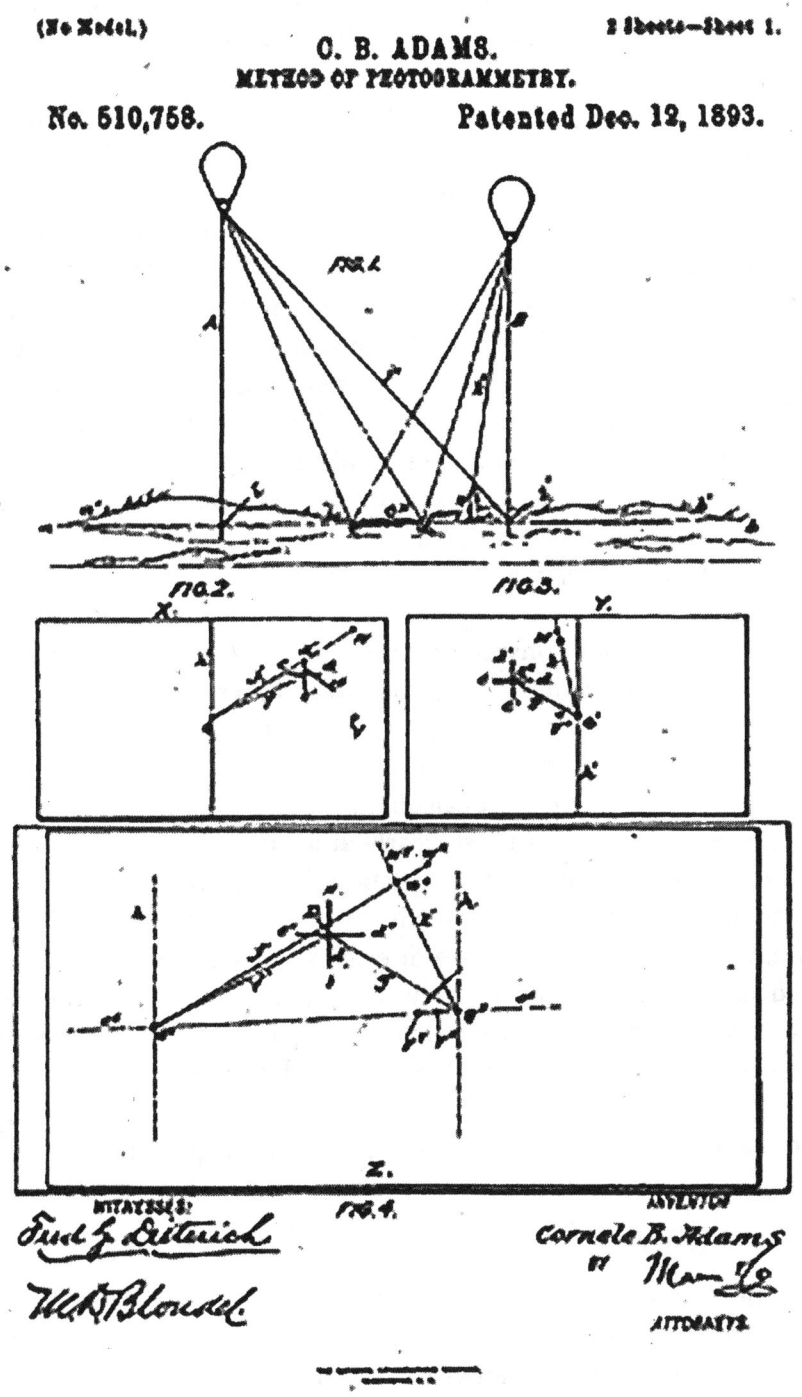

Figure 9.1 Photogrammetry technique via hot air balloon created by O. B. Adams (1893).

Source: U.S. Patent Office.

visualization (Mitchell 1992). William J. Mitchell (1992) argues that this type of geometric thinking as a technique for spatial rendering is rearticulated in the calculations of the digital computer: "The numerically encoded geometric models that are stored in computer memory and transformed into perspective views may be conceived and organized as collections of zero-dimensional lines, two-dimensional surfaces, three-dimensional solids, or combinations of these" (119–21). The Renaissance conception of space as reducible to geometric primitives is thus still operative in today's approaches to perspectival representation in digital systems. In addition, Leone Battista Alberti's perspectival system using vertical and horizontal lines, which constructed perspectival space as measurable and recordable for artists, reemerges as the "grid," which acts as both a tool and metaphor for the structure of modernist epistemologies. Elizabeth Patterson (2007) links the grid of painting and natural philosophy with the military–industrial systems of command and control and weapons systems: "The grid is a process of systematization. It orchestrates a reorganization of the image on the level of representation, dividing the image into minute units, segmented and modular—an organization seemingly outside the constraints of subjective perception. Based on sampling and quantization, it assumes that representation takes place through precise numeric values rather than steady gradation" (143). Imposing the regularity of the grid onto the spatial information of the world around us enables precise calculations of terrestrial phenomena and structures, which has been most clearly and expertly deployed through the systematic coordination of state action from a distance. We can see the rationalization of space most vividly today in the birth of drone warfare, whereby military craft are directed via databases of satellite and radar data toward human targets who appear to distant operators as grainy clusters of light flickering across grids of video-screen pixels. We need to ask, to what degree do VR and 3D technologies reproduce these systems that have historically rationalized space and made it amenable to command and control and other mechanisms of power?

Perceptual Research and the Quest for Verisimilitude

Beyond modern representational systems that rationalize space, VR and 3D technologies also emerge from trends in modern perceptual research that conceptualizes the human visual apparatus as a manageable set of inputs, outputs, and signal-processing systems. Understood as signals, perceptual stimuli can then be reproduced by artificial processes, producing simulations of real-world experiences. From this perspective, if they are sufficiently close to real-world experiences, the simulations could become indistinguishable from real-world phenomena for a human perceiver. Perceptual research has been based on modern scientific models of perception, which have shaped the information and communication technology used to encode, store, and transmit perceptual information, again, often for military or state purposes. For instance, the history of the MP3 audio-compression format, as outlined by Jonathan Sterne (2012), is entwined with earlier perceptual research that involved dissecting the ears of living cats in the late nineteenth century and was motivated by the need to transmit more signals over the limited bandwidth of telecommunication networks. The correspondence that this type of research established between biological systems of perception and electrical signals paved the way for the scientific conceptualization of the entire human sensorium as composed of an array of sensory inputs (Crary 1990). After the development of high-fidelity sound and image recording technologies in the early twentieth century, the next step was to synchronize and present these signals together in order to replicate all of the sensory dimensions of human perception.

Although methods of visual depiction and the invention of visual devices predate theories of perception, the era of modern scientific development saw increased efforts to capture "true-to-life" images of the world.[7] This quest for verisimilitude parallels the scientific rationalization of visual, aural, and haptic perception. Media historian Jonathan Crary (1990) has shown how discourses on optical devices, such as the camera obscura and stereoscope, articulate nineteenth-century ruptures from earlier models of vision, by reconstructing the "dominant model of what an observer was in the nineteenth century" (7). Through an analysis of the material practices and technological tools of vision, assumptions about the nature of vision and the notion of the observer can be reconstructed within networks of historical artifacts and discourses. Within these trends we can place a series of twentieth-century visual technologies that have moved, haltingly and often retrogressively (e.g., sixty years of low-resolution, "standard definition" broadcast National Television

---

[7] For instance, the nineteenth-century thaumatrope, a spinning disc that superimposes two discrete images, has been traced back to prehistoric times given new archaeological evidence. https://www.dailymail.co.uk/sciencetech/article-2207596/A-night-pictures-caveman-style-Prehistoric-artists-used-cartoon-like-techniques-make-paintings-move.html.

System Committee [NTSC] television is not an abnormality), toward increasing verisimilitude.[8] From 3D and widescreen cinema (e.g., *This is Cinerama!* released in 1952), to efforts at "smellovision," theme-park rides, and so on, complex spectacles have been engineered that immerse the viewer and attempt to transport him or her to "another world." Experiments, such as Ivan Sutherland's "Sword of Damocles" device that he developed in 1968, can be seen as a precursor to today's approach to VR in which a single user wears an apparatus that replaces sound and vision from the user's environment with the stimuli of a simulated world. This vision of VR almost became widely available in the 1980s and 1990s with a failed attempt by the electronics industry to bring VR to the consumer market.[9] At the same time, researchers in higher education were experimenting with other techniques, investing their time and money into very expensive, room-sized VR systems, such as Cave Automatic Virtual Environments (CAVEs; Cruz-Neira, Sandin, and DeFanti 1993), in which multiple users engage with the VR technology simultaneously. Ongoing trends that decrease cost and increase computer graphics processing power have brought VR back into the mainstream, reigniting debates about the benefits and risks of using VR to enhance human knowledge and experience (Bailenson 2018; Lanier 2017).

Taken together these histories of 3D and VR technologies can be seen to construct a new visual subject for the twenty-first century, one that is both centrally incorporated into technological systems (e.g., imagine the VR user with the headset fully engulfing his or her head) and yet is also kept at a distance from what is actually happening inside those systems (e.g., the fact that machine learning produces its own computer code that computer scientists often have no way of interpreting). Perceptual research and the quest for verisimilitude construct this new visual subject as split between, on the one hand, the imaging system, computer storage and processing/display algorithms, and on the other, the human observer, for whom data must be presented in a way that accounts for human perception and psychology. These trends can easily lead to "views from nowhere" that privilege machine vision over human perspective.

---

[8] This is not to say that the "quest for verisimilitude" is the dominant logic shaping the development of media technologies. Verisimilitude as an ideal to strive for in the development of media technologies has been inconsistently articulated in media discourse, often at odds with other discourses. High-definition television, for instance, took 30 years to go from prototype to widespread adoption (Winston 1996). Furthermore, Jonathan Sterne (2012) is quick to point out that the highly successful MP3 audio format defies the assumptions of the "quest for verisimilitude," showing instead that the success of this media format depended on other logics, such as how easily the MP3 file could be shared across computer networks and the evolving practices of media circulation and consumption that developed around it.

[9] For a brief history and prehistory of VR headsets, see Campbell (2017).

William J. Mitchell (1992) explains how 3D models are produced for various purposes that often leave behind the human observer:

> It may or may not be the case that the perspective station point corresponds to that of an actual observer or recording instrument. Sometimes the point of image synthesis is to get the image to match the world, sometimes it is to get the world to match the image, sometimes it is to predict what the world will be like at some moment in the future or to show what it might have been like if history had taken a different turn, and sometimes it is just to produce a convincing portrayal of a purely fictive place. (118–19)

Thus, we may ask ourselves, are we creating new knowledge that enables humans to understand the world, or *views from nowhere* that privilege disembodied and disconnected subjects?

The Return of VR in Academia

Having established the historical trends that have shaped 3D and VR, we can turn to recent developments in the field and see how they might impact libraries and other academic contexts. Beginning with the Kickstarter-funded release of the Oculus Development Kit I in the spring of 2013, inexpensive and user-friendly immersive visualization hardware has steadily entered the mainstream.[10] In addition to popular enthusiasm within the video-gaming community, VR technologies are seeing renewed and growing interest in academic contexts. Technology that was once confined to research laboratories is now available for use by consumers and academics. These HMDs (head-mounted displays) are far more affordable than the room-scale visualization systems that were once considered the cutting-edge equipment for VR research in the academy (e.g., CAVE systems). Academic libraries are providing access to VR in newly created makerspaces and digital scholarship centers, and through checkout services at library circulation desks. In an increasing number of colleges and universities, a broad range of stakeholders—including graduate and undergraduate students, research faculty, and library staff—have easy access to head-tracked, stereoscopic viewing hardware that provides the means to readily engage with 3D content for the purposes of enhancing research and learning.

---

[10] https://www.kickstarter.com/projects/1523379957/oculus-rift-step-into-the-game/.

Scholarly Applications and Benefits of VR

Researchers and students in disciplines concerned with spatial data are already finding uses for VR in their work. For example, in 2002, a team of archaeological researchers discovered new relationships among 250,000 components of a 3D-modeled excavation site by viewing the entire site in VR (Van Dam et al. 2002). More recently, in 2018 the Cancer Research UK Cambridge Institute started developing a highly detailed visualization of cancerous tumor growth for the purpose of understanding the spread of individual cancer cells.[11] VR and 3D content are also being used for research purposes in medicine (e.g., Andersen et al. 2016), architecture (e.g., Portman, Natapov, and Fisher-Gewirtzman 2015), geology (e.g., Donalek et al. 2014), and cultural heritage preservation (Bozorgi and Lischer-Katz 2020).

Research has shown how the capabilities of VR to immersively present spatial data can benefit a range of disciplines and tasks. In engineering fields, for example, researchers have explored the benefits of immersive visualization on product prototyping, enabling the identification of "assembly-related problems such as awkward reach angles, insufficient clearance for tooling, and excessive part orientation during assembly" (Seth, Vance, and Oliver 2011, 7). In the field of architectural design, students who were able to virtually inhabit and navigate through their design solutions during the design process were found to be more likely to achieve a higher final project score (Angulo 2013). Students in interior design courses may also benefit from using VR when designing spaces, with research suggesting that using VR for design can support "scale perception, error recognition, and communication" activities (Pober and Cook 2019, 24). Finally, neurosurgeons who worked with interactive, 3D monitors that employed stereoscopic depth cues were found to improve on their skills necessary for analyzing and evaluating vascular structures compared with neurosurgeons using 2D screens (Kersten-Oertel et al. 2014). These examples show the broad applicability and range of immersive benefits of VR technologies for research fields that rely on spatial analysis skills.

These widespread benefits of VR are linked to the technology's capability to simulate real-world depth cues and provide a highly immersive interface, which traditional computing platforms (i.e., mouse, keyboard, and monitor workstations) are incapable of rendering (Donalek

---

[11] This research is ongoing, and more information can be found here: https://www.cruk.cam.ac.uk/research-groups/imaxt-laboratory/.

et al. 2014; LaViola et al. 2017). Ragan et al. (2013) found that under controlled conditions, "participants performed significantly faster when the display provided both stereo and head-tracked rendering" when presented with small-scale spatial judgment tasks (895). By providing enhanced visual information through stereoscopic depth rendering and embodied interactions via headtracking and other sensors, VR has been shown to augment the analytic and pattern-recognition capabilities of human perception. Many of these studies emerge from the fields of electrical engineering and computer science, but recent research has sought to replicate the associated benefits in teaching and learning environments, with particular work being conducted in the context of academic libraries (e.g., Lischer-Katz, Cook, and Boulden 2018).

Virtual Reality in the Academic Library

VR is reemerging at a time when academic libraries are changing how they allocate their scarce resources. They are quickly shifting their focus from traditional collection development to the establishment of centralized, collaborative workspaces and technology-oriented service centers (Massis 2010). In the era of comprehensive online databases of journal articles, Google Scholar, and other online discovery and access portals through which much of the universe of contemporary peer-reviewed research literature is now instantly available, researchers are rarely visiting academic libraries for the purposes of solely locating secondary source material (Dewan 2012; Turner, Welch, and Reynolds. 2013; Van Orsdel and Born 2002). Instead, scholars are relying on academic libraries to provide meeting spaces, specialized computer software and hardware, research data management, digital scholarship support, and a range of other research and teaching services. Recognizing this shift in usage, academic libraries are investing in research and development initiatives that aim to provide new services and technologies, including virtual reality, to further support research and teaching (German and Namachchivaya 2013; Saunders 2015). VR stands out among these new services because it can impart special analytic and teaching benefits while providing access to important 3D research data that researchers are creating at an increasing pace.

Because academic libraries function as centralized hubs for scholarly activity and must be discipline agnostic, serving patrons from all research fields, they have the potential to be effective sites for hosting VR for a range of users (see Figure 9.2 for an example of how VR is being used

Figure 9.2 Students using virtual reality equipment at University of Oklahoma Library's Innovation @ The Edge.

to support student learning at the University of Oklahoma [OU] Libraries). By centralizing VR technology in the library, myriad academic units can readily access VR hardware without taking on the added operational overhead associated with staffing, maintaining, and upgrading rapidly evolving technological systems (Cook and Lischer-Katz 2019). Moreover, libraries themselves are starting to function as research sites in which the impact of VR on research and learning can be studied. Thus, academic libraries can serve as an "intermediary deployment zone," a centralized location through which to expand access to the documented benefits of VR to all disciplines through research and development activities.

Case Study of VR Deployment in an Academic Library

The effectiveness of VR as a teaching tool in higher education is quite promising, but there remains a lack of research that systematically evaluates the benefits of VR in naturalistic settings, that is, outside of controlled laboratory settings. In 2017, researchers at the OU Libraries conducted a study to see whether the documented benefits of VR found in laboratory

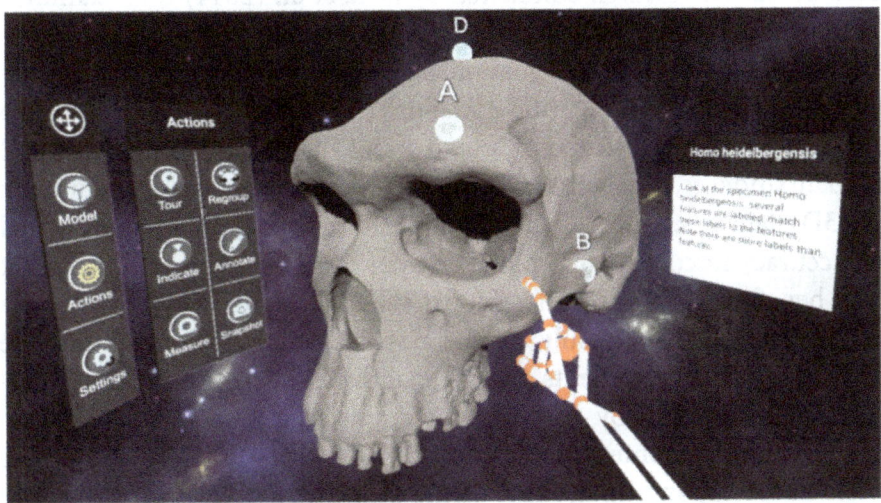

Figure 9.3 Anthropology student engaged in the VR-based course assignment.

studies could be transferred to a learning activity integrated into an introductory-level anthropology class (Lischer-Katz, Cook, and Boulden 2018). In the study, undergraduate students who were enrolled in an introductory anthropology course were given an extra credit assignment that made use of digital surrogates of fossilized hominid skulls deployed in VR. Researchers worked closely with the faculty member to design a classroom assignment that would support course learning objectives by engaging students in analytic tasks designed around the documented benefits of VR, including identifying, comparing, judging, and counting elements of the hominid skull models.

Following the VR activity (see Figure 9.3 for a screen capture of what these anthropology students saw during the activity), the students reported higher degrees of self-efficacy with regard to their ability to perform discipline-specific activities associated with spatial navigation and identification of fossil specimens, indicating the benefits of VR as a means of supporting students as engaged and empowered learners.

In this example, VR also enabled the library to provide wider access to the anthropological specimens as the existing physical skull replicas are too costly to provide for all of the students in the class. This supports existing research on 3D models that shows how they can enable digital access to physical specimens that are otherwise too distant, fragile, or rare to be handled directly (Limp et al. 2011). This study was designed based on earlier research conducted by Laha et al. (2014) that examined the impact of VR on participants' ability to quickly and accurately complete spatial tasks, with the goal of identifying "abstract task categories cutting across various scientific domains" (521). Participants in the Laha et al. (2014) study consisted of a mixture of fifty-six undergraduate and graduate students, each with no previous experience analyzing volumetric (i.e., 3D) data sets. Findings suggest that VR improved participants' speed and accuracy in completing spatial analysis tasks, and it seems likely that these benefits may be transferable to other disciplines that work with spatial materials. The results of these studies suggest that VR has the capacity to enhance students' spatial analysis abilities in a range of disciplines. Furthermore, by carrying out empirical research on VR in an academic library context, researchers at OU Libraries have shown the potential for expanding the role of the academic library into the future as a fruitful site for research and development that helps to establish and expand innovative, VR-based research tools.

Major Trends Shaping the Future of VR in the Library

The future of VR in the library will be shaped by three major trends currently unfolding: the rise of ubiquitous 3D/VR hardware, the development of vast collections of 3D assets, and the extension of traditional library discovery services through techniques of virtual browsing.

Ubiquitous Hardware

Futurists expect the uses of VR in everyday life and in academia to become less exotic and increasingly mainstream as VR technology diffuses throughout all sectors of society and becomes ubiquitous and potentially "disruptive." Cofounder of *Wired* and prolific futurist, Kevin Kelly (2017) situates VR at the end of a chain of widely disruptive technologies that we take for granted today, suggesting

> the first technological platform to disrupt a society within the lifetime of a human individual was personal computers. Mobile phones were the second platform, and they revolutionized everything in only a few decades. The next disrupting platform—now arriving—is VR. (231)

This statement anticipates the coming ubiquity of VR hardware and draws parallels between the rise of virtual experiences and other once-innovative technologies that have since become ubiquitous, such as smartphones and laptops. In spite of the dominant role played by the video game industry in its development today, VR now has the potential to become more than just another gaming platform. Rather, it is a fully interactive digital environment wherein the embodied user is able to engage with digital content in ways that more closely resemble how humans interact with physical objects in the real world (Prabhat et al. 2008).

Unlike traditional computer interface paradigms that rely on limited interface mechanisms often abstracted from intuitive bodily motions (e.g., clicks, swipes, etc.), VR makes full use of the embodied sensorimotor and proprioceptive capabilities of human beings (Stern, Wachs, and Edan 2008). This type of high-fidelity immersion—that is, an increasingly seamless linking of digital content and the human perceptual system via embodied interfaces—has profound implications for the future of academic libraries and their collections, especially as libraries begin to adopt 3D-scanning technologies and host 3D data sets (Lischer-Katz et al. 2019). However, as VR technologies become as common as smartphones and laptops, and on-site access to library collections becomes an underutilized library service, libraries will need to continually assess how to remain relevant in this evolving technological field, while staying true to their professional ethics.

Given their developmental histories as outlined earlier, VR and 3D technologies also run the risk of contributing to growing inequality in access to technologies for underrepresented groups. These technological trends raise ethical questions about how libraries will effectively support disabled and other underrepresented users who want to use these new complex devices, which make assumptions about the perceptual and physical capabilities of the user. In the short term, libraries will continue to provide access because the cost and complexity of VR systems is currently limiting VR diffusion among the consumer market, and this equipment should be accessible to all users, following accessibility standards.[12] Existing accessibility standards are not designed with VR in mind, so additional library research will be necessary in this field to ensure that VR is fully accessible to users with a range of perceptual and physical abilities (Clark and Lischer-Katz 2020).

---

[12] The Web Content Accessibility Guidelines (https://www.w3.org/WAI/standards-guidelines/wcag/) maintained by the W3C Web Accessibility Initiative offer specifications for designing digital resources with accessibility in mind.

Growing Vast Collections of 3D Assets

One area in which the future of VR technology and the mission of libraries significantly overlaps is the development of collections of scholarly 3D content. The size and scope of digital 3D asset collections is growing in parallel with the development of VR hardware and software. For instance, in July of 2018, Sketchfab—a commercial, community-based online hosting service for 3D content—surpassed three million individual models, rivaling the scale of the physical collections held by cultural heritage institutions.[13] Currently, only a small portion of these models consist of scholarly content that is produced in documented and transparent ways or is presented with the necessary metadata to ensure academic rigor and citability; however, more and more cultural heritage institutions, especially museums, are making selections from their collections available to encourage public engagement (Boyer 2016). Sketchfab currently supports easy web-based viewing of 3D models in low-cost portable VR headsets (like the smartphone-based Google Cardboard) without requiring the user to download additional plugins or invest in expensive visualization hardware, which is encouraging wider adoption of the platform. This publicly accessible 3D platform, while lacking the academic rigor of a curated, scholarly collection, effectively demonstrates the scalability of networked, VR-ready 3D asset collections.

Academically oriented 3D asset collections are also being developed individually within specialized disciplines. Consider Morphosource, an online repository dedicated to collecting morphological data sets (e.g., fossils) from fields like archeology, paleontology, and anthropology.[14] Unlike Sketchfab or other commercial platforms, Morphosource tracks specimen metadata, assigning a unique accession number for each upload to the site and linking each digital specimen back to the originating physical specimen. Making large sets of digitized scientific specimens available online provides ready access for many scholars to study the same specimens simultaneously. Making data sources publicly available helps to ensure transparency and reproducibility of research findings, such as those drawn from the measurement of fossil features, through the use of citable, persistent identifiers. When combining the large scale and ease-of-access provided by commercial platforms with the academic rigor of discipline-specific online repositories, it becomes easy to imagine future library collections that will contain vast quantities of well-curated scholarly 3D models.

---

[13] https://blog.sketchfab.com/over-three-million-3d-models-online/.
[14] https://www.morphosource.org/.

Virtual Browsing

VR also has the potential to shape the library of the future in terms of the ways in which patrons access traditional library collections. Consider the value of embodied browsing activity in the physical book stacks. Serendipitous information retrieval, or "the chance encountering of information," has been shown to benefit early-stage research and instruction, compared with common query-based search-and-retrieval paradigms (Foster and Ford 2003). A significant amount of potentially salient source material can be parsed efficiently in the physical book stacks by simple, intuitive body motions like craning the neck, bending down, or turning one's head. Each of these natural search behaviors can be replicated in virtual reality, which means that collections can be browsed and analyzed without needing to first learn the special keyboard combinations or software-specific interfaces necessary for using computer-based catalogs and other retrieval systems. As book collections are increasingly moved to off-site storage, academic libraries can maintain their capacity for rich information discovery by providing virtual browsing through VR (Cook 2018).

Virtual browsing in VR can also transcend the physical arrangement of the traditional library. The presentation of 3D assets in a virtual browsing environment need not be limited to mimicking the library stacks and reproducing their limitations as physical arrangements of books. Instead, perceptual cues developed in the field of data visualization, such as the use of semi-transparency, "fog," edge depiction, and other visual indicators, may support the display of scholarly materials beyond the typical bibliographic plane—that is, the physical library stacks with their grids of book spines as access points—to include the depth axis (z-axis) of the visual field, differentiating the relevance of search results based on visibility and the placement of resources in the background or foreground (Kersten-Oertel et al. 2014). Multiple layers of 3D models can be deployed simultaneously in VR, and users can make use of embodied locomotion (e.g., walking) to navigate through content in every direction in infinitely expandable space (Cook 2018). These approaches have great potential for making library collections more accessible to groups, such as children and disabled users who would otherwise have difficulty navigating the physical stacks, as the flexible interfaces of VR can be adjusted based on relevant human ergonomic factors. Through different combinations of sound, image, text, and haptic feedback, browsers of all abilities can be provided customized interfaces for navigating the stacks. Thus, virtual browsing in VR has the potential to expand upon traditional library services, maintaining the relevance of libraries and expanding their mission of equitable information accessibility to formerly excluded groups of patrons.

In summary, if VR follows the same adoption curve of personal computers and smartphones, and 3D digital asset collections continue to grow through streamlined, academically rigorous digitization processes, then—as is the case with virtual browsing—VR and 3D technologies will begin to shape the overall academic library experience.

Conclusions

What, then, will be the role of librarians and libraries in a world in which everyone has their own VR headset and ready access to vast 3D collections instantly accessible online? Given these current trends, we expect that VR hardware will be as ubiquitous as the smartphone and that the library will become responsible for the organization, preservation (see Lischer-Katz 2020), and accessibility of 3D digital collections of scholarly content. Rather than merely caretaking a storehouse for 3D models and other VR-ready content, librarians in the future will work alongside scholars across the disciplines to actively support research and instruction by developing new and more sophisticated applications that make use of the specialized features of VR. Academic libraries and librarians will one day oversee an entire 3D/VR research ecosystem that supports the full research lifecycle of 3D creation, analysis, publication, and curation (Limp et al. 2011).

3D and VR offer powerful tools for providing access to highly detailed simulations of things, places, and events in real, imagined, or reconstructed worlds,[15] such that future research may be primarily based on digitally captured 3D data, rather than on direct physical contact with the things themselves. Furthermore, the library of the future will have to support the research lifecycle of these new forms of data and provide access to them using rich, immersive technological platforms, such as VR, as well as augmented reality (AR) and "mixed reality" technologies that blend a user's perceptions of virtual spaces and objects with material aspects of the world.

---

[15] For an example of a reconstructed VR project, see Bryan Carter's Virtual Harlem project (Park et al. 2001).

At the same time, past experiences with visual technologies in Western contexts suggest the ways in which visual technologies can embed the epistemological and cultural assumptions of their creators in the form of assumptions about the nature of perceiving subjects, leading to exclusions in terms of the types of knowledge that can be produced and the range of knowing subjectivities that can be supported (e.g., excluding indigenous knowledge and conceptions of space-time, see Smith 2012). We certainly do not want to recreate the inequalities and exclusions, dominant worldviews, and power dynamics that plague scientific epistemologies from earlier eras; nor do we want to recreate the corporate boardroom in VR and the visual signifiers of global capitalism that Robert Markley (1996) warned of during the first wave of VR in the 1990s.

Furthermore, Bahrat Mehra (2015) cautions against libraries and library systems becoming "nothing more than mere tools to support political and corporate control that furthers a hegemonic agenda" (181). Instead, Mehra (2015) suggests a balance of social idealism and pragmatic realism, arguing that "aspects of the business model (e.g., outcome-based assessment, efficiency, user-centric services) have their place in library and information enterprises, but it is important not to forget the spirit of the social justice mission, which is to design systems and services that are equitable, meaningful, and empowering for marginalized and disenfranchised people" (181–82). Taking into account the cultural biases and corporate mentality that have shaped the development of these technologies, and taking steps to actively address them, can help to ensure that we consider the needs of traditionally marginalized groups as the library adopts VR and other emerging technologies.

Given the focus of VR technologies on the senses and the body, one glaring area that social justice sensitizes us to consider in the design of VR systems is the needs of disabled users. Given the library's mission of providing equitable access to information resources, librarians and library researchers need to take an active role in ensuring that VR can fully support users with different abilities.[16] A team of librarians and researchers at the Loretta C. Duckworth Scholars Studio at Temple University's Charles Library, led by digital scholarship librarian, Jasmine Clark, is developing the first VR program that will be compliant with existing accessibility regulations. In their VR case study, they identified

---

[16] Libraries may also have legal obligations to provide equal access, under such regulations as the American with Disabilities Act, state law, or institutional policies. Guidelines for federal agencies are codified in Section 508 of the Rehabilitation Act of 1973, https://www.access-board.gov/ict/#508-chapter-1-application-and-administration/.

"gaps in [library] staff knowledge of basic disability, as well as in DSC [Digital Scholarship Center] service policy when it comes to providing equitable services to visitors with disabilities" (Clark 2018, para. 6). In addition, the International Conference on Disability, Virtual Reality and Associated Technologies provides a forum for new research in this area, offering a source for librarians to identify the latest research on the use of VR by disabled users.[17] Librarians seeking to bring VR into their institutions need to follow developments in this field or they risk reproducing exclusions for a range of library patrons (Clark and Lischer-Katz 2020).

Given these challenges, how do librarians and their institutions move forward and act as leaders in this still nascent field? First, there is a clear need for managing, curating, and preserving VR and 3D data, and academic libraries are poised to take the lead in developing standards and best practices in this area. Second, libraries can use 3D/VR to expand access to existing library collections and services, as well as provide support for new applications, including a growing ecosystem of 3D/VR research data. Finally, new technologies need to be integrated into existing library services, while supporting the ethos of librarianship, in order to be sustainable and equitable. Librarians must closely monitor the continuing developments in the implementation of VR and 3D across different library communities, carry out research projects that critically interrogate the embedded assumptions of these technologies, and communicate effectively with a growing network of library researchers who are establishing the standards and best practices necessary for supporting VR in library contexts.[18]

The future of academic libraries is intimately linked to the future of emerging technologies and their application to research and teaching. In an age in which university budgets are being increasingly squeezed and academic units must continually defend their existence by demonstrating increasing "return on investment," the future of academic libraries de-

---

[17] The proceedings of this conference are available online: https://www.icdvrat.org/archive.htm. Much of the research in this area is focused on using VR to benefit disabled people, particularly in terms of its therapeutic possibilities.

[18] The library community is already taking a leadership role in the preservation of 3D and VR-related research data and learning materials. In 2018, three research projects were funded by the Institute of Museum and Library Services on the preservation of 3D data: Community Standards for 3D Data Preservation (Washington University, University of Iowa, and University of Michigan; https://osf.io/ewt2h/), Developing Library Strategy for 3D and Virtual Reality Collection Development and Reuse (Virginia Tech, Indiana University, and the University of Oklahoma; https://lib.vt.edu/research-teaching/lib3dvr.html/), and Building for Tomorrow (Harvard University; https://projects.iq.harvard.edu/buildingtomorrow/).

pends in large part on the ability of librarians to adapt to rapidly evolving scholarly and pedagogical practices and the rise of ubiquitous and constantly changing digital technologies. The emergence of new types of research methods, data, and pedagogies, and the continuing centrality of the library within academic life, require libraries and librarians to lead the way in this area, adopting organizational techniques and creating new administrative units (e.g. makerspaces, digital scholarship labs, visualization labs, etc.) that foster a culture of innovation, while still staying true to the essential library values of inclusion and equitable access to all forms of information.

Bibliography

Alder, Ken. "Making Things the Same: Representation, Tolerance and the End of the *Ancien Régime* in France." *Social Studies of Science* 28, no. 4 (1998): 499–545. http://www.jstor.org/stable/285489.

Andersen, Steven, Arild Wuyts, Peter Trier Mikkelsen, Lars Konge, Per Cayé-Thomasen, and Mads Sølvsten Sørensen. "Cognitive Load in Mastoidectomy Skills Training: Virtual Reality Simulation and Traditional Dissection Compared." *Journal of Surgical Education* 73, no. 1 (2016): 45–50.

Angulo, Antonieta. 2013. "On the Design of Architectural Spatial Experiences Using Immersive Simulation." In *EAEA 11 Conference Proceedings of the 11th Conference of the European Architectural Envisioning Association, Milan, Italy*, September 2013, 151–58.

Bailenson, J. *Experience on Demand: What Virtual Reality Is, How It Works, and What It Can Do.* New York: W.W. Norton, 2018.

Bowman, Doug A., and Ryan P. McMahan. "Virtual Reality: How Much Immersion Is Enough?" *Computer* 40, no. 7 (2007): 36–43.

Boyer, Doug. "Virtual Fossils Revolutionize the Study of Human Evolution." *Aeon*. Last modified February 25, 2016. https://aeon.co/ideas/virtual-fossils-revolutionise-the-study-of-human-evolution.

Bozorgi, Khosrow, and Zack Lischer-Katz. "Using 3D/VR for Research and Cultural Heritage Preservation: Project Update on the Virtual Ganjali Khan Project." *Preservation, Digital Technology, & Culture* 49, no. 2 (2020): 45–57. https://doi.org/10.1515/pdtc-2020-0017.

Campbell, Savannah. "'A Rift in Our Practices?': Toward Preserving Virtual Reality." MA thesis, New York University, 2017. https://miap.hosting.nyu.edu/program/student_work/2017spring/17s_thesis_Campbell_y.pdf/.

Clark, Jasmine. "Progressing Towards an Accessible VR Experience," Digital Scholarship Center (blog), Temple University Libraries, November 7, 2018. https://sites.temple.edu/tudsc/2018/11/07/progressing-towards-an-accessible-vr-experience/.

Clark, Jasmine, and Zack Lischer-Katz. "Barriers to Supporting Accessible VR in Academic Libraries." *Journal of Interactive Technology & Pedagogy* 17 (2020). https://jitp.commons.gc.cuny.edu/barriers-to-supporting-accessible-vr-in-academic-libraries.

Cook, Matt. "Virtual Serendipity: Preserving Embodied Browsing Activity in the 21st Century Research Library." *The Journal of Academic Librarianship* 44, no. 1 (2018): 145–49. https://doi.org/10.1016/j.acalib.2017.09.003.

Cook, Matt, and Zack Lischer-Katz. "Virtual Reality Integration in the Academic Library." In *Beyond Reality: Augmented, Virtual, and Mixed Reality in the Library*, edited by Kenneth Varnum. Chicago, IL: ALA Editions, 2019.

Crary, Jonathan. *Techniques of the Observer: On Vision and Modernity in the Nineteenth Century*. Cambridge, MA: MIT Press, 1990.

Crosby, Alfred W. *The Measure of Reality: Quantification and Western Society, 1250–1600*. Cambridge, UK: Cambridge University Press, 1997.

Cruz-Neira, Carolina, Daniel J. Sandin, and Thomas A. DeFanti. "Surround-Screen Projection-Based Virtual Reality: The Design and Implementation of the CAVE." In *Proceedings of the 20th Annual Conference on Computer Graphics and Interactive Techniques, Anaheim, CA*, 135–142. New York: Association for Computing Machinery, 1993.

Damerow, Peter. "The Impact of Notation Systems: From the Practical Knowledge of Surveyors to Babylonian Geometry," In *Spatial Thinking and External Representation: Towards a Historical Epistemology of Space*, edited by Matthias Schemmel, 93–118. Berlin: Edition Open Access, 2016. https://pure.mpg.de/rest/items/item_2368645/component/file_2368644/content.

Dewan, Pauline. "Are Books Becoming Extinct in Academic Libraries?" *New Library World* 113, nos. 1 and 2 (2012): 27–37.

Donalek, Ciro, S. George Djorgovski, Scott Davidoff, Alex Cioc, Anwell Wang, Giuseppe Longo, Jeffrey S. Norris, Jerry Zhang, Elizabeth Lawler, Stacy Yeh, Ashish Mahabal, Matthew J. Graham, and Andrew J. Drake. "Immersive and Collaborative Data Visualization Using Virtual Reality Platforms." In *Proceedings of 2014 IEEE International*

Conference on Big Data, Washington, DC, 609–14, Oct. 27–30, 2014. New York: IEEE.

Foster, Allen, and Nigel Ford. "Serendipity and Information Seeking: An Empirical Study." *Journal of documentation* 59, no. 3 2003): 321–40.

German, Lisa, and Beth Sandore Namachchivaya. *SPEC Kit 339: Innovation and R&D.* Washington, DC: Association of Research Libraries, 2013. https://publications.arl.org/Innovation-R&D-SPEC-Kit-339/.

Hall, Nathan, Juliet Hardesty, Zack Lischer-Katz, Jennifer Johnson, Matt Cook, Julie Griffin, Andrea Ogier, Zhiwu Xie, and Robert McDonald. 2019. "Challenges and Directions in 3D and VR Data Curation: Findings from a Nominal Group Study." *International Journal of Digital Curation* 14, no. 1 (2019): 150–67. http://www.ijdc.net/article/view/588/551.

Kelly, Kevin. *The Inevitable: Understanding the 12 Technological Forces That Will Shape Our Future.* New York: Penguin, 2017.

Kersten-Oertel, Marta, Sean J. Chen, and D. Louis Collins. "An Evaluation of Depth Enhancing Perceptual Cues for Vascular Volume Visualization in Neurosurgery," In *IEEE Transactions on Visualization and Computer Graphics* 20, no.3 (2014): 391–403.

Laha, Bireswar, Doug A. Bowman, and John J. Socha. "Effects of VR System Fidelity on Analyzing Isosurface Visualization of Volume Datasets." *IEEE Transactions on Visualization and Computer Graphics* 20, no. 4 (2014): 513–22.

Lanier, Jaron. *Dawn of the New Everything: Encounters with Reality and Virtual Reality.* New York: Henry Holt and Company, 2017.

LaViola, Joseph J., Ernst Kruijff, Ryan P. McMahan, Doug A. Bowman, and Ivan Poupyrev. *3D User Interfaces: Theory and Practice.* Boston: Addison-Wesley Professional, 2017.

Limp, Fred, Angie Payne, Katie Simon, Snow Winters, and Jack Cothren. "Developing a 3-D Digital Heritage Ecosystem: From Object to Representation and the Role of a Virtual Museum in the 21st Century," *Internet Archaeology* 30 (2011). https://doi.org/10.11141/ia.30.1.

Lischer-Katz, Zack. "Archiving Experience: An Exploration of the Challenges of Preserving Virtual Reality." *Records Management Journal* 30, no. 2 (2020): 253–74. https://doi.org/10.1108/RMJ-09-2019-0054.

Lischer-Katz, Zack, Matt Cook, and Kristal Boulden. 2018. "Evaluating the Impact of a Virtual Reality Workstation in an Academic Library: Methodology and Preliminary Findings." In *Proceedings of the Annual Meeting of the Association for Information Science & Technology*, Nov. 9–14, 2018, Vancouver, Canada, 300–08. Silver Spring, MD: Association for Information Science and Technology. https://asistdl.onlinelibrary.wiley.com/doi/10.1002/pra2.2018.14505501033.

Lischer-Katz, Zack, Jennifer Grayburn, Kristina Golubiewski-Davis, and Veronica Ikeshoji-Orlati. "3D/VR Creation and Curation: An Emerging Field of Inquiry." In *3D/VR in the Academic Library: Emerging Practices and Trends*, edited by Jennifer Grayburn, Zack Lischer-Katz, Kristina Golubiewski-Davis, and Veronica Ikeshoji-Orlati. CLIR Report 176, Arlington, VA: Council on Library and Information Resources, 2019. https://www.clir.org/pubs/reports/pub176.

Luhmann, Thomas, Stuart Robson, Stephen Kyle, and Jan Boehm. *Close-range Photogrammetry and 3D Imaging*. Berlin: Walter de Gruyter, 2014.

Markley, Robert. "Introduction: History, Theory, and Virtual Reality." In *Virtual Realities and Their Discontents*, edited by Robert Markley, 1–10. Baltimore, MD: Johns Hopkins University Press, 1996.

Massis, Bruce E. "The Academic Library Becomes the Academic Learning Commons." *New Library World* 111, nos. 3 and 4 (2010): 161–63.

Mehra, Bharat. "Introduction to Special Issue - Social Justice in Library and Information Science Services." *Library Trends* 64, no. 2 (2015): 179–97.

Mitchell, William J. *The Reconfigured Eye: Visual Truth in the Post-photographic Era*. Cambridge, MA: MIT Press, 1992.

Park, Kyoung S., Jason Leigh, Andrew E. Johnson, Bryan Carter, Jennifer Brody, and James Sosnoski. "Distance Learning Classroom Using Virtual Harlem" In *Proceedings of the Seventh International Conference on Virtual Systems and Multimedia*, Berkeley, CA, October 25–27, 2001, 489–98. New York: IEEE. https://ieeexplore.ieee.org/document/969704.

Patterson, Elizabeth M. "Visionary Machines: A Genealogy of the Digital Image." PhD diss., University of California, Berkeley, 2007.

Pober, Elizabeth, and Matt Cook. "The Design and Development of an Immersive Learning System for Spatial Analysis and Visual Cognition." In *Proceedings of Conference of the Design Communication Association*, Bozeman, MT, September 7–10, 2016. Bozeman, MT: Design Communication Association.

Pober, Elizabeth, and Matt Cook. "Thinking in Virtual Spaces: Impacts of Virtual Reality on the Undergraduate Interior Design Process." *International Journal of Virtual and Augmented Reality* 3, no. 2 2019): 23–40.

Porter, Theodore M. *Trust in Numbers: The Pursuit of Objectivity in Science and Public Life*. Princeton, NJ: Princeton University Press, 1996.

Portman, Michelle E., Asya Natapov, and Dafna Fisher-Gewirtzman. "To Go Where No Man Has Gone Before: Virtual Reality in Architecture, Landscape Architecture and Environmental Planning." *Computers, Environment and Urban Systems* 54 (2015): 376–84.

Prabhat, Andrew S. Forsberg, Michael Katzourin, Kristi Wharton, and Mel Slater. "A Comparative Study of Desktop, Fishtank, and CAVE Systems for the Exploration of Volume Rendered Confocal Data Sets." *IEEE Transactions on Visualization and Computer Graphics* 14, no. 3 (2008): 551–63.

Ragan, Eric D., Regis Kopper, Philip Schuchardt, and Doug A. Bowman. "Studying the Effects of Stereo, Head Tracking, and Field of Regard on a Small-scale Spatial Judgment Task." *IEEE transactions on visualization and computer graphics* 19, no.5 (2013): 886–896.

Saunders, Laura. "Academic Libraries' Strategic Plans: Top Trends and Under-recognized Areas." *The Journal of Academic Librarianship* 4, no. 3 (2015): 285–91.

Schemmel, Matthias. "Towards a Historical Epistemology of Space: An Introduction." In *Spatial Thinking and External Representation: Towards a Historical Epistemology of Space*, edited by Matthias Schemmel, 93–118. Berlin: Edition Open Access, 2016. https://pure.mpg.de/rest/items/item_2368645/component/file_2368644/content.

Scott, James C. *Seeing Like a State: How Certain Schemes to Improve the Human Condition Have Failed*. New Haven, CT: Yale University Press, 1998.

Seth, Abhishek, Judy M. Vance, and James H. Oliver. "Virtual Reality for Assembly Methods Prototyping: A Review." *Virtual Reality* 15, no. (2011): 5–20.

Smith, Linda Tuhiwai. *Decolonizing Methodologies: Research and Indigenous Peoples, 2nd Ed.* London: Zed Books, 2012.

Stern, Helman I., Juan P. Wachs, and Yael Edan. "Optimal Consensus Intuitive Hand Gesture Vocabulary Design." In *Proceedings of IEEE International Conference on Semantic Computing*. (2008): 96–103. New York: IEEE.

Sterne, Jonathan. *MP3: The Meaning of a Format*. Durham, NC: Duke University Press, 2012.

Turner, Arlee, Bernadette Welch, and Sue Reynolds. 2013. "Learning Spaces in Academic Libraries—A Review of the Evolving Trends." *Australian Academic & Research Libraries* 44, no. 4 (2013): 226–34.

Van Dam, Andries, David H. Laidlaw, and Rosemary Michelle Simpson. "Experiments in Immersive Virtual Reality for Scientific Visualization." *Computers & Graphics* 26, no.4 (2002): 535–55.

Van Orsdel, L., and Kathleen Born. "Periodicals Price Survey 2002: Doing the Digital Flip." *Library Journal* 127, no.7 (2002): 51–56.

Winston, Brian. *Technologies of Seeing: Photography, Cinematography and Television*. London: British Film Institute, 1996.

Wise, M. N. *The Values of Precision*. Princeton, NJ: Princeton University Press, 1997.

10

The New Wave of Digital Collections: Speculating on the Future of Library Curation

*Alex Wermer-Colan and
James Kopaczewski*

> As for the history of the future itself, unless it is understood to be a literary genre (Science Fiction), we often tend to abandon it to prophets and Cassandras, if not to the writers of bestsellers on the subject, without remembering that every present of time in which we move includes its own dimension of futurity, of fears and expectations, which (realized or not) at once accompany that present into the past along with it.
> —Frederic Jameson[1]

Across the academic disciplines, researchers, teachers, and librarians are increasingly concerned about blind spots in their data sets. For interdisciplinary academic fields, such as library curation and literary studies, the specter of copyright keeps in the shadows a wide range of corpora reflecting the diversity of twentieth- and twenty-first-century authors and works outside the traditional canon. The post-World War II "New Wave" of science fiction represents one such aporia, a significant, but inaccessible moment in cultural history, when a mass-market genre's conventions, from formulaic plots to stereotypical tropes, as well as

---

[1] Frederic Jameson, *The Antinomies of Realism* (New York: Verso Books, 2013).

its authorship and readership (predominantly White, heteronormative men), were thoroughly called into question. Since the sci-fi genre's inception in the late nineteenth century, it took nearly a century for New Wave (1964–1983) writers, such as Samuel R. Delany and Joanna Russ, to deconstruct and redeploy the genre, introducing taboo themes, while turning toward questions of the "near future," with an emphasis on the so-called "soft" sciences (such as anthropology, psychology, sociology).[2] In the 1960s and 70s, a range of minority, countercultural perspectives entered the fray, often garnering such major awards as the Hugo and the Nebula in recognition of their experiments with the stylistic strictures of the genre and their radical visions of alternate pasts and futures. Yet the vast majority of this valuable corpus of twentieth-century literature, like a large proportion of multicultural writing in English more generally, remains under the lock and key of copyright into the unforeseeable future.

As Frederic Jameson has persuasively argued since writing his pivotal work of cultural criticism, *The Political Unconscious: Narrative as a Socially Symbolic Act* (1981), genre fiction can offer a valuable lens through which to look at the broader culture that produces it.[3] To do so, however, Jameson reminds us, it is also important to analyze how genres, as a formulaic set of rules for plot and style, become sedimented in forms that determine how our culture can see itself, both its past and its future. Literary studies often focus on canon formation, but critics like Paul Kincaid have argued that identifying a canon for science fiction remains difficult, not least due to divergent popular definitions. Fans and critics dispute the historical or literary merit of specific works, yet the results continue to skew Anglocentric, White, male, and heteronormative. The genre has historically been slow to welcome new voices, particularly those of women, people of color, and writers who identify as LGBTQ. For all concerned, the stakes are high for finding new ways of expanding, measuring, and celebrating science fiction's diverse contours.

A more inclusive approach to genre formation can be approximated at scale using quantitative methods enhanced with computational tools for textual and cultural analytics. However, those who apply digital methods to contemporary literature are confronted with two primary obstacles: (1) copyright restrictions and (2) the undigitized, what Marga-

---

[2] Many critics cite Jules Verne's *Journey to the Center of the Earth* (1864) as the first canonical work of science fiction literature. The early periods of sci-fi are identified as the era of "Scientific Romances" (1864–1903), the "Radium Age" (1904–33), and the "Golden Age" (1934–1963). For New Wave writers, see Robert Heinlein, Katherine MacLean, Alfred Bester, Theodore Sturgeon, Judith Merril, Thomas M. Disch, James Triptree Jr., Philip K. Dick, William S. Burroughs, J. G. Ballard, Michael Moorcock, Roger Zelazny, Samuel R. Delany, Ursula Le Guin, Joanna Russ, and Octavia Butler.

[3] Frederic Jameson, *The Political Unconscious* (Ithaca, NY: Cornell University Press, 1981).

ret Cohen called "the great unread," a term borrowed by Franco Moretti to justify distant reading. These limitations in access to copyrighted works, especially out-of-print, mass-market materials, are evident even in large-scale repositories like the HathiTrust Digital Library. Although the Google Books project has created extensive digital research corpora, Ted Underwood, Ben Schmidt, and many other scholars warn it is missing more than can currently be measured, limiting research in such fields as historical genre analysis.[4] While HathiTrust contains a growing set of canonical "science fiction" literature (although limitations in Library of Congress subject metadata limit the breakdown of genre fiction), cross-checking Temple Libraries' Paskow Science Fiction Collection has shown that only a small percentage of the special collections materials are currently contained in HathiTrust's collection of 14 million books. Indeed, to study science fiction as a coherent, historical genre requires quantitative methods and big, representative data sets not least because the number of published works increased exponentially with the proliferation of magazine and paperback formats in the mid-twentieth century. Recent scholarly works of computational analysis on science fiction, such as Ted Underwood's "The Life Cycles of Genres" (2016) and the multiauthored study, "Towards a Poetics of Strangeness" (2017), provide a critical foundation for a cultural analysis of mass market genre fiction, yet both studies lack access to a data set representative of the diverse literary field.[5] Enlarging the available science fiction corpus will help bring into relief works and authors that were underappreciated when first released, creating a more thorough range of sources for scholars.

In the fall of 2018, Temple University Libraries's Digital Scholarship Center, now the Loretta C. Duckworth Scholars Studio, began the generative process of sorting through an uncatalogued set of duplicate books and magazines deaccessioned from the Paskow Science Fiction Collection held by Temple Libraries' Special Collection Research Center (SCRC). In total, the Paskow Collection contains around 12,000 science fiction paperback books, including materials compiled by both vocational donors as well as through limited exchanges with libraries.[6] The collection was originally established in 1972, when the SCRC acquired science fiction

---

[4] Ted Underwood, *Distant Horizons: Digital Evidence and Literary Change* (Chicago: University of Chicago Press, 2019).

[5] Ted Underwood, "The Life Cycles of Genres," *Journal of Cultural Analytics* 2, no. 1 (May 23, 2016): doi: 10.22148/16.005. https://culturalanalytics.org/article/11061-the-life-cycles-of-genres; Michael Simone et al., "Towards a Poetics of Strangeness: Experiments in Classifying Language of Technological Novelty," *Journal of Cultural Analytics* (September 8, 2017)/. https://culturalanalytics.org/article/11068-towards-a-poetics-of-strangeness-experiments-in-classifying-language-of-technological-novelty/.

[6] Finding aids for the Paskow Collection can be found here: https://library.temple.edu/collections/paskow-science-fiction-collection-science-fiction-and-fantasy/.

paperbacks from a Temple alumnus, the late David C. Paskow. During the 1980s and 90s, the former SCRC curator, Tom Whitehead, purchased materials from the Science Fiction Research Association, which had placed their materials under the care of the American Philosophical Society. Combined, these series of acquisitions helped to form the core of our duplicate sci-fi corpus.

During the early stages of cataloguing, digitizing, cleaning, and text mining our growing corpus of sci-fi lit, a mostly contingent labor force of postdocs, resident librarians, and graduate student workers collaborated to scope out the landscape of digital collections.[7] In light of the rapidly changing terrain of web-based data curation, we gradually conceived and developed a long-term digital research and curation project of sci-fi genre fiction, inspired by, and indebted to, what we consider a "new wave" of digital collections, heterogeneous in content and form, but unified in the effort to bridge humanistic and scientific approaches to data. Spanning a wide array of libraries and research institutions, this trend is evident in such illuminating textual analysis and visualization tools as Ben Schmidt's "Bookworm" module for the HathiTrust Research Center, Yale University Digital Humanities Lab's "Robots Reading Vogue" website, and Indiana University's Observatory on Social Media.[8] In an innovative fusion of these tendencies, Ben Schmidt's guided tour of the HathiTrust collection, "Creating Data: A Guided Tour of the Digital Library," provides a model for how web-based data curation through interactive scrollytelling.[9] The principles underlying this emerging trend in digital exhibition and curation are undoubtedly inspired by and constitutive of the "collections as data" movement.[10] Following the strategies developed by this data-oriented movement spanning collection

---

[7] Our team has included, but is not limited to Alex Wermer-Colan, James Kopaczewski, Rikk Mulligan, Margery Sly, Jasmine Clark, Jordan Hample, Matt Shoemaker, Luling Huang, Bethany Farrell, Jeff Antsen, Vivien Wise, Gabe Galson, Stephanie Ramsey, Holly Tomren, Matt Ducmanas, and Michael Carroll. We've built connections at many other universities and libraries, especially through the SciFi Collection Libraries Consortium (http://sfspecialcollections.pbworks.com/w/page/75814541/About%20the%20SciFi%20Collection%20Libraries%20Consortium%20 working with Jeremy Brett, Curator of the Science Fiction and Fantasy Research Collection at Texas A&M Libraries, Sarah Potvin, the Digital Scholarship Librarian at Texas A&M, and Elspeth Healey at Kansas University Libraries' Kenneth Spencer Research Library, with the goal of acquiring grant funds to expand the projects digitization, data sharing agreements, and data curation.

[8] See HathiTrust, "Bookworm." https://bookworm.htrc.illinois.edu/develop/; Yale University DH Lab; "Robots Reading Vogue." http://dhlab.yale.edu/projects/vogue.html; Indiana University, "Observatory on Social Media." https://osome.iuni.iu.edu/.

[9] Ben Schmidt, "Creating Data: A Guided Tour of the Digital Library." http://creatingdata.us/datasets/hathi-features/.

[10] Thomas Padilla, "Humanities Data in the Library: Integrity, Form, Access," *D-Lib Magazine* 22, nos. 3–4 (March 2016). https://www.dlib.org/dlib/march16/padilla/03padilla.html/.

development and digital scholarship, the SF project team has sought to establish multi-institutional partnerships, experimenting with innovative, accessible data-curation methods, and fostering discoverability and engagement with copyrighted corpora.[11] The sci-fi digitization project, although supplemental to the primary operations of the library, has also gradually served as a catalyst and vehicle for organizational restructuring, building new connections among departments, including the Digital Scholarship Center, the Special Collections Research Center, Library Technology Services, and Metadata and Digitization Services.

Working toward our vision of a coalition of speculative fiction collections developing shared digitization goals and workflows, we have worked within existing networks, engaging with research centers like the Stanford Literary Lab and the UChicago Text Lab, and with academic libraries like Texas A&M and University of Kansas that possess sci-fi holdings.[12] The SF Nexus, as the coalition has come to be called, also seeks to include available corpora online whenever possible, exploring paths for web-scraping online resources that fans and scholars have built since the 1990s, like Project Gutenberg, Internet Archive, and other "rogue" online archives, such as Luminist.org, that contain underappreciated works of science-fiction literature.[13] The SF Nexus largely formed out of a need to develop standard practices for legally exchanging copyrighted data sets for the purposes of "nonconsumptive" research. Research centers may also purchase private collections of mass-market books partially to acquire duplicates for digitization.

As we imagine the future of digital exhibits, we are experimenting with open-source, dynamic, and versatile web infrastructures adaptable to the shifting face of digital technology in the coming years. To do so requires building mutually beneficial bridges with other online repositories and databases, while we focus on designing a multifaceted resource for accessing copyrighted data through multimodal, embeddable tools

---

[11] Thomas Padilla, "On a Collections as Data Imperative," September 27, 2016. http://digitalpreservation.gov/meetings/dcs16/tpadilla_OnaCollectionsasDataImperative_final.pdf/.

[12] Significant collections of science fiction material are held at repositories, including Georgia Tech, Syracuse University, Texas A&M University, Toronto Public Library, University of California-Riverside, University of Illinois-Urbana, University of Iowa, University of Kansas, University of Michigan, University of Oregon, University of Liverpool, and many more universities across the globe. For examples of valuable digital archives, see The Internet Speculative Fiction Database, http://www.isfdb.org; The Luminist League, www.luminist.org; Project Gutenberg, "Science Fiction (Bookshelf)," https://www.gutenberg.org/wiki/Science_Fiction_(Bookshelf); and the Internet archive, "The Science Fiction and Fantasy Fiction Collection," https://archive.org/details/sciencefiction/.

[13] Abigail De Kosnik, *Rogue Archives: Digital Cultural Memory and Media Fandom* (Cambridge: MIT Press, 2016).

for computational analysis designed for inclusive usability.[14] With the limitations of text mining in mind, we remain invested in exploring, within the bounds of the law, computational methods for bypassing the limitations of copyright, from data capsules (remote computing for nonconsumptive research) to extracted features data sets (quantitative, disaggregated data and metadata derived computationally from corpora).[15] Through these methods, we've slowly enabled scholarly use: Brianna Blackwell's digitized University of Kansas master's thesis, "Memory in the Apocalyptic Archive: A Literary and Computational Textual Analysis of *A Canticle for Leibowitz*" (2019) depended on access to extracted features from Temple's corpus, as has recent research by Pomona College undergraduate student Tai Xiang (viewable at his Github repo, "Sentiments of Science Fiction" [https://github.com/tyxiang0530/Sentiments-of-Science-Fiction/]). To further support such ongoing research, by partnering with Indiana University on their Institute of Museum and Library Services (IMLS) grant-funded project, "Data Capsule Appliance for Research Analysis of Restricted and Sensitive Data in Academic Libraries," Temple University Libraries is currently prototyping and testing the technical infrastructure needed to support remote, full-text access for nonconsumptive research on the model pioneered by the HathiTrust Research Center. We've also documented our process by blogging at the early stages, and then creating an Omeka site to showcase the book covers and their histories, to serve as a foundation for a multimodal website.[16]

---

[14] Although we aim to use tools that can guide new users through the fundamentals of data analysis, it is important to be mindful of terminology around "ease" of learning curves. For more on this subject, see Paige C. Morgan, "The Consequences of Framing Digital Humanities Tools as Easy to Use," *College & Undergraduate Libraries*, (August 7, 2018): 211–31. https://www.tandfonline.com/doi/abs/10.1080/10691316.2018.1480440/.

[15] Eleanor Dickson et al., "Synthesis of Cross-Stakeholder Perspectives on Text Data Mining with Use-Limited Data: Setting the Stage for an IMLS National Forum," paper presented at IMLS National Forum on Data Mining Research Using In-copyright and Limited-Access Text Datasets: Discussion Paper, Forum Statements, and SWOT Analyses. https://www.ideals.illinois.edu/handle/2142/100055/.

[16] The science fiction digitization project has generated four blog posts for the Scholars Studio, including Alex Wermer-Colan's "Building a New Wave Science Fiction Corpus" (12/20/2017; https://sites.temple.edu/tudsc/2017/12/20/building-new-wave-science-fiction-corpus/) and "Modeling the New Wave: On Learning to Use Machines to Read Sci-Fi Lit" (4/26/2018; https://sites.temple.edu/tudsc/2018/04/26/modeling-the-new-wave-on-learning-to-use-machines-to-read-sci-fi-lit/); James Kopaczewski's "Digitizing Alternate History Narratives" (2/22/2018; https://sites.temple.edu/tudsc/2018/02/22/digitizing-alternate-history-narratives/); and Jeff Antsen's "Disaggregating Copyrighted Corpora: An R Script for Extracting and Structuring Textual Features" (7/18/2019; https://sites.temple.edu/tudsc/2019/07/18/curating-copyrighted-corpora-an-r-script-for-extracting-and-structuring-textual-features/). The Scholars Studio's Omeka site, "Digitizing Science Fiction" can be viewed here: https://lcdssgeo.com/omeka-s/s/scifi/page/digitizing-science-fiction. Finally, Temple Now covered the project in their news reporting just as digitization was stalled by the pandemic in Edirin Oputu's "Byte-size Books: Digitizing Temple University Libraries' Science Fiction Collection" (6/15/2020): https://news.temple.edu/news/2020-06-15/byte-size-books-digitizing-temple-university-libraries-science-fiction-collection/.

By supplementing analytic tools with thorough documentation and tutorials, the SF Nexus's web resources will aim to showcase how such innovative methods can enhance, without replacing, traditional hermeneutic approaches. As humanities teachers and researchers increasingly advocate for an interdisciplinary, mixed-methods practice, we are exploring how libraries can transform and exhibit their special collections. By tracing, then, the past, present, and possible futures of Temple's Paskow Science Fiction Collection, we attempt in this essay to reimagine how libraries in the digital age can enhance the discoverability and accessibility of privatized collections and data sets for researchers, teachers, and the public more broadly.

The New Wave of Sci-Fi: Rethinking the Alternate Realities of Libraries

> America is a nation of liars, and for that reason science fiction has a special claim to be our national literature, as the art form best adapted to telling the lies we like to hear and to pretend we believe.—Thomas Disch[17]

Just as speculative fiction offers a fitting medium through which we can interrogate our assumptions about and reimagine the future of fields like the digital humanities, the New Wave era of science fiction literature provides the pivotal period in the genre's history through which we can conceive of a futuristic generation of digital collections. Across media as diverse as cinema and music, the New Wave has designated a loosening of hardened forms that allows for a flourishing of new perspectives, expressions, and speculations. The actual term *New Wave*, when it was first used for the science fiction movement, was imported from the modernist movement in French film, the *nouvelle vague*. More so than in the medium of cinema, however, the New Wave of science fiction remains a hotly contested historical period and aesthetic category in the genre's evolution. The New Wave's periodization in the 1960s and 70s remains nebulous, often uninterrogated, with many critics identifying its origin with the coining of the term itself, in 1961, rather than according to the aesthetic qualities with which the movement became associated. In the 1950s, such writers as Alfred Bester, Katherine MacLean, Theodore

---

[17] Thomas Disch, *The Dreams Our Stuff Is Made of: How Science Fiction Conquered the World* (New York: Simon & Schuster, 2000).

Sturgeon, and William S. Burroughs, had already overturned many of the genre's conventions, in both form and content.[18]

Inspired during interviews with Samuel R. Delany—the 75-year-old Temple University emeritus professor, polymath, and renowned African American writer who was at the vanguard, first, of a queer lineage during the New Wave and, ever since, of speculative fiction, science fiction (SF) criticism, and American letters more generally—our work has moved into ever more speculative new directions.[19] After reflecting on the importance of libraries to his life and work, Delany offered a useful way to think through New Wave sci-fi in terms of its figuration of libraries, information, and their shared future. Delany first cited Jorge Luis Borges's foundational essay and story (respectively, "The Total Library" [1939] and "The Library of Babel" [1941]). At the fantastical peaks of his essay, Borges described what would be included in such a "total library," writing: "Everything would be in its blind volumes. Everything: the detailed history of the future ... the exact number of times that the waters of the Ganges have reflected the flight of a falcon ... the unwritten chapters of Edwin Drood ... the song the sirens sang, the complete catalog of the Library, the proof of the inaccuracy of that catalog."[20]

After alluding to this foundational text, Delany pointed toward a historical shift, from Isaac Asimov's vision of an *Encyclopedia Galactica* in his *Foundation* (1951) trilogy at the height of the "Golden Age," to his own novels published at the breaking point of the New Wave, *Trouble on Triton: An Ambiguous Heterotopia* (1976) and *Stars in My Pockets Like Grains of Sand* (1984).[21] In these two works, Delany charts the contours of a web-like network known as the *General Information* system, through which people across the universe use cyborgian gloves to jack in and instantaneously receive wide swathes of data, such as the entire poetic works of an imaginary epoch. Following the pinnacle of the Space Age

---

[18] See Alfred Bester, *Starburst* (New York: New American Library, 1958); Katherine MacLean, *Missing Man* (New York: Orion, 1975); Theodore Sturgeon, *More than Human* (New York: Ballantine Books, 1953); William S. Burroughs, *The Nova Trilogy* (1961–64).

[19] Wermer-Colan's interviews with Delany appeared in two parts in the *Los Angeles Review of Books*, "Stonewall, Before and After: An Interview with Samuel R. Delany" (July 6, 2019), https://lareviewofbooks.org/article/stonewall-before-and-after-an-interview-with-samuel-r-delany/ and "Promiscuous Autobiography on Facebook: An Interview with Samuel R. Delany, Part II" (January 10, 2020), https://lareviewofbooks.org/article/promiscuous-autobiography-on-facebook-an-interview-with-samuel-delany-part-ii/.

[20] Jorge Luis Borges, "The Total Library," 1939, https://libraryofbabel.info/Borges/TheTotalLibrary.pdf/.

[21] Isaac Asimov, *Foundation* (New York: Gnome Press, 1951); Isaac Asimov, *Foundation and Empire* (New York: Gnome Press, 1952); Isaac Asimov, *Second Foundation* (New York: Gnome Press, 1953); Samuel R. Delany, *The Einstein Intersection* (New York: Ace Books, 1967); Samuel R. Delany, *Trouble on Triton: An Ambivalent Heterotopia* (Middleton: Wesleyan University Press, 1996); Samuel R. Delany, *Stars in My Pockets Like Grains of Sand* (New York: Bantam Books, 1984).

at the end of the 1960s, such New Wave writers as Delany increasingly turned toward exploration of "inner space," precisely at a time when new media technologies were spreading their tentacles into all aspects of quotidian life (for instance, the Defense Advanced Research Projects Agency [DARPA] was originally established for space exploration in response to the launch of Sputnik and ended up inventing the network that is the foundation of the Internet). These proto-cyberpunk works, from Delany's Afrofuturist *Nova* (1968) and *Dhalgren* (1975) to J. G. Ballard's *The Atrocity Exhibition* (1969) and Philip K. Dick's *Valis* (1981), make legible the postindustrial fusion of cybernetics and psychedelia that, during an era of rising countercultural protest and new media technology, led speculative writers to critically interrogate the meanings and potentials of the "virtual."[22]

As New Wave writers from J. G. Ballard to Joanna Russ explored the structures of "inner space," they also often demurred at that strange compound noun *science fiction*, proposing instead the term *speculative fiction*."[23] If fantasy is the genre that explores the impossible, sci-fi and speculative fiction could trace the limits of the possible. In a 1984 interview, Russ, author of *The Female Man* (Figure 10.1) among a host of other SF classics, offered a useful example of the difference between science fiction and fantasy, mocking *Star Wars* for portraying spaceships that go "whoosh" as they travel through the void.[24] From this perspective, two main subgenres of speculative fiction can be deduced, according to their temporality: alternate-history narratives speculate on the past that could've been, whereas science fiction speculates about alternate worlds of the present and the future.

Alternate-history narratives, such as Martin Smith's *The Indians Won* (Figure 10.2), explore the ways that historical events could have turned out differently.[25] The content of these narratives span a dizzying array of topics from dystopian tales of a victorious Confederacy to Native Americans defending their sovereignty via nuclear weapons.[26] Although

---

[22] Samuel R. Delany, *Nova* (New York: Doubleday, 1968); Samuel R. Delany, *Dhalgren* (New York: Bantam Books, 1975); J. G. Ballard, *The Atrocity Exhibition* (London: Jonathan Cape, 1970); Philip K. Dick, *Valis* (New York: Bantam Books, 1981). For a detailed discussion on cyberpunk today, see Lee Konstantinou, "Something Is Broken in Our Science Fiction," *Slate* (January 15, 2019), https://slate.com/technology/2019/01/hopepunk-cyberpunk-solarpunk-science-fiction-broken.html/.

[23] See James Gunn and Matthew Candelaria, eds., *Speculations on Speculations: Theories of Science Fiction* (New York: Scarecrow Press, 2005).

[24] Samuel Delany and Joanna Russ, "A Dialogue: Samuel Delany and Joanna Russ on Science Fiction," *Callaloo* 22, Fiction: A Special Issue (Autumn 1984): 27–35.

[25] Martin Cruz Smith, *The Indians Won* (New York: Belmont Production, 1970).

[26] Harry Harrison, *A Rebel in Time: The South Will Rise ...* (New York: Tor Books, 1983); Martin Cruz Smith, *The Indians Won* (New York: Belmont Production, 1970).

Figure 10.1 Joanna Russ, *The Female Man* (1975).

Figure 10.2 Martin Cruz Smith, *The Indians Won* (1970).

on the surface these narratives tell preposterous, counterfactual stories, they uncover important distinctions between the ways that scholars and the general public digest historical knowledge. Recently, alternate-history narratives have made something of a comeback: Philip K. Dick's *The Man in the High Castle* (1962) has been adapted into a Netflix series and Colson Whitehead's *The Underground Railroad* (2016) has won a Pulitzer Prize.[27] Despite the reluctance of most historians to view alternate history as a legitimate source base, literary scholars and cultural critics have treated alternate-history novels as a serious field of inquiry.

Thomas Mallon, a critic for *The New Yorker*, notes that alternate history allows writers to "retouch destiny."[28] Alternate-history narratives offer a historically rich genre for cultural and literary scholars studying the social composition of traditional and New Wave science fiction readership and the diversification of New Wave authorship.[29] Jameson reminds us that alternate history is a window onto the way history is contingent and structured by material conditions, meaning that we shouldn't accept the present as natural or normal, but rather as a product of historical and political circumstances that could have been otherwise.[30]

The politics of future-oriented "speculative fiction" involves determining who gets to define what is and isn't possible. The subversive perspectives of New Wave writers in the 1960s delineated just such a political divide with older generations, one nearly as polarized as that between young protesters and "the establishment." New Wave authors were often socialist members of the New Left who criticized previous science fiction for being outdated, patriarchal, imperialistic, and overly idealistic about "progress." These heated debates, epitomized by the divide in SF writers supporting or opposing the Vietnam War, largely faded out by the late 1970s, as various lineages of science fiction, diverse politically and aesthetically, blended into new syntheses in theory and method, content and form. Like the New Wave, the term *speculative*

---

[27] Philip K. Dick, *The Man in the High Castle* (New York: Putnam, 1962); Colson Whitehead, *The Underground Railroad* (New York: Doubleday, 2016).

[28] Thomas Mallon, "Never Happened: Fictions of Alternate History," *The New Yorker* (November 21, 2011).

[29] We have digitized dozens of alternate-history narratives, including: Gregory Benford and Martin Harry Greenberg, *Hitler Victorious: Eleven Stories of the German Victory in WWII* (New York: Garland Books, 1986); Harlan Ellison, *I Have No Mouth & I Must Scream* (New York: Pyramid Books, 1958); Robert Moore Williams, *The Day They H-Bombed Los Angeles* (New York: Ace Books, 1961); Wilson Tucker, *The Lincoln Hunters* (New York: Rhinehart & Company, 1958).

[30] Frederic Jameson, *Archaeologies of the Future: The Desire Called Utopia and Other Science Fictions* (New York: Verso, 2005). Also see Kathleen Singles, *Alternate History: Playing with Contingency and Necessity* (Berlin: Walter de Gruyter, 2013); Frederic Jameson, *Postmodernism, or, The Cultural Logic of Late Capitalism* (Durham: Duke University Press, 1992).

fiction—although often serving strategic purposes in various rhetorical debates—itself became a contested category: during the 1950s, *speculative fiction* designated a subgenre of sci-fi, but by the mid-1960s, New Wave writers used the term to differentiate high literature from "pulp."[31] By the 1970s, the term took on a life of its own, becoming so ubiquitous that even its proponents let it fall by the wayside.[32] As our social relations become ever more dependent on computational algorithms for predictive modeling of our ecological, economic, and political futures, the slippery term *speculative fiction*, perhaps as anachronistic as the *New Wave*, offers our project a valuable framework with which to approach a critical outlook on the future of new media. The history and theory of library, archival, and information science is developing at unprecedented speed (and crises of all kinds are looming on the horizon, or becoming a reality); for this reason, to contextualize what has been, and could be, it would be wise not to forgo imagining the alternate histories, as well as the possible futures, of academic institutions and libraries.

Pulping Pulp for the SF Nexus: Digitizing the Wealth of Cultural Detritus

> Using the same standards that categorize 90% of science fiction as trash, crud, or crap, it can be argued that 90% of film, literature, consumer goods, etc. is crap. In other words, the claim (or fact) that 90% of science fiction is crap is ultimately uninformative, because science fiction conforms to the same trends of quality as all other artforms.—Theodore Sturgeon[33]

Theodore Sturgeon's oft-quoted dictum or law invoking the principle that 90 percent of everything, including science fiction, is "trash," was first delivered at a science fiction fan convention in Philadelphia.[34] While Sturgeon was responding to a common concern among sci-fi writers that the genre is characteristically judged by its worst examples, he also, begrudgingly, helps to remind us that to make sense of our culture and its industries, we cannot avoid the vast accumulation of "crud." The wide array of mass-market books, many of which are presumed to be

---

[31] Marek Oziewicz, "Speculative Fiction," in *Oxford Research Encyclopedias*, March 2017.
[32] See Carl Freedman, *Conversations with Samuel Delany* (Jackson: University Press of Mississippi, 2009).
[33] Theodore Sturgeon, "Onhand ... Offhand," *Venture* 1, no. 5 (September 1957): 49.
[34] Although competing origins for Sturgeon's law exist, the most reliable account comes from James Gunn, who attributes the law as first being pronounced at the World Science Fiction Convention in 1953.

Figure 10.3 A selection of duplicate paperbacks from the Paskow Collection.

of little "literary merit," still provides a crucial background for any "distant reading" of the genre's transformations during the post-WWII era.

In their aspirations to intellectual sophistication and literary merit, postmodern writers of the New Wave often took the occasion to parody the traditions of pulp science fiction. This transformative period in science-fiction literature can be explained in part by the mass-market industry's transformation as the Golden Age era of pulp magazines waned, and the "paperback revolution" brought the "pocket" book into popularity (Figure 10.3). In this new publishing terrain, as the New Wave swelled and crested, after breaking the formulaic conventions of the genre, this polyvocal corpora left in its wake vital subgenres, from cyberpunk to Afrofuturism. These experimental subgenres inspire our unconventional approach to collection development and curation: Instead of preserving rare physical objects, digitization can involve acquiring the mass-market, physical commodity in order to "destroy" it, breaking its bindings for the purpose of more efficiently producing a digital copy in a feed-sheet scanner.[35]

The SF Nexus aims to build bridges and standards to enable libraries to collaborate with digital scholarship centers for the digitization of mass-market genre fiction toward a crowdsourced archive for nonconsumptive research online. Our first waypoint focuses on the New Wave (roughly 1964–1983) movement to privilege the period of modernist experimentation that gave birth to speculative works by women, people of color, and LGBTQ writers. Our corpus also includes hundreds of works created before the New Wave; early corpus creation and curation concentrates on incorporating and highlighting, for instance, the significant number of women writers during the pulp era (1920s–1930s), estimated at around 30 percent. Part of our project involves an ongoing bibliographical analysis and index building that will extend this list by drawing on the work of SF critics like Rob Latham, Maureen S. Barr, Sarah Lefanu, Justine Larbalestier, Lisa Tuttle, and Lisa Yaszek to identify more women writers.[36] This scholarship and Tor.com's more recent "Fighting Erasure: Women SF Writers" series can help direct the selection of earlier writers.[37] In a similar fashion we are turning to the scholarship of André Carrington and Sami Schalk, along with editors, such as Nalo Hopkinson, Uppinder Mehan, and Sheree R. Thomas, to help widen our inclusion of writers of color, from indigenous to postcolonial SF.[38]

As the project grows through collaborations with librarians and archivists at special collections across the country, our workflow, stan-

---

[35] By the time the pandemic brought digitization to a halt, Temple Libraries had digitized almost 400 books, anthologies, and magazines representing the New Wave. We were processing our third batch of materials (over 200 more print materials spanning the wide range of mass-market paperbacks). Beyond novels, we have full runs of science fiction magazines, such as *Analog, Isaac Asimov's Science Fiction Magazine*, and *Orbitz*. In addition, by web-scraping Luminist.org and Internet Archive, we have also added hundreds of novels and thousands of magazine issues to our corpus. Recently, HathiTrust's Research Center made available a workset of science fiction literature, offering another avenue for analysis.

[36] See Rob Latham, ed., *Science Fiction Criticism: An Anthology of Essential Writings* (New York: Bloomsburg, 2017); James Gunn, Maureen S. Barr, and Robert Candelaria, eds., *Reading Science Fiction* (Basingstoke, UK: Palgrave, 2008); Sarah Lefanu, *In the Chinks of the World Machine: Feminism and Science Fiction* (London: The Women's Press Ltd., 1988); Justine Larbalestier, *Daughters of Earth: Feminist Science Fiction in the Twentieth Century* (Middleton: Wesleyan University Press, 2006); Lisa Tuttle, *Writing Fantasy & Science Fiction* (New York: Bloomsburg, 2005); Lisa Yaszek, "We Get the History of Women in Science Fiction 'Thoroughly Wrong,'" *Library of America*, September 7, 2018. https://loa.org/.

[37] Tor.com, "Women Writers," https://www.tor.com/tag/women-writers/.

[38] André Carrington, *Speculative Blackness: The Future of Race in Science Fiction* (Minneapolis: University of Minnesota Press, 2016); Sami Schalk, *Bodyminds Reimagined: (Dis)ability, Race, and Gender in Black Women's Speculative Fiction* (Durham, NC: Duke University Press, 2018); Nalo Hopkinson, *Brown Girl in the Ring* (New York: Hachette, 1998); Uppinder Mehan, editor, *So Long Been Dreaming: Postcolonial Science Fiction & Fantasy* (Vancouver: Arsenal Pulp Press, 2004); Sheree R. Thomas, ed., *Dark Matter: A Century of Speculative Fiction from the African Diaspora* (New York: Warner Books, 2000).

dards, and policies have been designed to serve as a flexible model for institutional collaborators seeking to contribute to the "collections as data" movement, from offering templates for data agreements to best practices for text postprocessing, as well as the ingestion of data into HathiTrust and the extraction of textual features for data curation. The model for digitization, for instance, was informed by a desire to minimize the inefficiencies and time commitment inherent in manual text cleaning and preparation. Toward this goal, we have tried to reconceptualize a model for optical character recognition (OCR) of scanned texts that can minimize grunt labor. We have decided against precise cleaning of texts, instead relying on automated OCR post-processing when possible, supplemented with text wrangling, toward the humble goal of achieving roughly less than a 5 percent OCR error rate.[39] Rather than spend the majority of our time curating a small set of perfect data, we aim to prioritize the curation of large data sets with error rates low enough to be statistically accommodated by large-scale computational analyses.

In the humanities, when we think or teach students about "data," we often imply a false sense of objectivity, a unity to our vision that transcends the "anecdotal." This digital curation project will not actively contribute to this illusion; rather, our digital exhibits should illustrate how we only see "data" through a glass darkly. As we speculate on the unexpected ways a "book" can be conceived as "data," we approach "data" as always already perspectival and partial, only a fragment of a greater, multidimensional whole, one that requires critical inquiry to comprehend with meaning and significance. A speculative digital collection's interactive interfaces for computational analysis serve, then, not just to give calculations on large sets of data, but to challenge how we think about the generative tensions between meaning and fact, narrative and information.[40]

As one telling example of how partial our "data" can be, during our research, we have struggled to clarify just how many science fiction books were published in the twentieth century. In fact, simply identifying the cover artists for each book and magazine issue in our holdings remains

---

[39] See Katie Rawson and Trevor Munoz, "Against Cleaning," 2016: http://curatingmenus.org/articles/against-cleaning/; David A. Smith and Ryan Cordell, "A Research Agenda for Historical and Multilingual Optical Character Recognition," 2018, https://ocr.northeastern.edu/report/; Ryan Cordell, "Why You (A Humanist) Should Care About Optical Character Recognition," January 10, 2019, https://ryancordell.org/research/why-ocr/.

[40] Fred Gibbs and Trevor Owens, "The Hermeneutics of Data and Historical Writing," in *Writing History in the Digital Age*, eds. Kristen Nawrotzki and Jack Dougherty (Ann Arbor: University of Michigan Press, 2013).

a challenge. Mass-market publication data is highly proprietary; the most cursory of data can be gleaned from industry sources, such as *Publisher's Weekly*, or national publishing guilds like The Publishers Association. Only specific publishing houses (namely, Del Rey, Bantam, Ace) identify the number of novels released each year, but they do not provide consistent data about sales. The inability to source accurate publication data speaks to a lost, alternate history of libraries, one where funding and the prioritization of resources over the last half-century would have allowed us to have, by now, more thorough book-history data. This gap also offers, as a backdrop to our distant reading, the negative outline of the "total library," a tantalizing dream that hovers interminably on the horizon of the landscape of digital collections.

The Total Library: Discovering the Meaning of Data

> History is one area that General Info is notoriously poor in imparting. —Samuel R. Delany[41]

The New Wave of science fiction literature, like the New Wave of cinema, consisted primarily in the modernist experimentation with form and content beyond previously prescribed formulas and limitations. The "new wave" of digital collections is likewise marked by an avant-garde political commitment to upturning the staid foundations of institutional rituals and styles, blurring dearly held boundaries in the exhibition and annotation of archival materials of cultural heritage, while reverse engineering web technologies designed by capitalism to serve the purposes of consumption. A "new wave" of digital collections is neither unwilling to destroy printed matter to digitize it, nor devoted to facsimile reproductions, turning away from "consumptive" forms of research to celebrate the array of critical perspectives on cultural objects afforded by computational methods of cultural analytics. Such a transformation may be at the heart of libraries and academia today, but it comes in part due to the force of external circumstances.

From recent advances in computational processing, to the integration of digital humanities methods and projects into the curriculum, from the crisis in labor at the heart of academic scholarship, to the transformation of the digital medium by cyberpunk levels of corporatization of databases and text-mining portals, the "new wave" of digital

---

[41] Delany, *Stars in My Pockets Like Grains of Sand*, 64.

collections has come at a vital and unsettling transition period in the history of social systems used for information circulation and curation. In this era of instability and change, the SF Nexus has been cautiously designed to grow over the coming years toward a model of library stewardship of data, adapting our design and infrastructure to new developments in collections curation.

While scoping out a framework for the SF Nexus, we established a series of principles motivated by "collections as data," informed by archival and information sciences, oriented out of the critical humanities, and constitutive of something as akin to a "Speculative DH." We intend for the project's experimental and speculative orientation to inform all future stages of its development. Currently available digital resources for science fiction trend toward online exhibits for such genre analysis, especially small data sets like the University of Calgary's exemplary resource, "The Stuff of Science Fiction."[42] Recent innovations in software programming for web-based cultural analytics, such as Bookworm, suggest a growing trend toward creating open-source, embeddable, portable tools used for online data curation.[43] What is needed today is not just a network of crowdsourced digitization, but also a relay point for the companion sites in the world of sci-fi and pulp fiction. The SF Nexus aspires to link siloed projects together to comprehensively supplement databases like the Corpus of Historical American English.[44] Furthermore, such sites can leave space to showcase creative experimentation in digital storytelling and research interfaces, where computer science and humanities students can display the result of projects.

Although digital tools for data mining can be integrated into the web resources for the SF Nexus over time, corpora should also be enriched with metadata profiles and offer extracted features of each text (such as bag-of-words, n-grams, named entities, part of speech, topic models, and word embeddings). As a form of metadata, disaggregated, interoperable data, from bag-of-words to word embeddings, can be shared with users. Such metadata descriptions can serve, then, as additional, calculable variables (selected through faceting by the user) in the algorithmic processes underlying computational hermeneutics.[45] Such modes of data

---

[42] University of Calgary, "The Stuff of Science Fiction," http://stuffofsciencefiction.ca/.
[43] See HathiTrust, Bookworm, https://bookworm.htrc.illinois.edu/develop/.
[44] Brigham Young University, "Corpus of Historical American English," https://corpus.byu.edu/coha/.
[45] For innovative metadata curation with HathiTrust, see Ted Underwood's project designed to provide page-level genre metadata for English-language volumes in HathiTrust, 1700–1922 and, in its current iteration, for HathiTrust's English-language digital library for post-1923 materials: https://github.com/tedunderwood/hathimetadata/.

curation, by enabling users to create analytic pipelines that synthesize data from various interactive interfaces, can augment the user's awareness of a historical corpora's multidimensional meanings.[46] The process of computational analysis helps us question and redraw the parameters of the speculative fiction genre, challenging preconceived notions of canonicity and revealing underexplored patterns integral to the marketing and production of speculative fiction in the post-WWII era.

The web curation of sci-fi books and magazines requires thinking through the multiplicity of ways a physical text, and the sci-fi genre more generally, can be approached as "data," from its aesthetic structure, to its marketing design, evident in the title, cover art, and blurbs. Researchers increasingly desire web-based tools to support distant readings of place and proper names in science fiction and fantasy, an exploration of the significance of its nouns and adjectives, the analysis of higher level discursive formations through topic models analyzed in their rise and fall over the publishing history, and large-scale stylistic statistical measurements classifying genres and subgenres. Recent affordances in cloud computing and replicable code, such as Jupyter Notebooks with Google Colab, suggest a relatively flexible mode of developing open-source, lightweight infrastructures without major web development. To curate geo-locating literary fiction, maps can be imported directly from illustrations in sci-fi novels, whereas interfaces already developed for programs like Voyant-tool's Dreamscape allow for interactive mapping of real and sci-fi fictional world building using encoded textual data. After running named-entity recognition on science fiction texts to identify place and proper names, maps can be populated with locations in alternate-history (most of which are real locations with counterfactual histories as seen in Howard Waldrop and Jake Saunders's *The Texas-Israeli War: 1999*; Figure 10.4) and near-future narratives taking place on Earth (a tool could also enable users to create their own maps of fantastical lands in space operas).[47]

As we look toward what will become central to our data curation, it is clear that machine learning represents, as it did for twentieth-century science fiction writers, the new frontier for the digital humanities and computational hermeneutics in natural language processing.[48] We ap-

---

[46] For an example of cultural analytics documentation, see Richard Jean So, Hoyt Long, and Yuancheng Zhu, "Race, Writing, and Computation: Racial Difference and the US Novel, 1880–2000," *Journal of Cultural Analytics* 3, no. 2 (January 11, 2019). doi: 10.22148/16.031. https://culturalanalytics.org/article/11057/.

[47] Howard Waldrop and Jake Saunders, *The Texas–Israeli War: 1999* (New York: Ballantine Books, 1974).

[48] Bethany Nowviskie, "Reconstitute the World," *Bethany Nowviskie*, blog entry, June 12, 2018, http://nowviskie.org/2018/reconstitute-the-world/.

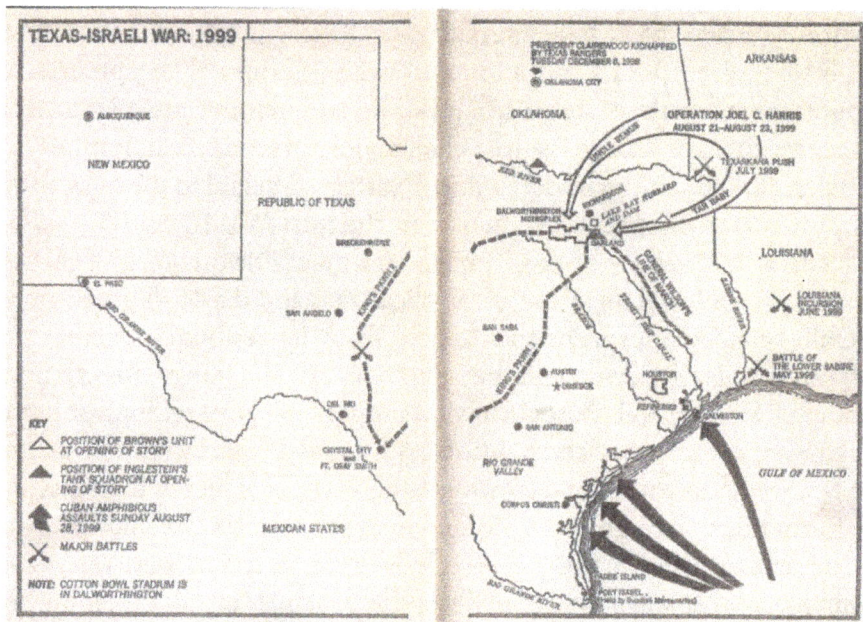

Figure 10.4 An alternate-history map of an Israeli invasion of post-apocalyptic independent Texas.

Howard Waldrop and Jake Saunders, *The Texas–Israeli War: 1999*. (New York: Ballantine Books, 1974).

proach this "magical" method with critical skepticism, recognizing that it is at best an optimized process of pattern recognition whose meaning can only be understood through the construction of theoretically coherent data sets and whose results are skewed by bias in algorithms and training data. Although we've been developing word-embedding data sets for download and analysis by skilled researchers, our future experimentation and research focuses on showcasing the significance and utility of computational pattern recognition. This requires, however, teaching users how to approach embedding models as multidimensional representations of textual meaning.

Although studies have demonstrated the usefulness of word-embedding algorithms (such as Word2Vec and Fasttext) for small corpora, the jury is still out on optimizing the algorithm to produce the most reliable results, no doubt in part because of the relativist nature of these models. The qualitative methods of literary hermeneutics are necessary to explicate such networked relations of semantic meaning, reduced in dimensionality for the purpose of visualization. Comparing word embeddings of speculative fiction, in other words, requires a speculative approach, at once extrapolative, critical, and mathematical. At the core of New Wave speculative fiction lies political and ethical questions about the role of language and technology; formalist contortions of generic formulas and tropes served to help answer that question, as writers extrapolated (through "intuitive" predictive analytics) from available data of present and past conditions in order to create models of alternate worlds, guiding readers to heuristic and critical insights into their own, more real, world.

We can only speculate, for now, on what methods of qualitative interpretation will be developed to come to terms with these new modes of quantitative modeling. Although already demonstrating meaningful, even profound results for cultural studies, vector space modeling for word embeddings remains a remarkably speculative field (debates rage as to the most effective parameterizations, validations, and optimizations). After properly curating coherent data sets (such as dystopic, utopic, and heterotopic subgenres), iterative explorations of connotations and extrapolations of symbolic relations can be illustrated through a variety of two-dimensional graphic representations, such as cluster dendrograms of hierarchical semantic relations or t-distributed stochastic neighbor embedding (t-SNE) projections allowing for reduced dimensionality and spatialized translation of meaning through vector geometry. By supplementing a speculative, critical approach to vector space models with the enhanced experience offered by digital media (from websites to immersive technology), researchers can better translate their findings to fellow researchers, while guiding students to comprehend and experience the constitutive tension between qualitative and quantitative approaches, between narrative and information, meaning and "data." Through these portals, users, and students in classrooms, will find new opportunities to learn that such multidimensional data, like our cognitive constructions of abstract concepts, loses something in translation when flattened to two or three dimensions to be visualized (Figure 10.5).

Especially in the case of mass-market genre fiction, the object of study should be measured not just as a "text," but as a commodity, whose production and marketing forces shape their development lexically and graphically. The interplay among visual marketing, the paratextual blurbs, and the text becomes a crucial intersection point for cultural analysis and digital curation. To research the possibility of embedding an interface for the computational analysis of book covers, we've experimented with machine-learning algorithms to conduct image analysis on sci-fi book covers. While slowly digitizing high-quality images of book

Figure 10.5 Word-embedding cluster dendrogram of Samuel R. Delany's *Trouble on Triton*.

covers from the Paskow collection, we also downloaded 100,000 science fiction book covers from the Internet Speculative Fiction Database, as well as a data set of 200,000 book covers, constituting 20 genres categorized by Amazon. With Yale DH Lab's user-friendly tool, Pix-Plot, we've tested the limits of the pretrained Alexnet image-model to classify, cluster, and project in three-dimensional space the wide range of cover-art designs. In an interactive 3D visualization, users will be able to explore the range of graphic designs and aesthetic styles used on the sensational covers of sci-fi paperbacks and magazines, examining how they are distributed by temporal origin, such as during the radical cultural changes that occurred in America at the end of the 1960s (Figure 10.6).

Conclusions: The Future of Cultural History

> Utopias afford consolation: although they have no real locality there is nevertheless a fantastic, untroubled region in which

they are able to unfold; they open up cities with vast avenues, superbly planted gardens, countries where life is easy, even though the road to them is chimerical. Heterotopias are disturbing, probably because they secretly undermine language, because they make it impossible to name this and that, because they shatter or tangle common names, because they destroy "syntax" in advance, and not only the syntax with which we construct sentences but also that less apparent syntax which causes words and things (next to and also opposite one another) to "hold together." This is why Utopias permit fables and discourse: they run with the very grain of language and are part of the fundamental dimension of the fabula; heterotopias (such as those to be found so often in Borges) desiccate speech, stop words in their tracks, contest the very possibility of grammar at its source; they dissolve our myths and sterilize the lyricism of our sentences.— Michel Foucault[49]

Speculating on the future of library curation requires a reckoning with alternate histories and future realities for libraries. Alternate realities for libraries opens space to imagine the infinite ideal of the Total Library and invites provocative historical questions, such as what if the Library of Alexandria hadn't burned? Speculating on the future of library curation also forces us to rethink collecting practices. Libraries have inherently,

Figure 10.6 New Wave science fiction novels generated through Tensorflow with Yale DH Lab's Pix-Plot.

---

[49] Michel Foucault, *The Order of Things: An Archaeology of the Human Sciences*. 2nd ed. (New York: Vintage, 1994).

yet often inaccurately, speculated on who future users might be, how the widest number can be included in access initiatives, and what those users might desire from the library's resources and staff. In effect, library collection and curation remains an educated gamble on the future. The "new wave" of digital collections, and our minor contributions to it, seek to push library curation as well as academic scholarship to grapple with such speculative premises.[50] In this vein, Speculative DH requires asking as many questions as providing answers, shaking our acceptance of the actual as normal and inevitable in order to come to terms with what could have been different. What if libraries had collected pulp and not prioritized canon at the expense of diverse voices and genres? How would the library of the future look different if it were truly decolonial? How do data curators highlight marginalized voices against the backdrop noise of mass culture? Solutions to such questions will remain elusive in the near future, but the practice of speculating on the future of library curation offers the promise of bringing us closer to the possibilities and impossibilities opened up by the idea of a total library.

In his essay, "Cybernation and Culture" (1966), Marshall McLuhan argues that, unlike "the mechanical age" and its "fragmenting and dissociating" effects, the "electronic age of cybernation is unifying" (97). For McLuhan, artistic conscience is "focused on the psychic and social implications of technology," and artists are progenitors of "models of the new environments and new social lives that are the hidden potentials of new technology" (98). In his optimism that future technology will be able to build a global commons, McLuhan even naively cites a *Fortune* article from August 1964 written by Tom Alexander, entitled "The Wild Birds Find a Corporate Roost," recounting how big businesses had been retaining science fiction writers to help predict and invent new technological environments in the coming decades.[51] By asking science fiction writers for guidance as they sought to speculate on the future (in both senses of the word, conceptually and economically), corporations hoped to anticipate the evolution of technology and economy, in order to make smarter investments. These same corporations today are less likely to turn

---

[50] Another premise we still need to tackle, that of the "future history" of the library, is best captured by another beautiful passage, similar to this essay's opening epigraph, from the conclusion of Frederic Jameson's *The Antinomies of Realism*. He argues that "the historical novel of the future (which is to say of our own present) will necessarily be Science-Fictional inasmuch as it will have to include questions about the fate of our social system, which has become a second nature. To read the present as history, so many have urged us to do, will mean adopting a Science-Fictional perspective of some kind" (298).

[51] Marshall McLuhan, "Cybernation and Culture," in *On the Nature of Media: Essays in Understanding Media*, ed. Richard Cavell (Berkley, CA: Gingko Press, 2016); Tom Alexander, "The Wild Birds Find a Corporate Roost," *Fortune*, (August 1964): 130–34, 164, 166, 168.

to writers and filmmakers, of course, than data analytics and "machine learning," hoping to discover in predictive modeling the patterns of capital and society. For an age in which financial investments and political policies alike depend increasingly on extrapolative methods of data analysis for such predictive modeling, we would do well to remember the two-sided nature of the word *speculation*, referring not only to "abstract or hypothetical reasoning on subjects of a deep, abstruse, or conjectural nature," but also to "engagement in any business enterprise or transaction of a venturesome or risky nature, but offering the chance of great or unusual gain."[52] Just as scientists try to raise warnings of global warming, the right-wing embraces data analytics to cynically justify the burning of oil at the expense of a future that can be dismissed as likely unsaveable.[53]

As we are still in the young adulthood of the digital humanities, we are witnessing a transformation in the ways cultural critics approach their objects of study. On the one hand, from Pierre Bourdieu to Franco Moretti, cultural studies and the digital humanities have been infused with a commitment to the use of quantitative methods to give substance to a sociological perspective.[54] Against the background of that work, a new generation of scholars in literary humanities is exploring the subtler shades of literary meaning that computational hermeneutics can bring into light, with a turn toward a formalist emphasis on pattern recognition, and a structuralist investment in discourse analysis for ideology critique.[55] In keeping with these transformations, the "new wave" of digital collections would be wise to seek to bypass the divide between quantitative sociology and qualitative hermeneutics in the curation and visualization of historical, cultural big data, while ensuring replicable workflows, reproducible practices, and, to the extent possible, interoperable, open data.

As the literary field available for corpus analytics widens, approaching asymptotically the "total library," we have speculated on such an ideal as including not just the various editions of every work of a genre, and their composition histories, but also their reception histories, all

---

[52] These definitions were taken from a search for speculation in the *Oxford English Dictionary*. https://www-oed-com.libproxy.temple.edu/view/Entry/186112?redirectedFrom=speculate#eid/.

[53] Juliet Eilperin, Brady Dennis, and Chris Mooney, "Trump Administration Sees a 7-Degree Rise in Global Temperatures by 2100," *Washington Post*, September 28, 2018. https://www.washingtonpost.com/national/health-science/trump-administration-sees-a-7-degree-rise-in-global-temperatures-by-2100/2018/09/27/b9c6fada-bb45-11e8-bdc0-90f81cc58c5d_story.html/.

[54] Pierre Bourdieu, *Distinction: A Social Critique of the Judgment of Taste* (Cambridge, MA: Harvard University Press, 1987); Franco Moretti, *Distant Reading* (New York: Verso, 2013); Franco Moretti, *Atlas of the European Novel, 1800–1900* (New York: Verso, 1999).

[55] Andrew Piper, *Enumerations: Data and Literary Study* (Chicago: The University of Chicago Press, 2018); Ted Underwood, *Distant Horizons*.

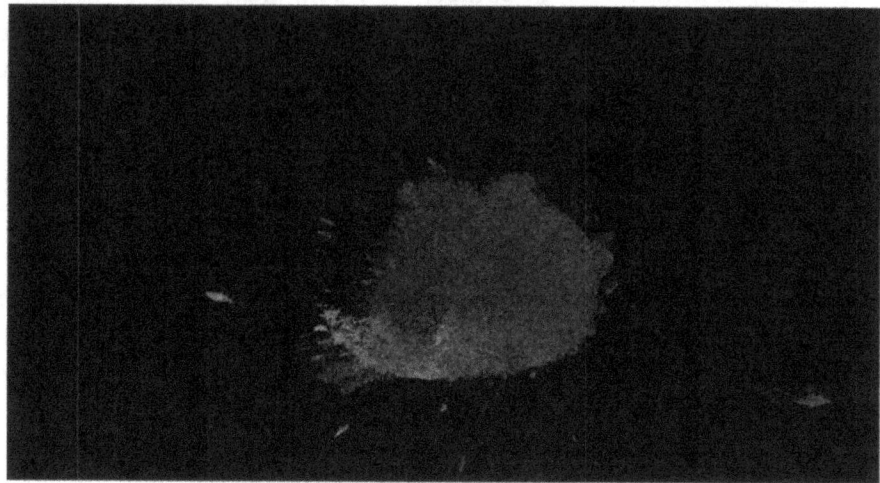

Figure 10.7 A cluster of 100,000 science fiction book covers resembles a constellation in the universe of the total library.

computationally readable and available for closer hermeneutic analysis. This dream of a digital library would allow, among other things, dynamic faceting between embedded analytic tools and full-text facsimile resources. Building toward this promise within phases of relative priority (aiming to improve access to messy data before perfecting and filling in data sets, for instance), digital collections curators and developers today can benefit from remaining speculative in their approach to the future of technology. Waiting for new forms of web development and curation to become feasible, this work requires patience and flexibility, trying to carefully surf a wave far bigger than one can handle, doing a balancing act so as not to get out of control, or fall behind and fluster. By remaining open to changes in the tide, we wait to learn from others and the changing digital environment, keeping our momentum going and our focus steady on the fantasy of the "total library," as we seek to change how we use technology to teach us how to think (Figure 10.7).

Ten years before Tim Berners-Lee coined the term *world wide web*, Samuel Delany—in his proto-cyberpunk novel, *Stars in My Pockets Like Grains of Sand* (1984)—adopted the metaphor of the "web" or "matrix" to articulate his theory of language and meaning, one that evolved through his speculative approach into a vision of information technology that we would be wise to consider when curating narratives and information on the Internet today.[56] Our exploratory approach has sought to bring into relief the insights and visions of an earlier era, so that we can better understand our own. While being attentive to our primary communities' most treasured practices, we hope to draw interest to our site not just from the diverse fan bases of sci-fi lit, but also from the wide range of students and teachers interested in today's sci-fi methods of digital analysis. A speculative method of curation, complemented with lesson plans and course syllabi for implementation in classes, can serve to make more accessible and ubiquitous the wide range of methods central to cultural and social studies, while broaching the divide between the sociology of literature and formalist criticism. We hope, in this way, that our research and curation project can help a "new wave" of digital collections bring into relief the constitutive tension between qualitative and quantitative methods and their content, between narrative and information, meaning and "data," with the aim of enabling a wide range of users to enjoy the process of realizing and articulating a more complex, political critique of our society's real and conceivable, pasts, presents, and futures.

Bibliography

Ashley, Michael. *The History of the Science Fiction Magazine, Vol. 3: 1946–1955*. Chicago: Contemporary Books, 1977.

Battles, Matthew. *Library: An Unquiet Story*. New York: W. W. Norton & Co., 2015.

Bode, Katherine. "The Equivalence of Close and Distant Reading; or, Toward a New Object for Data-Rich Literary History." *Modern Language Quarterly* 78, no. 1 (2017): 77–106.

Borges, Jorge Luis. "The Total Library." 1939. https://www.amazon.com/Total-Library-Non-Fiction-1922-1986-Classics/dp/0141183020.

Bould, Marc, Andrew Butler, Adam Roberts, and Sherryl Vint, eds. *The Routledge Companion to Science Fiction*. New York: Routledge, 2009.

Bourdieu, Pierre. *Distinction: A Social Critique of the Judgment of Taste*. Cambridge: Harvard University Press, 1987.

———. *The Rules of Art: Genesis and Structure of the Literary Field*. Redwood City, CA: Stanford University Press, 1996.

Carlson, Jake, and Lisa Johnston. *Data Information Literacy: Librarians, Data, and the Education of a New Generation of Researchers*. West

---

[56] For Delany's theory of language as a web, see Samuel R. Delany, *Longer Views: Extended Essays* (Middletown, CT: Wesleyan University Press, 1996).

Lafayette, IN: Purdue University Press, 2015.
Carrington, Andre. *Speculative Blackness: The Future of Race in Science Fiction*. Minneapolis: University of Minnesota Press, 2016.
Chu, Seo-Young. *Do Metaphors Dream of Literal Sleep?: A Science-Fictional Theory of Representation*. Cambridge, MA: Harvard University Press, 2011.
De Kosnik, Abigail. *Rogue Archives: Digital Cultural Memory and Media Fandom*. Cambridge, MA: MIT Press, 2016.
Cox, Ana Marie. "Space the Nation: The Future Is Female—and Black, and Disabled." *SyfyWire* (January 22, 2019). https://www.syfy.com/syfywire/space-the-nation-the-future-is-female-and-black-and-disabled.
De Kosnik, Abigail. *Rogue Archives: Digital Cultural Memory and Media Fandom*. Cambridge, MA: MIT Press, 2016.
Del Ray, Lester. *The World of Science Fiction: The History of a Subculture, 1926–1976*. New York: Ballantine Books, 1979.
Delany, Samuel R. *Longer Views: Extended Essays*. Middleton, CT: Wesleyan University Press, 1996.
Disch, Thomas. *The Dreams Our Stuff Is Made of: How Science Fiction Conquered the World*. New York: Simon & Schuster, 2000.
Faniel, Ixchel, and Ann Zimmerman. "Beyond the Data Deluge: A Research Agenda for Large-Scale Data Sharing and Reuse." *International Journal of Digital Curations* 6, no. 1 (August 2011): 58–69.
Foucault, Michel. *The Order of Things: An Archaeology of the Human Sciences*. New York: Vintage, 1966.
Freedman, Carl. *Conversations with Samuel Delany*. Jackson: University Press of Mississippi, 2009.
Gavin, Michael. "Vector Semantics, William Empson, and the Study of Ambiguity." *Critical Inquiry* 44, no. 4 (2018): 641–73.
Gibbs, Fred, and Trevor Owens. "The Hermeneutics of Data and Historical Writing." In *Writing History in the Digital Age*, edited by Kristen Nawrotzki and Jack Dougherty. Ann Arbor: University of Michigan Press, 2013.
Gunn, James, Maureen S. Barr, and Robert Candelaria, eds. *Reading Science Fiction*. Basingstoke, UK: Palgrave, 2008.
Gunn, James, and Matthew Candelaria, eds. *Speculations on Speculations: Theories of Science Fiction*. New York: Scarecrow Press, 2005.
Hopkinson, Nalo. *Brown Girl in the Ring*. New York: Hachette, 1998.
Jameson, Frederic. *Archaeologies of the Future: The Desire Called Utopia and Other Science Fictions*. New York: Verso, 2005.

———. *The Antinomies of Realism* New York: Verso Books, 2013.
———. *The Political Unconscious: Narrative as a Socially Symbolic Act.* Ithaca, NY: Cornell University Press, 1981.
Jockers, Matthew. *Macroanalysis: Digital Methods and Literary History.* Bloomington: University of Illinois Press, 2013.
Latham, Rob, ed. *Science Fiction Criticism: An Anthology of Essential Writings.* New York: Bloomsbury, 2017.
Larbalestier, Justine. *Daughters of Earth: Feminist Science Fiction in the Twentieth Century.* Middleton, CT: Wesleyan University Press, 2006.
Lefanu, Sarah. *In the Chinks of the World Machine: Feminism and Science Fiction.* London: The Women's Press Ltd., 1988.
Leonard, Peter. "Mining Large Datasets for the Humanities." Paper presentation, Lyon, France, 2014. http://library.ifla.org/930.
Link, Eric Carl, and Gerry Canavan, editors. *The Cambridge Companion to American Science Fiction.* New York: Cambridge University Press, 2015.
Mallon, Thomas. "Never Happened: Fictions of Alternate History." *The New Yorker*, November 21, 2011. https://www.newyorker.com/magazine/2011/11/21/never-happened.
McCaffery, Larry, ed. *Across the Wounded Galaxies: Interviews with Contemporary American Science Fiction Writers.* Urbana: University of Illinois Press, 1990.
Mehan, Uppinder, ed. *So Long Been Dreaming: Postcolonial Science Fiction & Fantasy.* Vancouver: Arsenal Pulp Press, 2004.
McLuhan, Marshall. "Cybernation and Culture," in *On the Nature of Media: Essays in Understanding Media*, edited by Richard Cavell. Berkley, CA: Gingko Press, 2016.
Moretti, Franco. *Distant Reading.* New York: Verso, 2013.
———. *Graphs, Maps, Trees: Abstract Models for Literary History.* London: Verso, 2005.
Morgan, Paige C. "The Consequences of Framing Digital Humanities Tools as Easy to Use." *College & Undergraduate Libraries* (August 7, 2018): 211–31.
Nowviskie, Bethany. "Speculative Collections," blog entry by Bethany Nowviskie, October 27, 2016. http://nowviskie.org/2016/speculative-collections.
Padilla, Thomas. "Humanities Data in the Library: Integrity, Form, Access." *D-Lib Magazine* 22, nos. 3–4 (March 2016).
———. "On a Collections as Data Imperative." Paper presented at the conference, Collections as Data, September 27, 2016.http://digital-

preservation.gov/meetings/dcs16/tpadilla_OnaCollectionsas DataImperative_final.pdf.

Piper, Andrew. *Enumerations: Data and Literary Study*. Chicago: The University of Chicago Press, 2018.

Rawson, Katie, and Trevor Munoz. "Against Cleaning." July 6, 2016. http://curatingmenus.org/articles/against-cleaning/.

Rieder, John. *Colonialism and the Emergence of Science Fiction*. Middletown, CT: Wesleyan University Press, 2008.

Schalk, Sami. *Bodyminds Reimagined: (Dis)ability, Race, and Gender in Black Women's Speculative Fiction*. Durham, NC: Duke University Press, 2018.

Simeone, Michael, Advaith Gundavajhala, Venkata Koundinya, Anandh Ravi Kumar, and Ed Finn. "Towards a Poetics of Strangeness: Experiments in Classifying Language of Technological Novelty." *Cultural Analytics* 2, no. 1 (September 8, 2017). doi: 10.22148/16.015

Singles, Kathleen. *Alternate History: Playing with Contingency and Necessity*. Berlin: Walter de Gruyter, 2013.

So, Richard Jean, Hoyt Long, and Yuancheng Zhu, "Race, Writing, and Computation: Racial Difference and the US Novel, 1880–2000." *Journal of Cultural Analytics* 3, no. 2 (January 11, 2019). doi: 10.22148/16.031. https://culturalanalytics.org/article/11057.

Sturgeon, Theodore. "Onhand ... Offhand." *Venture* 1, no. 5 (September 1957): 49–50.

Tennen, Dennis Yi. "Towards Computational Archaeology of Fictional Space." 49, no. 1 (2018): 119–47.

Thomas, Sheree R., ed. *Dark Matter: A Century of Speculative Fiction from the African Diaspora*. New York: Warner Books, 2000.

Todorov, Tzvetan. *The Fantastic: A Structural Approach to a Literary Genre*. Ithaca, NY: Cornell University Press, 1973.

Tuttle, Lisa. *Writing Fantasy & Science Fiction*. New York: Bloomsbury, 2005.

Underwood, Ted. *Distant Horizons: Digital Evidence and Literary Change*. Chicago: The University of Chicago Press, 2019.

———. "The Life Cycles of Genres." *Journal of Cultural Analytics* 2, no. 2 (May 23, 2016). doi: 10.22148/16.005. https://culturalanalytics.org/article/11061-the-life-cycles-of-genres.

Wilkin, Matthew. "Genre, Computation, and the Varieties of Twentieth-Century U.S. Fiction." *Journal of Cultural Analytics* 2, no. 2 (November 1, 2016). doi: 10.22148/16.009. https://culturalanalytics.org/article/11065-genre-computation-and-the-varieties-of-twentieth-century-u-s-fiction.

Yaszek, Lisa. "We Get the History of Women in Science Fiction 'Thoroughly Wrong." *Library of America*, September 7, 2018. https://loa.org. https://loa.org.

V

Networks, Collaboration, Community

11

The Collection Is the Network: Collection, Collaboration, and Cooperation at Network Scale

Daniel Dollar, Jeff Kosokoff, and Sarah Tudesco

It is 2030 and faculty arrive at their university for new faculty orientation. During the introduction to workings of the university library, they watch demonstrations of intelligent discovery systems, powered by machine learning that connects them with vast networks of analog and digital collections. They take out their mobile devices and explore the systems used to find texts that are foundational to their research. Searches return lists of important works regardless of whether the works are locally owned or licensed, and many are available because the research community has made them open to all. When they find what they want, they see different options. For a print title, they see an option that will deliver the material in less than 48 hours. If they want, they can borrow the item and keep it as long as they need. If the title is available in a digital format, the download is simple and seamless. If it is not immediately available digitally, the user connects to a suite of digital services that helps them get a basic digital reading copy or a digitized object that is optimized for computational analysis. From the point of view of the researcher, users get what they want, when they want, and in the format that they need. The faculty need not be concerned with whether the materials are owned or licensed by their local institution. Instead, they are served by a network that is the result of years of collaboration among large academic libraries—libraries that work together to build, organize, and maintain collections to support the unique and specialized research needs of scholars in the twenty-first century.

Academic libraries exist to serve the scholarly community with access to collections as a fundamental service. During the twentieth century, academic research libraries evolved into large, complex organizations that supported access to analog collections. Significant investment of institutional resources went into building collections with the goal of providing ready, convenient access to affiliated scholars. Physical proximity to collections and traditional circulation was a priority, research institutions were protective of their collections, and many institutions would limit what and with whom they shared. In the United States, the academic centers where doctoral-level studies developed and flourished all had major research library collections at their core (Abbott 2011). These large academic research libraries optimized themselves to acquire, organize, store, and preserve massive corpora of physical information sources. Librarians and their institutions frequently used collection size as a quality measurement alongside unrealized aspirations of building a *comprehensive* collection. In reality, not even the largest academic library could achieve this goal. In the analog world, individual research libraries began to bridge the local and global information environment through collaboration in acquisitions, cataloging, and resource sharing.[1] Nevertheless, the physical nature of scholarship prevented a truly seamless experience across siloed library collections.

The debut of the Mosaic web browser on January 23, 1993, was a seminal moment (Gillies and Cailliau 2000). From that point forward, the desire for scholars to connect with information quickly and seamlessly would help spur the move from analog to digital collections that has transformed libraries. In the succeeding decades, scholars have witnessed a rapid increase in the availability of digital resources: journals, monographs, images, data sets, and archival materials. Engagement with physical collections has decreased as more material, both historic and current, is made available online. Circulation, a traditional library metric for collection use, continues to decrease (Linden, Tudesco, and Dollar 2018).

---

[1] In this chapter, *resource sharing* refers to a wide variety of ways in which libraries share collections and services. This includes interlibrary loan, scan-and-deliver, shared staff, and cooperatively developed and deployed software.

Publication output has increased as the Internet continues to transform and facilitate publication and dissemination. Even before the advent of the Internet, librarians understood the impracticality of any single academic research library acquiring comprehensively (Putnam 1929). Instead, research libraries depend on networks to enable scholars to access global research collections of significant breadth and depth. The network is the foundation used by libraries to reorient their thinking and advocate for the principle that facilitating access to collections is a fundamental service to our scholars. What we have locally matters less, and what we can provide regardless of ownership matters more (Antleman 2017). Where scholars once built their research habits around a library at the core of their information universe, now they use a library that positions itself as a hub focused on facilitation of access across a networked information ecosystem, much of it based in libraries that will serve researcher needs (Dempsey and Malpas 2018). Libraries are embracing their role as advocates and facilitators for a more open scholarly communication landscape through a variety of collection development activities, including making locally created or held scholarly materials freely available. This is a major shift for academic research libraries as they move away from building collections primarily on what is acquired to an emphasis on providing broad access to scholarship and digital objects produced at the institutional level to the wider global community (Dempsey 2017).

Although the information environment is evolving rapidly, publishers still distribute much of their scholarly output in print and large academic research libraries are a key market for these materials. The continued growth of these print collections places considerable strain on library spaces. Library buildings typically occupy prime campus real estate, often near the center of campus. These are spaces that serve multiple needs as scholars seek collections as well as spaces to study and staff to assist them with research, writing, and digital projects. Scholars may also need access to basic and specialized equipment, from copiers to high-performance scanners. Library staff need space to work and collaborate with scholars and colleagues. The institutions need library spaces to reflect the ideals of the institution, which may include awe-inspiring reading rooms lined with beautiful historic texts. And finally, the libraries need space to house physical collections—making them accessible and browsable to the community.

Most large academic research libraries do not discard their collections to make room for new materials. Between the pressures of a growing print collection and projects to repurpose traditional stacks to meet other needs, high-density storage facilities have become an important part of the landscape. They provide efficient, secure, and environmentally optimized storage for collections. The construction and operation of such facilities requires significant financial investment. The wealthiest academic libraries are looking to cooperate in this area. At the University of California, this has taken the form of two storage locations, one run by the University of California, Los Angeles (UCLA), and a second operated by Berkeley. Princeton, New York Public Library, and Columbia have a shared storage complex called *ReCAP (Research Collections and Preservation Consortium)*. Harvard, which is reaching capacity at its high-density storage location, has now joined ReCAP. Duke and UNC-Chapel Hill have shared off-site storage. These partnerships have made it possible for many institutions to keep their print collections intact. Smaller institutions have not been so fortunate. It has been fairly common practice for collections to be dramatically downsized due to the demands mentioned.

The largest collections are incomplete, and the broadest bibliographic diversity of North American academic libraries is held collectively within the collections of all libraries (Lavoie, Malpas, and Shipengrover 2012). The breadth and depth of bibliographic holdings contained in American and Canadian libraries is represented in Figure 11.1. Published by Lavoie, Malpas, and Shipengrover in 2012, and updated by Lavoie in 2018, it shows that no one region holds all of the publications in North American libraries. Even the largest regional metropolitan area, Bos-Wash (Boston–New York–Washington mega-region), contains less than two thirds of all publications within the entire network (Lavoie 2018).

In order to preserve and maintain our collective bibliographic diversity, "shared print" programs have emerged. Within these programs, which have been implemented at various levels of geography across the country, libraries commit to retain and share specific copies of a particular book or journal title. This protects against the risk of deaccessioning titles out of existence. By distributing the burden, all libraries benefit from the commitment made by participants to retain titles in these accessible shared print networks. The collective collection stays large and diverse, even as each institution buys less print and retains fewer copies. Current efforts, presently being advanced by The Partnership for Shared Book Collections, are looking to find ways to bring together the various regional and subnational shared book programs to leverage even higher scales of network cooperation.

Alongside shared print programs that bring together existing collections, institutions continue to explore collaborations for prospective col-

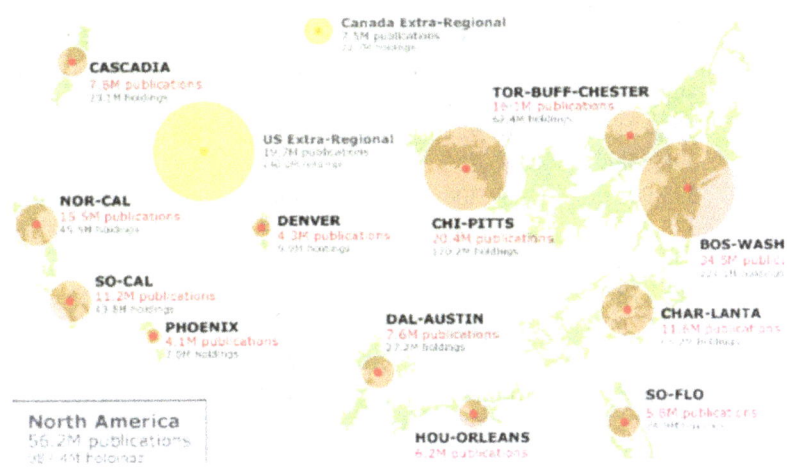

Figure 11.1 The North American mega-regional collective book collections (Lavoie 2018).

lection development initiatives through multi-institutional cooperation. Duke and UNC-Chapel Hill cooperate to build a single German-language collection with minimal duplication. The Ivy Plus Libraries Confederation has taken a modest step in this direction by collecting Brazilian materials through a cooperative plan in which each institution takes materials from one or two states and thus realizes broad national coverage. The Big Ten Academic Alliance's BIG Collection Initiative expands the idea of a single, multi-institutional collection at scale in ways that are similar and in many ways more ambitious than the steps taken over many years by the University of California system schools and their California Digital Library.[2] Taken together, such networks of collections will be able to provide higher levels of completeness, and the onus is shared through coordination.

Although interdependence has grown, academic research libraries remain rooted in their respective institutions. Libraries are charged to

---

[2] The University of California system and its California Digital Library have shared storage facilities, a shared print holdings retention program, consortial licensing, and shared cataloging programs. The Big Ten's BIG Collection is a system-wide collaboration that also aims to coordinate major collections in broad ways. See https://www.btaa.org/library/big-collection/the-big-collection-introduction/.

Table 11.1. Yale Circulation Data: 14-Year Overview of Local and Network Usage

Year	Local	Network	Total	Network %
2007	392,895	58,872	451,767	13
2008	395,121	62,928	458,049	14
2009	398,658	65,230	463,888	14
2010	393,903	69,806	463,709	15
2011	378,789	74,548	453,337	16
2012	356,743	79,648	436,391	18
2013	343,178	86,359	429,537	20
2014	308,269	89,257	397,526	22
2015	289,674	88,483	378,157	23
2016	270,949	84,643	355,592	24
2017	235,635	71,077	306,712	23
2018	225,993	74,843	300,836	25
2019	213,711	80,210	293,921	27
2020	148,821	58,189	207,010	28

be responsive to local needs/conditions, including community requests, and continue to acquire primary source materials apace. However, as research needs become more complex and discovery systems become more effective, libraries increasingly rely on partnerships at the network level to support local needs. Even the libraries with the most extensive collections recognize that researchers win when they have access to the largest pool of information, and the library of all libraries, that is, the "collective collection," is certainly more comprehensive than any one library could hope to acquire. Evidence that researchers are using the network is demonstrated by circulation data from Yale University Library (Table 11.1). The data show that usage of local collections is trending down, whereas usage of network collections, that is, items borrowed through resource sharing programs like BorrowDirect, is trending up. Since 2018, over one quarter of all the materials checked out by the Yale community were provided through the library resource sharing network, even during the COVID-19 disruptions of 2020.

Researchers can only gain access to things they can find. Much important ongoing work seeks to create better systems to facilitate discovery. Combined catalogs have been a part of the academic library ecosystem for a long time. Examples include the Triangle Research Libraries Network (Duke, UNC-Chapel Hill, North Carolina Central University, and North

Carolina State University), the Five College Consortium (Amherst, Hampshire, Mount Holyoke, Smith, and University of Massachusetts), UBorrow from the Big Ten Academic Alliance Libraries, and many, many more. These shared catalog programs facilitate access to materials for researchers through a combined discovery-and-request interface that leverages reciprocal borrowing policies. Within the Ivy Plus Libraries Confederation,[3] work is proceeding on a shared index to enable simpler discovery of its collective holdings. With tight integration to a request and delivery system, this will make it more seamless for scholars to discover and gain access to the collective collection in ways that feel as generous as access to locally held collections.

Resource sharing and openly available resources are key to our shared future, and libraries increasingly focus efforts on how to increase the speed and accuracy of interlibrary loan requests. The BorrowDirect system employed by the Ivy Plus Libraries Confederation uses real-time availability to put holds on available books in partner libraries and streamlines fulfillment. This greatly reduces staff time needed to manage the process, and books arrive within a few days instead of a couple of weeks. The network can obviate small and large distances. Libraries are increasingly looking at how we can share all parts of our digital holdings, and digitization on demand is making it possible to quickly share even rare materials held only in archives and special collections. Increasingly, and perhaps because materials are often housed in remote high-density facilities, libraries are scanning their own materials for their scholars through scan-and-deliver services in order to facilitate access to local collections. The network makes it possible to leverage this kind of service at greater scales, and so it matters less where an item is kept. This reinforces a perspective that makes information access a primary aim, which makes ownership look more like one among many possible means to support that access.

Digitization and born-digital materials provide their own challenges and opportunities, and librarians' work has evolved to include new areas related to licensing and copyright. In an increasingly online environment, libraries have moved to cooperate on negotiating deals for collective licensing of electronic collections. Libraries are working together to advo-

---

[3] The Ivy Plus Libraries Confederation is a cooperative effort that aims to build capacity to manage and develop collections, share their collective materials, and take a leadership role in developing a more efficient and effective information landscape. The members are Brown, Columbia, Cornell, Dartmouth, Duke, Harvard, Johns Hopkins, MIT, Princeton, Stanford, University of Chicago, University of Pennsylvania, and Yale.

cate for more reasonable licensing terms, seek ways to make more content freely available, educate producers and consumers of information about their rights, and claim fair-use rights. We are seeing some amazing possibilities in shared digital collections and preservation. The Google Books program provided the seed content for the creation of the Hathi-Trust Digital Library. HathiTrust, begun in 2008 as a collaboration of the universities of the Big Ten (including the University of Chicago) and University of California system, has grown into a partnership of more than 180 academic libraries. This communal digital collection allows public reading of out-of-copyright materials, enables computational analysis of a massive corpus of information without regard to copyright status, was made available to support libraries on an emergency basis during COVID-related disruptions and closures, and supports access to all materials for print-disabled users. By pooling resources libraries can create a great system and work collectively on projects to improve access to the network-level collection. HathiTrust quickly developed into a digital library of immense proportions with more than 17 million volumes and has now emerged as a leader in print preservation through the HathiTrust Shared Print Program, enticing libraries to identify and commit to retain more than 5.6 million print titles out of the approximately 8.4 million titles that correspond to digital versions in the HathiTrust Digital Library.

Although the HathiTrust Digital Library, Google, Facebook, Amazon, and Twitter are all markers of major transformations in the information landscape, librarians recognize the interwebs we experience today will look like incunabula a generation or two from now. We should not plan as though our networked library information landscape will look, feel, or work as it does today. Discovery will work better, the legal landscape will improve, and resource sharing and other fulfillment systems for physical and digital materials will enable much better services. We need to keep in mind that in a rapidly changing landscape we are just at the beginning—as a library community of practice and as a society—we are at a relatively primitive moment when it comes to applying technology to how we identify, deliver, and use information.

As we plan for a vastly improved electronic information environment, we also must ensure appropriate preservation and access for older technologies. From a library collection perspective, as in society at large, new media formats transform previous formats, but frequently do not obviate their predecessors. The role of newspapers changed when radio arrived. Newspapers and radio changed with the rise of broadcast television. On-demand technologies and the web changed newspapers, radio, and television. Because our researchers demand it, libraries continue to support many use cases for printed books, and not all of those important uses are by connoisseurs and Luddites. From a use and preservation perspective, digital and print are both important, and they support different uses; they complement each other no matter which version was born first.

As William Gibson said, "The future is here, it just isn't evenly distributed."[4] Many libraries are already realizing bits and pieces of the 2030 vision imagined earlier. More information is available to researchers everywhere while collective collections maintain and increase their scale, scope, and diversity. Materials are shared more broadly and more seamlessly; digital versions and print versions play their unique roles in the lives of scholars with fewer glitches. What does the future of the research library look like? If the trends discussed continue, the future looks much more evenly distributed and open, an increasingly substantial amount of the world's scholarly output will be freely available in electronic form, and what is not open will be ever more quickly deliverable upon request. The location of collections will matter less than their ease of discovery and distribution. A network of large, shared-print consortia will work to keep the print corpus available to researchers and students at academic institutions across the globe and through time. The tensions that surround digital texts will begin to loosen as cost models adapt, technology improves, and scholars continue to become more acculturated to reading online. In a positive view of the future, libraries will utilize new technologies, such as machine learning, to set up a robust, distributed infrastructure that ensures scholars can connect to the primary and secondary source material they need, when they need it, in the format in which they want it (Litsey and Mauldin 2018). Resources that were previously put in service of building and maintaining siloed collections will be deployed in areas that optimize and enhance the networked community. The ability to nimbly manage collections by connecting to these networks will be essential to meet the unique needs of scholars. In turn, scholars will continue to reorient their thinking, develop new models of scholarship, and utilize software tools to discover novel ways of engaging with texts and data. Librarians and scholars will work together as we adapt to new formats, new networks, and new tools that will result in new

---

[4] This is the conventional restatement of Gibson's idea, and Gibson seems to have been discussing this idea since the early 1990s. See https://quoteinvestigator.com/2012/01/24/future-has-arrived/.

scholarship. Researchers will have more streamlined and optimized access to a research library collection made of all library collections, an information service created, curated, and preserved collectively at network scale.

Bibliography

Abbott, Andrew. "Library Research Infrastructure for Humanistic and Social Scientific Scholarship in America in the Twentieth Century." In *Social Knowledge in the Making*, edited by Charles Camic, Neil Gross, and Michele Lamont, 43–87. Chicago: University of Chicago Press, 2011. http://home.uchicago.edu/aabbott/Papers/RISS.pdf.

Antleman, Kristen. "Stocks to Flows. *CNI Fall 2017 Project Briefings*, December 8, 2017. https://www.cni.org/topics/digital-curation/from-stock-to-flows.

Arizona State University Libraries. "The Future of the Academic Library Print Collection." (2017). https://lib.asu.edu/sites/default/files/marketing/ASU%20Whitepaper%20-%20Which%20Books.pdf.

Bowen, William. "The 'Cost Disease' in Higher Education: Is Technology the Answer?" *Ithaka Lectures*. October 2012. http://www.ithaka.org/sites/default/files/files/ITHAKA-TheCostDiseaseinHigherEducation.pdf.

Dempsey, Lorcan. "The Emergence of the Collective Collection: Analyzing Aggregate Print Library Holdings." In *Understanding the Collective Collection: Towards a System-wide Perspective on Library Print Collections*, edited by Lorcan Dempsey, Brian Lavoie, Constance Malpas, Lynn Silipigni Connaway, Roger C. Schonfeld, JD Shipengrover, and Günter Waibel, 1–10. Dublin, Ohio: OCLC Research, 2013. http://www.oclc.org/content/dam/research/publications/library/2013/2013-09intro.pdf.

———. "Library Collections in the Life of the User: Two Directions." *LIBER Quarterly* 26, no. 4 (2017): 338–59. http://doi.org/10.18352/lq.10170.

Dempsey, Lorcan, and Constance Malpas. "Academic Library Futures in a Diversified University System." *Higher Education in the Era of the Fourth Industrial Revolution*, edited by Nancy Gleason. Singapore: Palgrave Macmillan, 2018. https://doi.org/10.1007/978-981-13-0194-0_4.

Dempsey, Lorcan, Constance Malpas, and Mark Sandler. *Operationalizing the BIG Collective Collection: A Case Study of Consolidation vs Auton-*

omy. Dublin, OH: OCLC Research, 2019. https://doi.org/10.25333/jbz3-jy57.

Gillies, James, and Robert Cailliau. *How the Web was Born: The Story of the World Wide Web*. Oxford: Oxford University Press, 2000, 239.

Hazen, Dan C. "Rethinking Research Library Collections: A Policy Framework for Straitened Times, and Beyond. *Library Resources and Technical Services* 54, no. 2 (2010): 115–21. http://nrs.harvard.edu/urn-3:HUL.InstRepos:4111039.

Lavoie, Brian. "How Information About Library Collections Represents a Treasure Trove for Research in the Humanities and Social Sciences." The London School of Economics and Political Science (LSE) Impact of Social Sciences Blog. Posted on September 19, 2018. http://blogs.lse.ac.uk/impactofsocialsciences/2018/09/19/how-information-about-library-collections-represents-a-treasure-trove-for-research-in-the-humanities-and-social-sciences.

Lavoie, Brian, and Constance Malpas. *Stewardship of the Evolving Scholarly Record: From the Invisible Hand to Conscious Coordination*. Dublin, OH: OCLC Research, 2015. https://doi.org/10.25333/C3J63N.

Lavoie, Brian, Constance Malpas, and JD Shipengrover. *Print Management at "Mega-scale": A Regional Perspective on Print Book Collections in North America*. Dublin, OH: OCLC Research, 2012. http://www.oclc.org/research/publications/library/2012/2012-05.pdf.

Levine-Clark, Michael. "Access to Everything: Building the Future Academic Library Collection." *portal: Libraries and the Academy* 14, no. 3 (2014): 425–37. https://muse.jhu.edu/article/549201.

Linden, Julie, Sarah Tudesco, and Daniel Dollar. "Collections as a Service: A Research Library's Perspective." *CRL: College & Research Libraries* 79, no. 4 (2018): 86–99. https://crl.acrl.org/index.php/crl/article/view/16612.

Litsey, Ryan, and Weston Mauldin. "Knowing What the Patron Wants: Using Predictive Analytics to Transform Library Decision Making." *Journal of Academic Librarianship* 44, no. 1 (2018): 140–44. https://doi.org/10.1016/j.acalib.2017.09.004

Malpas, Constance, and Brian Lavoie. *Right-scaling Stewardship: A Multiscale Perspective on Cooperative Print Management*.Dublin, OH: OCLC Research, 2014. http://www.oclc.org/content/dam/research/publications/library/2014/oclcresearch-cooperative-print-management-2014.pdf.

Putnam, Herbert, "American Libraries in Relation to Study and Research." *The Library Journal* (September 1, 1929): 693–98.

12

Refworld: Future Frontiers for Special Collections Libraries

Rachael Dreyer

Much has been made over the changing future of libraries at large, the evolving access points to informational, educational, and recreational resources. When discussing the future of libraries, special collections are often omitted from the conversation, in part due to the technological landscape that has impacted how all libraries deliver services and content. The parent libraries in which special collections and archival repositories reside are often focused on services and electronic resources. Makerspaces, 3D printing, collaborative commons for digital projects (Figure 12.1): These are perceived as the essential components of our modern academic library and these services are expected to foster and develop the skills that the modern professional marketplace requires of students.

Where, then, does a special collections library fit, when much of what a special collections library offers falls outside the bounds of modern academic libraries (Figure 12.2)? How can we ensure that we are relevant to existing and evolving academic and scholarly needs? As general library collections become more homogenous, through electronic database holdings and the ability to share resources among consortium members, special collections develop greater status as a library's only truly unique collection; special collections librarians must not squander this opportunity to impact the research environment. As service providers, reference

Figure 12.1 Knowledge Commons in the Pattee Library, Pennsylvania State University.

Photo credit: Wilson Hutton, Pennsylvania State University Libraries, flickr.com.

and public service archivists and special collections librarians encounter the effects of policies and practices, and witness how these factors contribute to a student, faculty, or community stakeholder's experience. For this reason, those who provide end-user services are uniquely situated to offer suggestions for future practices. Therefore, any discussion of how special collections can maintain centrality and scholarly relevance needs to begin with this cradle of academic inquiry. Although not an all-encompassing summary of potential methods used to center special collections and archives in the middle of the education and research mission of a parent institution, this chapter explores the future of special collections libraries and archives from a reference practitioner's perspective. The author explores the need to embrace developing technologies and to enhance partnerships with those engaged in new areas of scholarship and teaching. Emerging trends that surround collecting and acquisitions in the special collections and archives field are also addressed, with special emphasis on the need to create more inclusive and representative collections and to contribute to the creation of user communities. Last, the chapter explores the need to balance resources for reference between

Figure 12.2 Students and professor in the Old Main Library, ca. 1890.
Photographic Vertical File, Special Collections Library, Pennsylvania State University Libraries.

physical spaces and online services amid the rising expectations for digital access to rare and original materials.

The Scarcity of Rare and Unique Materials

As academic libraries license the same online journals and databases, purchase the same university press titles, and coordinate deselection through shared print retention agreements and repositories, special collections and archives become the resource that sets each library apart from its peers. Although many larger libraries purchase books using similar approval plans and subscribe to electronic journal packages, rare and unique materials held in special collections are difficult to duplicate. Each institution has an individualized collecting policy that reflects the research needs and interests of its stakeholders in the university environment; collection strengths reflect historical priorities and depict institutional history. Indeed, "[a]t its core, the goal of the academic repository is to support teaching, learning, and original research. The rare, unique, and primary resources of the repository and its work in appraisal, preservation, arrangement, and description provide the foundation for critical and creative study that promotes the creation of new knowledge and understanding of society, culture, and history."[1] The rare and unique holdings contained in special collections libraries are an area of distinction for the parent institution.[2] No special collection is like another; each is shaped by the expertise, interest, and personalities of those who founded it and carry on the stewardship of the collections entrusted to their care. However, an item does not contain research value merely because it is rare. For researchers, rare and unique collections represent an opportunity to engage in singular scholarly inquiry; for special collections librarians, these rare and unique materials represent specialized expertise in these particular subject areas that they are able to share with researchers through a collaborative research process. For institutions, rare and unique materials represent the unique support they contribute to the growth and development of human knowledge.[3] Although rarity may enhance the attraction of special collections holdings, value emerges when special collections librarians make these holdings available so researchers may interact with these materials.

Teaching and Learning Collaborators

One of the central pillars of any university's purpose is its teaching and learning mission; consequently, engaging actively and directly with the current instructional environment is one way we maintain the scholarly relevance of a special collections library. The students who earn degrees from the university should know about special collections because they have used collections, visited exhibits, and benefited from remote research assistance; this would provide evidence that we have enhanced the learning and teaching missions of our institution through information literacy support and instruction. However, the question of what information

---

[1] Christian Kelleher, "Archives Without Archives: (Re)Locating and (Re)Defining the Archive Through Post-Custodial Praxis," *Journal of Critical Library and Information Studies* 1, no. 2 (2017): 1–30, quote on p. 5. doi:https://doi.org/10.24242/jclis.v1i2.29/.

[2] Though it might seem obvious, it is important to remember that researchers access these rare and unique materials at a public service point and interact with special collections staff when doing so.

[3] Lisa Carter, "It's the Collections that Are Special," *In the Library with the Lead Pipe* 11 February (2009). http://www.inthelibrarywiththeleadpipe.org/2009/its-the-collections-that-are-special/ (accessed August 31, 2018).

Figure 12.3 Researcher using the card catalog in Central Library, undated.

Photographic Vertical Files Collection, Eberly Family Special Collections Library, Pennsylvania State University.

literacy *is* for this new generation of students and scholars means that we must adapt our instructional toolkit to the current educational landscape. Whereas these primary source research skills used to encompass the use of a card catalog (Figure 12.3), the use of a call number system to locate a desired volume (Figure 12.4), or the ability to locate both primary and secondary sources for a research paper, the requirements of digital literacy have increased exponentially. Online tools, such as finding aids and digital collections, allow much of the research to take place outside of the reading room. Yet the bulk of our holdings are analog and will remain so, which means we still bring students into our spaces to enhance their understanding of how the resources in special collections can enrich their student/scholar experience. This hybrid experience, which combines both analog and digital resources from book and manuscript holdings, is the ideal; as instructors, we want to demonstrate the primacy of all formats in the research experience. But this ideal future is far off on the horizon. How do we centralize our position within the current and ongoing curriculum?

Instruction is one of the most effective ways to connect with both faculty and students; working with faculty helps library instructors adapt to emerging current research and teaching trends. However, many of

Figure 12.4 Card catalog in the Pattee Library.
Photographic Vertical Files, Academics and Research.

these instruction sessions target traditional special collections research skills, such as navigation and search strategies for online finding aids and catalog records. Research skills are evolving as the possibilities of current scholarship expand into new arenas; students are employing new tools and software in the research process, many of which are unfamiliar to special collections librarians. To remain strong collaborators, "librarians also need to be aware of the key skills being taught and learned such as visual and data literacy."[4] Traditional special collections research remains the same in many respects; we continue to provide service for analog collections and the navigational tools that provide information about those resources.

However, our instructional toolkit needs an update to incorporate the new tools and strategies employed by digital humanities scholars because this user population will continue to grow. "There is a bridge

---

[4] Raymond Pun, "Conceptualizing the Integration of Digital Humanities in Instructional Services," *Library Hi Tech* 33, no. 1 (2015): 134–42, quote on p. 141.

connecting DH and instructional services. ... By producing and promoting these resources ... the Library is continuously meeting the need of the scholarly community: scholars are analyzing text, data and metadata in their respective fields in the humanities differently, repositioning their findings and exploring new avenues of research."[5] Indeed, digital humanities experts are natural collaborators in many ways, as "[s]ome of the more conceptually challenging and politically oriented work from within archival studies has reached out into the humanities by necessity."[6] Special collections librarians must find a way to leverage emerging partnerships and to reorient instructional models to adapt to the interconnectedness of scholarship and instruction. As one digital humanities librarian posits, "digital humanities instruction should be thought of as a two-step instructional process—adding value to [skill-based teaching] with a focus on further developing research questions, managing data, and refining methodology."[7] This describes what librarians have always done to varying degrees, but introduces different emphasis on new tools and data-analysis skills. We might facilitate this reorientation toward the digital humanities through several strategies. Special collections librarians join instructional faculty as full instructors, teaching full-semester courses such as the First-Year Seminar or graduate research methods. Another possibility entails active involvement in the coordination and facilitation of summer institutes or intensives, centered on the topic of research tools and methods as they apply to digital humanities; "librarians may teach credit-bearing courses at some institutions, [but] this option is not available to all librarians. The intensive format offers librarians an opportunity to re-imagine and explore their role in academic instruction."[8] A third option involves a semester-long commitment without becoming the instructor of record for a credit-bearing course: the embedded special collections librarian/archivist. Embedding special collections librarians in a course achieves more effective collaboration and offers an immersive opportunity to experiment with unique content and new methods of scholarly analysis. These types of collaboration ensure the centrality and relevancy of special

---

[5] Ibid.
[6] Marika Cifor and Stacy Wood, "Critical Feminism in the Archives," *Journal of Critical Library and Information Studies* 1, no. 2 (2017): 1–27, quote on p. 17: https://doi.org/10.24242/jclis.v1i2.27/.
[7] John E. Russell and Merinda Kaye Hensley, *College and Research Libraries* 78, no. 11 (2017): 588–91, 600, quote on p. 589. Accessed August 20, 2018. https://crln.acrl.org/index.php/crlnews/article/view/16833/18427/.
[8] Susan Powell and Ningning Nicole Kong, "Beyond the One-Shot: Intensive Workshops as a Platform for Engaging the Library in Digital Humanities," *College & Undergraduate Libraries* 24, no. 2–4 (2017): 516–31. Accessed August 20, 2018. https://doi-org.ezaccess.libraries.psu.edu/10.1080/10691316.2017.1336955/.

collections libraries to the teaching and learning mission of our parent institutions because "the library has emerged as ... a core academic resource, and one that remains a sustainable resource continually adapting to the changing world."[9] The special collections library must also adapt and incorporate new instructional and collaborative strategies to demonstrate that it is both essential and sustainable in the learning environment.

The synergy between information literacy and digital humanities explorations provides special collections libraries with an opportunity to connect two user populations (emerging student scholars with digital humanities experts) with one another. We need to envision the special collections reading room as a hub of research conversations, serving as the nexus for exciting collaborative scholarship between new groups of learners. Although traditional forms of scholarship continue, in order to maintain cultural and scholarly relevance as research moves into the digital realm, collaborating more closely with digital humanists is one way to avoid falling into the stereotype of the dusty and disused reading room.

To banish this common stereotype, special collections and archives professionals need to engage in collaborative partnerships, as active participants, not passive members. Although our unique collections draw researchers to us, we also need to assume an active role in recruiting researchers and instructors as collaborators. And through years of involvement with the scholarly life of the university, we have ideas about emerging areas of scholarship and inquiry that are well suited to collaborative explorations. In considering collaborative partnerships, libraries should look to other emergent areas in the library and on campus. Partnerships evolve naturally when both sides can experiment together.[10] If there is a Makerspace in the library, incorporate bookbinding or book repair workshops into the program schedule. If 3D printing facilities exist, work to develop a way to print a 3D replica of a publisher's binding or to print bookplates, or even, as our library did, print replicas of game pieces so that recreations of historic games in the rare books collection could be played by visitors to an exhibition about educational toys. In addition, one of our Penn State Special Collections curators created a 3D print of a cuneiform tablet so that it could be passed around, handled, and

---

[9] Jennifer Gunter King, "Extended and Experimenting: Library Learning Commons Service Strategy and Sustainability." *Library Management* 37, no. 4/5 (2016): 265–74, quote on p. 272.

[10] The "Editing the Eartha M. M. White Collection" project provides an example of a partnership that involved digital humanities as well as special collections, and describes how the initial partnership offered opportunities to improve in subsequent iterations of the project. Clayton McCarl, "Editing the Eartha M. M. White Collection: An Experiment in Engaging Students in Archival Research and Editorial Practice," *The Journal of Academic Librarianship* 44, no. 4 (2018): 527–37.

Figure 12.5 Students handling 3D-printed copy of cuneiform tablet in the Special Collections Library.

Photo by the author (2018).

examined closely by students (Figure 12.5); activities that would never be possible with the original tablet. Creating this surrogate from an artifact from a collection that was highly requested served a preservation need as well as an educational and outreach need.

We can encourage students to make use of the 3D printing equipment, but in order to fully understand it, we need to be comfortable with using it ourselves; acquiring these and other emerging technology skills needs to be part of our current professional competencies. We need to develop proficiency with them or we risk losing touch with our researchers, for those with questions about how to apply new, emerging research tools to our rare and unique collections will seek answers from the reading room reference desk. Clearly, special collections librarians need to be knowledgeable about emerging research processes if our collections are involved. Bringing these technologies into mainstream archival literacy expectations allows us to center special collections in the teaching-and-learning mission of the institutions we serve.

Corrective, Collaborative Collecting

In recent years, libraries have engaged in close analysis of existing practices, services, and collections through the application of critical theory.

The critical librarianship movement contributes to action toward an inclusive approach to serving all library stakeholders, and influences professional practice in the special collections and archives environment as well. In a special collections library of the future, critical special collections librarianship informs evolving practices at all service points, for example, collecting initiatives that serve to offer an alternative to the dominant narrative, evaluating physical and online service points to ensure that they are accessible to all, questioning the hiring practices that reinforce existing power structures within special collections and archival workspaces. Critical practices in archives and special collections libraries have impacted collection development in visible ways, encouraging institutions to reexamine traditional collecting practices and to actively seek materials from underrepresented communities and donors who would contribute a more inclusive and representative historical legacy. Critical practices allow special collections to explore alternate approaches to collection-building that provide more open and transparent collecting practices. If we approached our collecting efforts as "a living digital community archive that documents and preserves the local heritage of its community as it is happening, rather than an after-the-fact historical archive,"[11] we can decenter the archive as the ultimate authority and therefore bring additional voices and perspectives into our holdings.

To aid in this work of dispersing archival authority and supporting archival inclusion, we can expand our definition of the custodial relationship between records and their creators, and those who facilitate access to them. As other archival theorists have explained, marginalized communities often feel that institutions acquire their records and then the communities themselves lose the ability to manage their own histories. As we examine and dismantle existing power structures, we should also consider archival practices to be structures as well. Gerald Ham introduced the postcustodial approach in 1980; for nearly forty years, there have been discussions and limited praxis with the postcustodial[12] model

---

[11] Andrea Copeland, "Public Library: A Place for the Digital Community Archive," *Preservation, Digital Technology & Culture* 44, no. 1 (2015): 12–21, quote on p. 16.

[12] Postcustodial theory is "[t]he idea that archivists will no longer physically acquire and maintain records, but that they will provide management oversight for records that will remain in the custody of the record creators." Society of American Archivists. "Postcustodial Theory of Archives." A Glossary of Archival and Records Terminology, accessed August 15, 2018. https://www2.archivists.org/glossary/terms/p/postcustodial-theory-of-archives/. In the custodial model, individuals or organizations donate their records to an archive, and an archive then takes control of the records: The collection is arranged so that it can be easily navigated by users, it is described in a publicly accessible format, and it is stored securely. Gift agreements also include the transfer of copyrights, should researchers wish to publish or use an image from the collection in a project.

of archival collecting. However, it is one approach to portraying a more complex, multifaceted history in our holdings and it can provide communities with ownership of their own historical legacy, while dispersing archival authority from an established institution. How does this work? Communities themselves maintain control of their physical records, and therefore their history, and provide access to physical collections, while a larger partner institution provides a platform for descriptive tools and connects the community's collection with researchers interested in the community's history. It is no small thing to transfer the entirety of a person's life or work, or the recorded history of an organization; it is understandable that many communities are hesitant to turn this documentation over to an institutional body in perpetuity. With digital surrogates, the options become ever more feasible: Communities and individuals can retain originals while institutions make digital versions available. Indeed, "the post-custodial paradigm disaggregates archives from the strictures of custody and enables archivists and archival repositories to look beyond institutional boundaries to engage in new ways with records, creators, subjects, and users."[13] Many crowd-sourced community archiving projects have taken such an approach,[14] but this model has yet to gain traction within the wider research environment at archives and special collections libraries. In some cases, "[m]anuscript repositories, including academic collections ... may be even more strongly tied to custody than archives repositories, because the manuscript repository's identity is highly dependent on the uniqueness of its holdings."[15] Nonetheless, unhitching ownership from access and description opens the door to collaborative collecting with new and diverse donors. This can also redistribute resources between larger, financially secure institutions and smaller, less established or funded institutions. Collaborative, postcustodial arrangements strengthen the position of cultural heritage institutions, and therefore the communities that they represent, but it also reorients the process toward access, rather than ownership, of collections. Furthermore, postcustodial collection arrangements can help introduce new user communities to the archives as donors, but as researchers as well.

What role, if any, do public-facing special collections staff play in collaborative and inclusive collecting? More than other special collections

---

[13] Kelleher, "Archives Without Archives," 26.
[14] The Culture in Transition project is one such example of a community history project and illustrates one example of a postcustodial approach in practice. See https://metro.org/cit-toolkit/ for more information. The University of Texas Libraries' Human Rights Documentation Initiative is another example; to learn more, visit https://legacy.lib.utexas.edu/hrdi/about/.
[15] Kelleher, "Archives Without Archives," 14.

team members, reference desk staff experience the gaps and deficiencies in special collections' holdings acutely; when an institution lacks representation about a topic a scholar or student wants to investigate, they see first-hand the demoralizing effect on the researcher. Unfortunately, many of our holdings do not reflect inclusive and diverse history: It is often researchers who are exploring topics related to underrepresented communities who are most frequently disappointed. Involving public-facing archivists and special collections librarians in outreach efforts to gain trust and support from community organizations and cultivating donor relationships makes logical sense because of this firsthand experience with users' interactions with our collections. Public-facing professionals must make time in their workdays to engage in outreach efforts to cultivate these donor relationships—for example, taking part in resource fairs, visiting historical societies, engaging with student groups, and offering tours or lectures to civic organizations. Reference dialogue offers an opportunity to discuss ideas and suggestions for future collecting and research endeavors. Those who work most directly with the public also enjoy opportunities for casual conversations with researchers. These conversations can be informative for both researchers and special collections librarians, particularly about the depth and breadth of certain areas of the repository's holdings. In order to harness the valuable data communicated during these interactions, create spaces for conversations with researchers and the reference team about how their research projects might inform collecting efforts. This could take the form of a brief exit interview as part of the reference interaction or a suggestion box with recommendation cards that researchers submit anonymously at the end of their research visit, or even a webform for researchers to use to suggest areas in which we need to enrich our holdings. Indeed, many faculty members are already comfortable making suggestions and requests for acquisitions based on the semester's syllabus. Because this practice exists unofficially, it could be formalized and adapted so that all researchers have equal ability to influence collecting efforts. Serendipity is responsible, in part, for collecting efforts; potential archival donors contact us because they feel that their materials have worth and enduring value. As public-facing professionals, we must work to cultivate relationships with our community and with our researchers, encouraging them to share the histories of their communities and lives, particularly if our catalogs and finding aids come up short on their topic of focus. Through even small and welcoming interactions at the reference desk, we make strides toward ensuring that everyone feels empowered to approach the reference desk with collection development ideas.

Research Spaces and Services

When we consider special collections and archival scholarship, and the space in which this work is conducted, there have been few changes to the physical service points at which archivists and librarians encounter those in need of research assistance. "When planning spaces for digital scholarship, academic libraries focus on furniture, hardware, and software. People, including employees who will work in the space and patrons who will occupy and use the space, are often a secondary focus."[16] Special collections libraries and archives cannot become full partners in digital scholarship endeavors if our physical spaces lack basic amenities of the digital era, such as adequate numbers of electrical outlets to power devices used by researchers to perform their work. When comparing images of reading rooms of the past (Figure 12.6) and present, it is remarkable how similar they seem. Though furniture and upholstery may get an update, the basics of the reading room remain the same.

Just as we must address the changing flow of reference traffic from physical to online spaces, we must heed the changes in how scholarship is conducted to ensure our infrastructure can continue to support scholarly work in the coming years. Putting the blended innovation landscape to full advantage for the special collections environment supports "[a] fully interactive environment that exists at the overlap of the physical and digital worlds."[17] To create this interactive and blended setting, special collections libraries should survey their current users to ensure that current configurations and infrastructure support users' research methods.

Makerspaces and 3D-printing labs, collaboration spaces, and computer labs have remade the traditional academic library. Indeed, "the infrastructure of [library] environments have rapidly evolved to reflect the learner's needs, whether that is filling a gap in knowledge, space to collaborate with peers, or opportunity to receive aid from an expert."[18] Yet no evolutionary shift has touched the reading room; most reading rooms include a reference desk used by a staff member to supervise researchers, tables, and chairs (Figure 12.7).

---

[16] Rachel Wexelbaum, "Assessing Safe Spaces for Digital Scholarship in the Library," *LIBRES: Library and Information Science Research Electronic Journal* 26, no. 1 (2016): 14–30, quote on p. 15.

[17] Shirley Dugdale and Brian Strawn, "Crafting an Innovation Landscape." *Planning for Higher Education* 45, no. 2 (2017): 2–15, quote on p. 12.

[18] Tiffany Chow, "Design Implications: How Space can Transform the Library and its Public," *Progressive Librarian* no. 36/37 (2011): 71, quote on p. 72.

Figure 12.6 A researcher in the Rare Books Room in the Pattee Library.
The Pennsylvania State University. Photographic Vertical File, Academics and Research.

Copiers or scanners may be available, but that will likely be the extent of any vestiges of the twenty-first century: Reading rooms resemble their predecessors of earlier decades. Many of the reasons cited for not updating reading room layout and policies have mentioned the safety and security of the materials. Yet an updated approach to reference services actually offers increased security. For example, the roving reference model ensures that public service archivists and special collections librarians are engaged with their environment, rather than the work on their desktop computers. Instead of sitting at a desk, librarians wander the space with portable computing devices, offering impromptu reference consultations, directional assistance, or technical support. Removing the desk entirely takes out a perceived barrier between the researcher, which makes the reading room more accessible and inviting, but also creates clearer sight lines. If we as professionals make it too difficult to use

Figure 12.7 View from the reference desk in the Eberly Family Special Collections Library, Paterno Library.

Photo by the author (2018).

collection materials for modern research, we run the risk of alienating researchers and rendering our collections "use-less." After all, we collect, preserve, and curate materials so that they can inform the research projects of students and scholars. Creating inclusive spaces sometimes means addressing physical space, in addition to intellectual space, and we need to take proactive measures to ensure our collections are accessible from the first point of contact.

Changes to the special collections research experience extend past physical reading rooms as well. The proliferation of digital content has worked dramatic changes on the research encounter, with effects on access as well as instruction, and even on the collections we acquire. In our current research environment, digital access to all contents of an archive is something that many researchers and students expect. Managing expectations and providing education for how resources are allocated for digitization projects are now part of routine reference interactions. The impact of expectations for digital access on public services creates tension in several areas. First, special collections libraries and archives are always going to have some portion of their holdings that are only available in physical form, even as we gain an increasing amount of born-digital primary source material. Second, as more of our finding aids are published online as Encoded Archival Description (EAD), four collections are increasingly discoverable by more people, though the actual material may be analog. Third, reference staff receive requests for information and for digital surrogates from these collections, which are described (but not available online), causing remote reference to increase rapidly. Consequently, we need to orient ourselves in such a way that we maintain balanced and well-resourced services and examine existing practices closely. This might mean that all images available through online portals allow high-resolution downloads. It may mean that we manage copyright and permissions with Creative Commons licenses to ensure full transparency about how images can be used in subsequent works. Furthermore, if these direct means of supplying downloads and rights information are not available, it could also entail cross-training between departmental units to ensure that digital images can be retrieved and delivered to end users in an efficient way. Each institution will need to evaluate its digital infrastructure to assess the possibilities, but one thing is clear: The traditional service model, in which a user discovers an image through a digital collection and then must contact the library or archives directly, impedes access to our collections. Our physical footprint limits in-person reference traffic; we have a certain number of tables and chairs available to accommodate researchers. On the other hand, there is nothing to constrain the growth of our virtual reference traffic. Yet our service model tilts toward providing onsite reference services to researchers. For example, the majority of the reference work conducted by the Research Services team from our Eberly Family Special Collections Library occurs in virtual environments. Various experimental reference services tie in directly to specific services offered by our team, or provide opportunities to explore service expansion. For instance, we are exploring the possibility of remote video reference for consultations as well as for intensive, magnified examination of rare books or archival material during instruction sessions. Future special collections reading rooms will be even further oriented toward a flipped reference service model; as finding aids, digitized content, digital projects, and platforms proliferate, many more researchers discover special collections' holdings. This is the desired result of increasing the accessibility of our rare and unique collections. At the same time, when many researchers discover primary or special collections sources during an initial search, they do require additional assistance to incorporate these sources into their work, which creates additional backlogs for public service archivists and special collections librarians. In considering an effective service model, special collections leadership must consider that workloads need to be calibrated and staffing levels need to be redistributed or increased to maintain effective public services for stakeholders with whom we interact at all access points. We must balance our service points in order to ensure that we can provide access to all the formats represented in our holdings to all researchers who wish to use them. Just as with analog research methods, "[d]ifferent researchers are involved in the use of digital means of work to different degrees and for different purposes, resulting in diverse experiences with and outcomes from the use of digital tools."[19] Achieving balance between all service points and formats is one way that we ensure equal access for both onsite and remote researchers; in both service provision and acquisitions, we strive to maintain a "format-agnostic"[20] approach.

Final Thoughts

Although not an exhaustive list of all the strategies that special collections libraries might employ to modernize their service models, the approaches outlined here identify several ways to incorporate special collections into the teaching-and-learning mission of universities. As information literacy skills change and research methods evolve, special collections need to take a proactive approach if we are to maintain that centrality. Within special collections, the reference desk and reading room assume a core position as well; each researcher encounters a member of the reference staff whether inquiring about digital access, asking for details about a letter in our holdings, or finding out how to schedule an instruction session. Indeed, public-facing special collections librarians are uniquely situated to establish partnerships with various stakeholders for research and instruction, to reach out to potential donors to increase inclusivity and address the iniquity of archival underrepresentation in the collections, and to recommend recalibrations of existing reference service models. Ensuring that public services remain aligned with existing and emerging needs is critical for special collections' continued relevancy. As professionals and special collections institutions, we must pursue an active and engaged role in the academic community to ensure that our instruction, collections, spaces, and services meet the evolving needs of current and

---

[19] Panayiota Tsatsou, "Literacy and Training in Digital Research: Researchers' Views in Five Social Science and Humanities Disciplines," *New Media & Society* 20, no. 3 (2018): 1240–59, quote on p. 1254.
[20] Stanford University Libraries. "Web Archiving." Collection Development, accessed August 30, 2018. https://library.stanford.edu/projects/web-archiving/collection-development/.

future researchers. We must remember that though our special collections are wonderful, unique assets, value does not emerge from the rarity of our holdings, but from how successfully we collaborate and engage with members of our stakeholder communities.

Index

Page numbers in *italics* refer to illustrations.

A

abolition movement, 14
   and African American women, 15, 19
   in Salem, Massachusetts, 9–11
abolition of slavery, 9, 10
   and Female Anti-Slavery Society of Salem, 10; *see also* Remond, Nancy; Remond, Sarah
   and Hamilton Hall, 10
academic freedom, 82
academic libraries, 75–79, 246, 248
   and changes in American higher education, 75, 79–82, 128–29
      case study of Ohio University, 86–91
   during the Colonial era, 77–78
   and digitization, 223–37
   first university, 77
   history of, 75–79
   as "intermediary deployment zone," 196
   librarians and, 247
   as prime campus real estate, 247
   and response to change, 82–86
   special collections of, 83–85, 127–28, 130
      changing attitudes toward, 127–140
      diversity in, 248, 253
         Native American Literature Collection at Amherst College, 93–107
      importance of networks on, 246–54

academic libraries (*continued*)
   print programs of, 248
   and virtual-reality technology, 185–205; *see also* rationalization of space; 3D-scanning technologies
      and academia, 193–98
      trends in, 198–202
      immersive media, 187–93
access to special collections, 185, 234
   access and use, 85, 88–92, 132–37
   changing attitudes toward, 127–40
   official statements regarding, 131–32
accessibility, 124, 217
   authentic, 111–25
   diverse representation in special collections, 112
ACRL/RBMS Guidelines Regarding Security and Theft in Special Collections, 131
Adams, Frederick B., 33
Adams, Randolph 129, 132
Aedes Althorpianae, 29; *see also* Althorp; Dibdin, Thomas Frognall; Spencer, 2nd Earl of
Afric-American Female Intelligence Society, 5
African American history and culture, 15, 112, 113, 119, 121–25
   collecting and preserving materials, 112
      Digitizing African American Archival Materials Across University of Minnesota

African American history and culture (*continued*)
    Collections (DAAAUMN), 112–25
    underrepresentation in archives and special collections, 112–25
African American women, 5, 15, 117; see also Female Literary Society for African American women, Minerva Literary Society
Afro-American Historical Society, 14
Alberti, Leone Battista, 190
Alcott, Louisa May, 3, 14
Alexander, Edward Porter, 111
Alexandrian Library, 76
Althorp, 29; see also Dibdin, Thomas Frognall; Spencer, 2nd Earl of
American Antiquarian Society, 154
American economy, 8, 78
American Enlightenment ideals, 153
American higher education, 75, 128
    changes in over time, 79–82
    and support of academic libraries, 75–79
    and virtual reality, 185–205
American Historical Association, 81, 132
American libraries, 151
    expanded access, 85
    expanded collections, 83–85
        physical buildings, 83–85, 87, 247
    professionalization of librarianship, 82–83
    response to changes in higher education, 82–86
American Library Association (ALA), 82, 130, 162
    Code of Ethics, 187
    Condensed Rules for an Author and Title Catalog, 83
American Philosophical Society
American Philosophical Society (*continued*)
    as caretaker of Paskow Science Fiction Collection, 214
    Indigenous Subject Guide, 95
    membership of Mary Hyde Eccles, 42
    Proceedings of, 42
The American Negro Historical Society, 14
American rare book collections, 118, 129, 135–36
American Revolution, 4, 7, 8, 14
Amherst College, 97
    Amherst College Digital Collection, 99
    Native American Literature Collection, 97–107
analog collections, 106, 245, 246, 261, 262, 272
analog-to-digital collections, 246
analytic tools, 185, 217, 236
antebellum activism, 9, 12
antebellum America, 8, 16–18
    women of, 3, 7–9, 12, 14, 17, 18
anti-slavery literature, 3, 11
Apostles of Culture, 20
Archbishop Marsh's Library, 33
archival description, 116; see also Encoded Archival Description (EAD)
archival literacy, 265
archival repositories, 257, 267
archival theory, 116
archive, 76, 115, 117, 119, 156
    digital, 119, 158, 160, 161, 252, 266
    physical, 26, 106, 113–18, 120, 123, 127, 130, 138, 185, 201, 247, 252, 259, 266, 267, 271, 272
Archives Space, 123
archivists, 112, 117, 118, 122, 140, 152, 158, 225, 258, 267, 269, 272; see also Society of American Archivists

Index

Arundel Castle, 34
Asimov, Isaac, 218
   Foundation trilogy, 218
Association of College and Research Libraries (ACRL), 130, 133, 135, 139
   ACRL/RBMS Guidelines Regarding Security and Theft in Special Collections, 131, 133, 135, 139
   Competencies for Special Collections Professionals, 139
   Rare Book Collections, 135
Association of College and Research Libraries/American Library Association, 130
   Rare Book and Manuscript Section (RBMS), 130, 131, 134, 137, 140
      RBM: A Journal of Rare Books, Manuscripts, and Cultural Heritage (formerly *Rare Books and Manuscript Librarianship*), 137, 139
Association of Tribal Archives, Libraries, and Museums, 100
athenaeums, 4, 6, 9
   Boston Athenaeum, 9, 11, 12
   Salem Athenaeum, 9–11
      Elizabteh Hawthorne as member, 10
The Atlantic Monthly, 11
Auchinleck, 36, 44, 45; *see also* Auchinleck, 8th Laird of
   The Book of Company at Auchinleck, 46
Auchinleck, 8th Laird of, 46; *see also* Auchinleck
augmented reality, 202
authentic accessibility, 113, 121, 125

B
backlogs of unprocessed collections, 114, 115, 116, 121, 138, 272
ballads, 119, 120
Ballard, J. G.
   The Atrocity Exhibition, 219
   "inner space," 219
Baltimore Library Company, 4
Barker, Nicolas, 32, 38, 54, 55, 56
   The Bookman, 55
Beatty, Sir Alfred Chester, 33
   Chester Beatty Library, 33–34
   Chronicle of Akbar the Great: a description of a manuscript of the Akbar-Nama illustrated by the Court painters, 343
Beinecke Rare Book and Manuscript Library at Yale, 26, 46
Bellenden-Ker, William, 7th Lord Bellenden, 27
Berners Lee, Tim, 236
Berger, Sydney, 132
Bester, Alfred, 217
biases against people of color and marginalized groups, 94
Bibliographical Society of America, 42
bibliomania, 25, 27, 29, 30, 32, 34
   Book Auction Bibliomaniacs, 32
bibliophiles, 26, 36, 40, 43
"Bibliotheca Mejicana," 175
Bibliotheca Spenceriana, 29; *see also* Althorp; Dibdin, Thomas Frognall; Spencer, 2nd Earl of
Big Ten Academic Alliance, 249, 251
   BIG Collection, 249
Birds of America, 49, *50*
Bishop, William, 86
Black men and women; *see also* social libraries
   intellectual opportunities for, 3, 4, 5, 8
   and Sunday schools, 17
Blackwell, Brianna, 216
Bliss, Mrs. Richard
   first card cataloguer of The Ladies Library, 13

Bodleian Library at Oxford University, 51, 77, 179, 180
Boke of Good Manners, 28
book history, 136
book making, 32
book production, 32
bookman, 135, 136
Bookworm module, 214; *see also* Schmidt, Ben
born-digital materials, 152, 159, 161, 162, 251; *see also* digital collections
born-digital primary source material, 271
Borges, Jorge Luis, 218
  "The Library of Babel," 218
  "The Total Library," 218
BorrowDirect, 250
Boston, 3, 5, 14, 15, 248
Boston Library Society, 11
Boston Public Library, 5
Boswell, James, 42, 43
  diaries, 45
  Private Papers of James Boswell, 46
"Boyer Report," 128; *see also Reinventing Undergraduate Education: A Blueprint for America's Research*
Brant, Sebastian
  Das Narrenschiff (Ship of Fools), 29, 30, *31*
  Jamieson 1874 reprint, 30
British Library, 26, 47
  David and Mary Eccles Centre for American Studies, 36
  Endangered Archive Programme, 177
  Lady Eccles Oscar Wilde Collection, 46
British peerage, 34
British Royal Library, 51, 76
Brizdle, Barbara, 168
broad access to scholarship and digital objects, 247

Brookfield, Lord William, 58
Brown, John Carter, 135
Brown vs. Board of Education, 22
Brudenell, Edmund, 43
building collections, 246, 247
Burley, Susan, 10; *see also* Salem Book Club
Burroughs, William S., 218

C
California Digital Library, 160, 249
call number system, 94, 261
Cancer Research UK Cambridge Institute, 194
card catalog, *261*, 261, *262*
Carnegie, Andrew, 25, 87
Carnegie Library, 87
Carrington, André, 225
Cather, Willa, 14
Cave Automatic Virtual Environments (CAVEs), 192
Center for Research Libraries (CRL), 162
Centre national de la recherche scientifique, 180
Charles, Prince of Wales: A Birthday Souvenir Album, 51
Charleston Library Society, 12, 13
Chester Beatty Library, 33
Chronicle of Akbar the Great: a description of a manuscript of the Akbar-Nama illustrated by the Court painters, 34; *see also* Beatty, Sir Alfred Chester
circulating libraries, 3–7, 9, 13, 15, 86
civil rights movement, 119, 128, 140
Civil Society, 9
Civil War, 4, 5, 8, 11, 15, 18, 19, 20, 78, 79
classic liberal arts, 77, 80, 91
Coalition for Networked Information, 162
Coleridge, Samuel Taylor, 48

Index

Collaborating for Impact: Special Collections and Liaison Librarian Partnerships, 139
collecting and preserving materials, 112
collection development, 96, 99, 112, 195, 224, 247, 266, 268
collections; *see also* special collections
  digital, 113, 116, 120, 202, 245, 246, 252, 261; *see also* Amherst College, Digitizing African American Archival Materials Across University of Minnesota Collections
    aggregators, 123–24
    new wave, 214, 217, 227, 234, 235, 237
  electronic, 215, 257
  and scholarly pursuits, 84
collections of scholarly 3D content, 200
Colonial era of higher education, 77–78
Colonial female readers, 3, 4, 8
Colored Reading Society, 15
common school education, 16; *see also* Sabbath schools
computational analysis, 213, 216, 226, 229, 231, 245, 252
computational tools, 212, 216, 227
computer algorithms, 95, 223
computer interface paradigms, 199
computer science, 195, 228
computer-generated 3D visualizations, 186
Confederate Imprint Collection, 12; *see also* Parkman, Francis; Coolidge, Algernon
Coolidge, Algernon, 12; *see also* Confederate Imprint Collection; Parkman, Francis
Cooper, James Fennimore, 96
copyright, 211, 212, 251, 272
  law, 100

copyright (*continued*)
  out-of-copyright materials, 252
  restrictions, 211, 212, 216
Cornell Hip Hop Collection, 96
Cornell University, 81, 84
Council on Library and Information Research Cataloging and Digitizing Hidden Special Collections and Archives, 112
country house libraries, 25, 29, 35; *see also* Roxburghe Club
Crapo, Stanford Tappan, 40; *see also* Eccles, Mary Morley (née Crapo) Hyde, Viscountess
"Creating Data: A Guided Tour of the Digital Library," 214
Creative Commons Attribution, 181
Creative Commons licenses, 272
critical theory, 265
Crowell, Edith Hall, 13
cultural heritage, 34, 46, 101, 106, 139, 182, 186, 194, 200, 227, 267
Currer, Frances Mary Richardson, 38, 39, 40
curriculum, 79, 81, 227, 26
  changes resulting from Morrill Land Grant Act, 80–82, 128
  of Colonial colleges, 77–78, 85
    liberal arts, 77, 79, 80, 81, 91
    model of lectures and recitations, 77
  libraries as support for, 75, 77, 82
  of library schools, 83, 85
Cutter, Charles
  classification system of, 83
  Rules for a Dictionary Catalogue, 83
CyberCemetary, 161
cybernetics, 219

D

Da Vinci, Leonardo, 188
D'Arcy McNickle Center for American Indian and Indigenous

D'Arcy McNickle Center for American Indian and Indigenous Studies at the Newberry Library (*continued*)
　　Studies at the Newberry Library, 101
Das Narrenschiff (*Ship of Fools*), 29, *31;* see also Brant, Sebastian
Data Capsule Appliance for Research Analysis of Restricted and Sensitive Data in Academic Libraries, 216
Data Refuge project, 160–61
data sets, 179, 198, 199, 200, 211, 213, 215, 216, 217, 226, 228, 230, 231, 236, 246
　　exchanging copyrighted data sets, 215
　　extracted features data sets, 216
David and Mary Eccles Centre for American Studies at the British Library, 47; *see also* Eccles, David McAdam Eccles, Mary Morley (née Crapo) Hyde
de Botton, Alaine, 26
　　Status Anxiety, 26
de Worde, Wynken, 29
Deer Woman: An Anthology, 102, *104*
Delany, Samuel R., 212, 218, 219, 23
　　Nova, 218
　　Stars in My Pockets Like Grains of Sand, 236
　　Trouble on Triton: An Ambiguous Heterotopia, 218
Demilt, Elizabeth, 13
depository distribution system, 155
Depository Library Act of 1962, 151n2, 154
Desbans, Edme-Louis, 53; *see also* Wrightsman, Jayne
　　Placets de l'officier Desbans, 53, *54*
Describing Archives: A Content Standard (DACS), 116

descriptive equity, 121, 122, 125
Dewey, Melvil, 79, 85, 86, 129
　　Dewey's classification system, 83
　　first library school, 83, 129
　　Library School Accession Rules, 83
　　Library School Shelflist Rules, 83
Dewey Decimal System, 95
Dhalgren, 219
Dick, Philip K., 212n2, 219n22
　　The Man in the High Castle, 222
　　Valis, 219
Dickens, Charles, 13, 96
digital accessibility, 116, 197
The Digital Atlas of Native American Intellectual Traditions, 100
digital collections, 113, 116, 118, 119, 158, 202, 261
　　aggregators, 123
　　"born digital," 152, 159, 161, 162, 251
　　creation of, 113, 120, 214
　　and librarians, 211, 214, 225, 251, 252, 253
　　"new wave," 211, 217, 227, 234–35, 237
　　rights issues and, 120
　　speculative future of, 236
　　surrogates, 129, 185, 197
　　3D, 185, 186, 188, 190–95, 197–99, 200–04, 232, 257, 264, *265*, 269
　　traditional service model, 160, 272
　　and US Government Publishing Office, 157, 158
digital content, 106, 199, 271
digital deposit, 152, 155, 158
digital dissemination, 152; *see also* digital deposit
digital exhibition and curation, 214, 215, 226
digital humanities, 106, 217, 227, 229, 235, 262–64
　　Yale University Digital Humanities Lab, 214, 232

Index

digital object identifier, 157, 158
digital objects, 118, 123, 245
digital preservation in the twenty-first century, 26, 161
Digital Public Library of America, 100, 117, 118, 119
digital reading copy, 245
digital resources, 246, 261, 228
digital revolution, 91
digital scholarship, 195
   centers, 193, 204, 205, 225
   librarian, 203
digital surrogates, 185, 267
digital technology; *see also* 3D-scanning technology, 215
digitization, 99, 100, 112, 113, 117, 118, 120, 121, 125, 131, 202, 215, 225, 226, 228, 251, 271
digitized object, 58, 245, 272
digitized records, 113, 117, 125
Digitizing African American Archival Materials Across University of Minnesota Collections (DAAAUMN), 112, 118, 121, 125
direct digital dissemination, 152
discoverability, 112, 115, 125, 215, 217
Donald and Mary Hyde Collection of Dr. Johnson and Early Modern Books and Manuscripts, 36, 44; *see also* Eccles, Mary Morley (née Crapo) Hyde; Harvard University
double elephant, 49
Douglass, Frederick, 10
Downtown Collection at New York University, 96, 97
The Downtown Book, 97
Duarte, Marisa
   Network Sovereignty: Building the Internet Across Indian Country, 105

Duke of Roxburghe, John Ker, 27, 28
Dürer, Albrecht, 30

E

early American republic, 3, 4
early European modern bookbinding, 34
Early Republic, 7, 15, 18
East Asian Collection, 33
East India Marine Society, 10
Easton Neston, 39, 48, 49; *see also* Hesketh, Christian ("Kisty") Mary (née McEwen)
ebooks, 185
Eccles, David McAdam, 36, 43, 46
Eccles, Mary Morley (née Crapo) Hyde, 33, 35, 36, 40, *41*, 42–47
   Dean Farm, 36, 44; *see also* Hyde, Donald
   Donald and Mary Hyde Collection of Dr. Johnson and Early Modern Books and Manuscripts at Houghton Library, 44, *45*
   James Boswell's Book of Company at Auchinleck, 36, 42, 43, 44, 46
   Lady Eccles Oscar Wilde Collection at the British Library, 46, 47
   as member of the American Philosophical Society, 42
   as member of the Roxburghe Club, 42-43
   and Pierpont Morgan Library and Museum, 47
Egypt, 76
Eisenberg, Pablo, 97, 99
   Eisenberg collection, 97, 98
electrical engineering, 195
electronic information environment, 252
elegant book bindings, 32
Eliot, C. W., 81

embodied understanding, 185
Emerson, Ralph Waldo, 3, 13
Encoded Archival Description (EAD), 272
End of Term harvest, 160
end-user services, 258
Entry, Source, and Manuscript Record, 169
Environmental Data and Governance Initiative (EDGI), 161
Eshton Hall, 40
Esther Inglis's Les Proverbes de Salomon, 56; *see also* Getty, Lady Victoria
exponential growth of library collections at universities, 128

F
fair-use rights, 252
Fales, DeCoursey, 96
FDSys, 155
    Govinfo.gov, 155, 156, 158
Feldman, John, 168
female academies, 8
Female Anti-Slavery Society, 10, 11
female education, 7
female literacy, 16
Female Literary Society, 5, 15
female personhood, 8
female suffrage, 9, 19, 21
feminization of librarianship, 129
Fettercairn House, 46
Fields, Annie Adams, 12
fifth Earl of Rosebery, Philip Archibald, 33
finding aids, 114–17, 121, 123, 124, 131, 167, 194, 261–62, 268, 271
1st Baron Aldington, and Araminta, 51
first female member of the Roxburghe Club, 40

First Nations authors, 94
First World War, 21
Fischer, Agustin, 175
Five College Consortium, 97, 101, 251
Five College Native Studies program, 97, 101
flat-file database, 167
Floors Castle, 27; *see also* Roxburghe Club
folksonomies, 124, 125
FOLIO (Future of Libraries Is Open), 106
Forten, Charlotte, 10–11, 14
Foundations for Evidence-Based Policymaking Act of 2018, 160
Four Oaks Farm, 42, 44; *see also* Eccles, Mary Morley (née Crapo) Hyde
Fourteenth Amendment, 19, 21
    and significance for women, 19, 21
Francis, Lee, 102
Franklin, Benjamin, 4, 78; *see also* Junto, Library Company of Philadelphia
free Blacks, 10, 11
Freedom of Information Act, 158
frontier violence, 93
Frost Library, 97
fugitive documents, 155
Fuller, Margaret, 3, 12, 14
Fuller, Timothy, 3
fully interactive digital environment, 199
future of libraries; *see* libraries

G
Garrison, Dee
    Apostles of Culture, 20
Garrison, William Lloyd, 10
gender
    limitations to library access because of, 6, 9, 14, 18, 21

gender (*continued*)
   success of social libraries for women, 19–20, 22
genre fiction
   digitization of, 225, 231
genre formation, 212
Georgetown University, 97
German style of education, 80
Getty, Lady Victoria, 38, 40, 55
   as Roxburghe Club member, 56
      Esther Inglis's Les Proverbes de Salomon, 56, 56
Getty, John Paul, Sr., 55
Getty, Mark, 56
Getty, Sir J. Paul, Jr., 33, 55
   Wormsley Estate
      Wormsley Library, 55–56
Getty Museum and Research Institute, 55
GI Bill, 128
Gilbert Lyceum, 14
Gilded Age, 19, 96
Gilded-Age collecting, 96
Goodhue, Sarah Parker, 13
Google Books project, 213, 252
government information, 151, 156
   current efforts to provide access, 159–62
   current environment and access, 156–59
   distribution of, 152
   history of access to, 153–56
   Preservation of Electronic Government Information, 162–63
Government Printing Office (GPO), 154-163
Government Publications Office, 154n17
Govinfo.gov, 155
GPO Access Act, 154–55
Green, Samuel Swett, 86
Greene, Mark A., 114

Greek Alexandrian Library, 76
Grolier Club, 42–44
Guggenheim Company, 33
Guidelines for Efficient Archival Processing in the University of California Libraries, 115

H

Hall, Jacquelyn Dowd, 140
Hamilton Hall, 10; *see also* Remond, John
haptic feedback, 191, 201
Harper, Frances Ellen Watkins, 3, 14
Harvard University, 26, 77, 84, 85, 248
   and C. W. Eliot, 81
   Houghton Library, 26
      Donald and Mary Hyde Collection of Dr. Johnson and Early Modern Books and Manuscripts, 36, 44, 45
Harwood, Edward, 30
   View of the various editions of the Greek and Roman classics, 30
HathiTrust Digital Library, 163, 213, 214, 216, 226, 252
   Bookworm, 214, 228
Hawksmoor, Nicholas, 48
Hawthorne, Nathaniel, 7, 10, 12
head-mounted displays, 186, 193
headtracking, 195
Heber, George Henry, 32
Heber, Richard, 36, 40
Heber, Thomas, 32
Hesketh, Christian ("Kisty") Mary (née McEwen), 35, 37, 48–51, 61
   The Country House Cookery Book, 49
   For King and Conscience: John Graham of Claverhouse, 49
   Officer of the Order of the British Empire, Deputy Lieutenant, 35, 48
   Viscount Dundee, 1648–1689, 49
Hesketh Collection, 49

Hesketh Collection (*continued*)
Birds of America, 49, 50
Hesketh, 2nd Baron of (Frederick Fermor-Hesketh), 48, 37, 48
high-density storage facilities, 248, 251
Hilton, Sylvia, 13
historically Black college or university (HBCU), 123
Honma, Todd, 94
Houghton Library, *see* Harvard University
Howard University, 95
hubs for scholarly activity, 195
Hugo Awards, 212
human perceptual system, 199
Huntington Library, 26
Hyde, Donald Frizell, 33, 42
Donald and Mary Hyde Collection of Dr. Johnson and Early Modern Books and Manuscripts, 44, 45
Hyde, H. Montgomery, 46

I
immersive media technologies, 185, 187, 194, 202, 231, 263
quest for verisimilitude, 190–93
rationalization of space, 188–90
incunabula, 29, 30, 34, 252
Indiana University, 216
Indiana University's Observatory on Social Media, 214
Indigenous Comic Con, 102
indigenous peoples, 93, 94, 99, 100, 105, 107
indigenous scholarship, 101, 225
Indigenous Subject Guide, 95
industrial magnates, 128
information dissemination, 152
information dissemination products (IDPs), 154, 157
information literacy, 260, 261, 264, 273
information technology, 95

Inglis, Esther, 56, *57*
calligraphy of, 56
Esther Inglis's Les Proverbes de Salomon, 38, 56
inner space, 219
Institut de la recherche et d'histoires des textes (IRHT), 179–80
Institute of Museum and Library Services, 100, 162, 179, 204n18, 216
intellectual emancipation of women, 7
intellectual rights, 120
International Conference on Disability, Virtual Reality and Associated Technologies, 204
International Conference of Indigenous Archives, Libraries, and Museums, 103, 105
Internet Archive, 160, 215
Iqbal-namah'i Jahangiri, 178
Isham, Ralph, 44, 46
Private Papers of James Boswell, 46
Ivy Plus Libraries Confederation, 249, 251

J
Jackson, William, 33
Jameson, Frederic, 212
The Political Unconscious: Narrative as a Socially Symbolic Act, 212
jazz artists, 58, 116
Jefferson, Thomas, 55, 78, 135
John Rylands Library at the University of Manchester, 29
Johns Hopkins model, 80, 81
Johns Hopkins University, 80
Johnson, E. Pauline (Tekahionwake), 94
Flint and Feather, 94
Legends of Vancouver, 94
Johnson, Samuel, 43; *see also* Eccles, Mary Morley (née Crapo) Hyde

Johnson, Samuel (*continued*)
   Letters, 42, 45
Johnston, Jane, 3, 12
Johnston, John, 3, 12
joint-stock associations, 4
Jordan, June, 111
The Journal of Academic Librarianship, 139
junior colleges and technical schools, 128
Junto, 4, 13; *see also* Franklin, Benjamin

K

Kautz Family YMCA Archives, 122
Kelly, Kevin, 198; *see also* Wired
Kenny, Maurice, 94
   Dead Letters Sent and Other Poems, 94
   Feeding Bears: New Poems, 94
keywords, 115, 117, 118, 119
Kincaid, Paul, 212
King, Marion, 13
King Ashurbanipal, 76
King's College, London, 48
Koninklijke Bibliotheek, 172, 173
Kugelberg, Johan, 96

L

The Ladies Library, 28
Ladies Literary Society, 5
Lady Eccles Oscar Wilde Collection at the British Library, 36, 46, 47; *see also* Eccles, Mary Morley (née Crapo) Hyde
Lafayette, Marquis de, 10
land ownership, inheritance, and wealth creation, 25
legacy data, 171, 175, 182
Legal Information Preservation Alliance's (LIPA) Chesapeake Project, 161
Lenox, Nancy, 10; *see also* Remond, John; Remond, Nancy

letter-press photographic relief engraving, 32
Lewis, Edith, 14
liberal arts, *see* curriculum
The Liberator, 11
librarians
   academic, 82, 152
   and access to information, 130–32, 140, 158
   and efforts toward equality in information technology, 95
   reference, 85, 86, 269
   and special collections, 117, 127, 129, 154, 157, 246, 257, 258, 260, 262, 263, 265, 268, 270, 272, 273
   and virtual reality, 187, 202–05
   women as, 5, 13, 19, 20
librarianship, 20, 113, 127, 130, 134, 140, 266
   feminization of, 129
   as male- to female-dominated profession, 129
   and new technologies, 204
   as a profession, 75, 82–83, 91, 93, 128
   Library Journal, 83
   Rare Book Librarianship, 137
   Rare Books and Manuscripts Librarianship, 137
libraries, 4, 25, 163
   academic, *see* academic libraries
   Association of College and Research Libraries, 133, 135, 139
   circulating, 4, 5, 6, 7, 9, 13, 15
   and critical theory, 266
   depository, 155, 156, 157
   Depository Library Act of 1962, 154
   digital, *see* digital collections
   and digitization, 223–27
   as educational institutions, 5, 8, 16, 128
   embrace of technology, 128, 130
   and 3D/virtual reality technologies, 186–88, 190–93

libraries (*continued*)
　　195–98, 227, 233
　　future trends, 198–205, 214, 217–23
　family holdings and, 8
　future of, 199, 204, 211, 215, 233–37, 253, 257–58
　history of, 4, 12, 76, 88–91, 151
　and interlibrary loans, 251
　in Ireland, 25, 33, 35; *see also* Roxburghe Club
　　country house libraries, 25, 27, 29, 32, 40
　membership, 9
　　Boston Athenaeum, 11, 12
　　Salem Athenaeum, 9, 10, 11
　and online tools, 261
　partnerships, 252
　primary source, 140
　and print preservation, 253, 271
　public lending, 5, 15, 16, 18–22, 134
　public services offered, 85, 130, 271, 273
　rare book, 129, 134
　　Rare Book and Manuscript Section of the Association of College and Research Libraries (RBMS), 130, 131, 132, 134, 137, 139, 140
　research, 13, 76, 138, 152, 159, 246–47, 249, 250
　　African American studies, 19
　royal, 52
　social, 4, 6, 13, 14, 15
　special collections, 260, 263, 264, 267, 273
　structural racism and, 94–95, 111–12
　subscription, 4, 12, 14
　as support for scholarly pursuits, 76
　tribal, 105, 106
library as place, 85, 269
　as centralized, collaborative workspaces and technology-

library as place (*continued*)
　　oriented service centers, 195
　specialized equipment needed by scholars, 247
library collections, 84, 201, 257
Library Company of Philadelphia, 4, 13
Library of Congress, 33, 94, 95, 113, 160
　and racist policies, 95
　Reading Room, 86
Library of Congress Classification system, 83
Library of Congress Name Authority Files (LCNAF), 124
Library of Congress Subject Headings, 117, 124
Library of Congress subject metadata, 213
library curation, 211
library education, 129; *see also* Dewey, Melvil
　first school of, 83
Library Journal, 82, 83
The Library of Trinity College Dublin, 33
library science, 83, 122
library services, 85, 187, 202, 204
library taxonomies, 124
Library Trends, 134, 136
The Life and Opinions of Tristam Shandy, Gentleman, 48
limited editions versus mass printing, 32
Lindley, Bridget, 48; *see also* Hesketh, Christian ("Kisty") Mary (née McEwen)
Linked Open Data, 106
literacy, 5
literary salon, 3, 10
literary societies, 4, 5, 6, 14, 20, 88
　Black, 14, 15, 18, 21
　Gilbert Lyceum, 14

literary societies (*continued*)
  White, 14
literature, 6, 8, 14, 78, 127
  eighteenth-century, 43
  English, 42
  Native American Literature Collection at Amherst College, 93–107
  related to library scholarship, 133, 135, 136, 138, 140
  research, 195
  science fiction, 212–213, 215, 217, 223, 224, 227, 237
Local Contexts project, 105
LOCKSS (Lots of Copies Keeps Stuff Safe–USDOCS, 158
Longfellow, Henry Wadsworth, 12
  The Song of Hiawatha, 12
Loretta C. Duckworth Scholars Studio, 203, 213; *see also* Temple University
Lowell, James Russell, 33
Luminist.org, 215
lyceum movement, 8, 12

M

machine learning, 192, 229, 231, 235, 245, 253
Machine-Readable Cataloging (MARC), 106
MacLean, Katherine, 217
MacMullen, Grace, 13
Madison, James, 153
makerspaces, 193, 257, 269
Malahide Castle, 44, 45, 46
Manhattan, 3, 44, 53, 96
Manning, Mary, 10
manuscript data, 168, 169, 177–81
Mapping manuscript migrations, 179–81
Marchmont, 48; *see also* Hesketh, Christian ("Kisty") Mary (née McEwen)

Marcus, Cecily, 113
Marlay, Charles Brinsley, 33
Marsh, Archbishop Narcissus, 34
mass market, 6, 211, 213, 215, 223, 224, 227, 231
master and doctoral degrees in library science, 83, 122
Maximilian I of Mexico, 175
McEwen, Sir John, 48; *see also* Hesketh, Christian ("Kisty") Mary (née McEwen)
McEwen, Robert Finnie, 48
McGregor Plan, 132
McLuhan, Marshall, 234
mega-libraries, 91
Mehra, Bahrat, 203
Meissner, Dennis, 114
Melville, Herman, 13
metadata, 100, 113, 117, 118, 119, 167, 177, 180, 200, 213, 228, 263
metadata aggregator, 167
metadata enhancement, 121
Metropolitan Museum, 38, 51, 52
Minerva Literary Society, 5; *see also* Female Literary Society for African American women
minimal processing, 114
Mitchell, William J., 193
modern academic library, 257
Modern Language Association, 81
Mohawk authors, 94, 95, 98
Monday Evening Club, 9
Monk, Thelonious, 58
Montagu, Elizabeth, 43
moral piety, 78
More Product, Less Process, 114–15
Morgan, John Pierpont, 33
Morgan, John Pierpont, Jr., 33
Morley, Emma Caroline, 40; *see also* Eccles, Mary Morley (née Crapo) Hyde
Morphosource, 186, 200
Morrill, Justin, 80

Morrill Acts of 1862 and 1890, 128
Morrill Land Grant Act of 1862, 80
Morris, Edith K., 13
Mosaic web browser, 246
museum curators, 111
Museum of Houston, 51

N

National Archives and Records Administration [NARA], 156, 159
National Digital Information Infrastructure Preservation Program, 159
National Digital Platform, 100
National Digital Stewardship Alliance (NDSA), 159
National Endowment for the Humanities, 169
National Leadership for Libraries Planning Grant, 100
national libraries, 77
National Library of Ireland, 33
Native American authors, 12, 94, 97
Native American collection, 12
Native American Literature Collection, 97, 99, 100, 103; see also Amherst College
Native Realities Press, 102
Native Studies, 97, 100, 101
The Nebula Awards, 212
Negro Society for Historical Research, 14
new republic, 13, 16, 78
New Wave, 212, 223, 224
  authors, 212, 212n2, 219, 222, 223, 224
  of digital collections, 214–17, 227, 234, 235, 237
    SF Nexus, 215, 223, 225, 228
  of science fiction, 211, 217–24, 225, 227, 231
New York Athenaeum, 10

New York City, 5, 16–17; see also Manhattan, Sabbath Schools
  and African American female literacy, 5, 14
New York Female Union Society to Promote Sabbath Schools, 17
New York Philomathean Society, 14
New York Society Library, 4, 13
  influence of women on, 13
New York University, 96
Newport, Rhode Island, 4, 12, 13
Nineteenth Amendment, 21
1993 GPO Access Act, 154
Noble, Safiya, 95
  Algorithms of Oppresssion: How Search Engines Reinforce Racism, 95
nouvelle vague, 217; see also New Wave novels, 6, 222, 227, 229

O

Occom, Samson (Mohegan), 98
  A Sermon, Preached at the Execution of Moses Paul, An Indian, 98
Ohio University, 76, 86
  as academic library, 87, 88–91
Ojibwa, 3, 12
online databases, 129, 156, 195, 215, 228
online environment, 113, 125, 186, 200, 225, 246, 251, 253, 259
online finding aids, 117, 131, 167, 261, 262, 271
optical character recognition, 226
Oxford University, 17, 34
  Bodleian Library, 51, 77, 179, 180

P

paperbacks, 21
  covers of, 232
  Paskow Science Fiction Collection, 213, 214, 217, *224*, 232

Index

paperbacks (*continued*)
   "revolution," 224
Parkman, Francis, 12
The Partnership for Shared Book
   Collections, 248
Paskow, David C., 214
Paskow Science Fiction Collection, 213,
   214, 217, *224*, 232
*Past or Portal? Enhancing Undergraduate
   Learning through Special
   Collections and Archives*, 139
Patent and Trademark Resource
   Centers, 160
Peabody, Elizabeth Palmer, 3, 12
perceptual information, 191, 199
perceptual research, 187, 190–93
persistent uniform resource locator
   [PURL], 157
Personal Observation, 172–75; *see also*
   Schoenberg Database of
   Manuscripts (SDBM)
Petty-Fitzmaurice, Lieutenant-Colonel
   Henry William Edmund, 33
Philadelphia, 5, 11, 12, 15, 223
Philadelphia Library Company of
   Colored Persons, 4, 14
Phillipps, Sir Thomas, 181
Philosophical Library, 9
Phoenix Society, 15
photogrammetry, 188, *189*
Pierpont Morgan Library and Museum,
   26, 47, 55, 136
Placets de l'officier Desbans, 38, 53, 54,
   54; *see also* Desbans, Edme-
   Louis; Wrightsman, Jayne
plain text, 174
Plummer, Caroline, 10
portal: Libraries and the Academy, 139
Porter, Dorothy, 95
postcustodial approach, 266, 266n12,
   267
postwar boom of the 1950s and 1960s,
   the, 128

practical education, 128
pre-modern manuscripts, 167, 177–81
preservation, 114, 131, 265
   versus access, 134-35, 137, 138, 140
   cultural, 76, 194
   digital, 26, 129, 202, 252, 253
   of electronic government
      information, 151– 156
      Digital Library Federation, 159
      National Archives and Records
         Administration, 156–57, 158,
         159, 160, 161
      National Digital Information
         Infrastructure Preservation
         Program, 159
   of knowledge, 82
   Legal Information Preservation
      Alliance, 161
   Preservation of Electronic
      Government Information,
      162
   rare book, 32, 259–60
   ReCAP (Research Collections and
      Preservation Consortium),
      248
   of special collections, 131, 136
   of 3D and virtual-reality collections,
      204
Preservation of Electronic Government
   Information (PEGI) Project,
   162
Princeton University, 84, 248
Princeton University Press, 36, 42n36
print culture, 7
printed materials, 6
private book clubs, 4
professionalization of librarianship, 75,
   82–83; *see also* librarianship
professionalization of scholarship, 83,
   129
Progressive Era, 21
public domain, 99, 100, 106
public lending library, 11, 18–20, 22,
   163

The Publishers Association, 227
Publisher's Weekly, 227
pulp fiction, 223, 224, 225, 228, 234
Pynson, Richard, 29

Q

Queen Elizabeth II: A Birthday Souvenir Album, 51; see also Roberts, Lady Jane
quest for verisimilitude, 187, 190–93

R

race, 9
   and access to literacy, 22
   as barrier, 21
   Library of Congress Subject Headings and, 124
   search terms and, 121–25, 229
      descriptive equity, 121–23
   segregation in libraries, 18
   SF Nexus and, 225
   social and subscription libraries and, 6, 9, 14, 16–18
racial bias, 95
Rāmamālā Library, 177
Ransom, Harry, 96, 97
The Ransom Center, 96
Rare Book and Manuscript Section (RBMS), 130
rare book collections, 33, 42, 127, 129, 135, 140
   Amherst College, 99, 101
   book preservation and, 32
   creation of, 129
   digitization of, 118
   Roxburghe Club and, 42
      Baron de Rothschild and, 58
      Lord Hesketh and, 48
      Mary Hyde Eccles as collector of, 42–48
   technology and, 264, 265, *265*
rare book librarians, 127, 133, 134, 135
   technology and, 137–38, 272

rare book librarians (*continued*)
   women as, 136
rare books, 140
   access to, 26, 127, 129, 130, 132, 133, 136, 137
   literature about, 136–37, 138
rationalization of space, 188–90; see also immersive media technologies; perceptual research; quest for verisimilitude
reading clubs, 8
Reading Room Society, 14
reading rooms, 3, 14, 261, 264, 269, 270, 273
   access to, 127
re-binding, 32
ReCAP (Research Collections and Preservation Consortium), 248
Reconstruction, 5, 14, 19, 21
Red Planet, 102
Redwood Library, 4, 13; see also libraries
"The Ladies Library," 13
reference desk, 86, 91, 265, 268, 269, 273
reference staff, 86, 272, 273
Reinventing Undergraduate Education: A Blueprint for America's Research Universities, 128; see also "Boyer Report"
Remond, Charles, 10
Remond, John, 11
   and desegregation of schools, 10, 11
   Hamilton Hall, 10, 15
Remond, Nancy (née Lenox), 10, 11, 15
Remond, Sarah, 10
Renaissance, 77, 188, 190
repository, 44, 112, 115, 118, 131, 155, 161, 167, 259, 260
   online, 200
Republic of Ireland, 25

Index

"republic of letters," 6, 7, 22
research, 80
   importance of in American higher education, 80–82, 84, 85, 87, 91, 128
Resource Description Framework (RDF), 181
   Schoenberg Database of Manuscripts as research tool, 169, 175, 177–82
research lifecycle, 202; *see also* Schoenberg Database of Manuscripts
respects des fonds, 116
rise of desktop publishing, 155, 157
rising automation, 136, 259
Riviere & Sons, 47, 47; *see also* Riviere, Robert
Riviere, Robert, 47
Roberts, Lady Jane, 35n31, 37, 40, 51–52
   Curator of the Print Room at Windsor Castle, 51
   Drawings by Holbein from the Court of Henry VIII: Fifty Drawings from the Collection of Her Majesty Queen Elizabeth II, 52
   Enlightened Princesses: Caroline, Augusta, Charlotte, and the Shaping of the Modern World, 52
   Five Gold Rings, a Royal Wedding Souvenir Album, 51
   Leonardo da Vinci: Anatomical Drawings from the Royal Library, Windsor Castle, 51
   1000 Years of Royal Books and Manuscripts, 52
   Windsor Castle: The Museum of Fine Arts, Houston, 17 May–16 August 1987, 52
Roberts, Sir Hugh Ashley, 37, 51
Robinson, Dr. John Martin, 34
Rosebery, 5th Earl of (Philip Archibald Primrose), 33
Rothschild, Hannah Mary, de, Honourable, 57–59
   Commander of the Order of the British Empire, 57
   first woman chair of the Board of Trustees for the National Gallery in London, 58
   great aunt Kathleen Annie Pannonica de Koenigswarter, Baroness de Koenigswarte, 58, 58n76
   The Jazz Baroness, 58
Rothschild, Ferdinand de, Baron, 58
   Waddeso Manor, 58
Rothschild, Victor, 58
Rothschild Foundation, 58
roving reference model, 270
Roxburghe, third Duke of (John Ker), 27; *see also* Roxburghe Club
   A Catalogue of the Library of the late John, Duke of Roxburghe, 28
Roxburghe Club, 25–27, 29, 32, 33
   archives, 34
   bibliomania and, 29, 30, 32
   gender distribution in, 34
   Irish libraries and, 33
   women of, 35–40
      Eccles, Mary Morley (née Crapo) Hyde, 35, 36, 40–48
      Getty, Lady Victoria (née Holdsworth), 55–57
      Hesketh, Christian ("Kisty") Mary (née McEwen), 35, 37, 48–51
      Roberts, Lady Jane (née Low), 51–52
         Royal Librarian, 51-52
      Rothschild, Honourable Hannah Mary, 39, 57–59
      Wrightsman, Jayne (née Larkin), 38, 52–55
Royal Botanical Society, 33

Royal Botanical Society (*continued*)
Leonardo da Vinci: Anatomical Drawings from the Royal Library, Windsor Castle, 51
Ruggles, David, 3
Ruskell, Helen, 13
Russ, Joanna 212, 219
The Female Man, 219, *220*

S
Sabbath schools, 6, 16–18; *see also* schollars; *see also* Sabbath schools
Saint-Aubin, Gabriel Jacques de, 53
Placets de officier Desbans, 54; see also Wrightsman, Jayne
Salem, Massachusetts, 9
  anti-slavery movements in, 9
  desegregation, 9
  Female Anti-Slavery Society, 11
  intersection of gender and race in nineteenth century, 9–11
  knowledge and learning, 9
Salem Athenaeum, 9–11
Salem Book Club, 10; *see also* Burley, Susan
Salem Normal School, 11
Salome, 47, *47*; *see also* Wilde, Oscar
scan-and-deliver services, 251
Schalk, Sami, 225
Schmidt, Ben, 214
  Bookworm module for HathiTrust Research Center, 214, 228
  "Creating Data: A Guided Tour of the Digital Library," 214
Schoenberg, Larry, 168, 182
  as private manuscript collector, 167
  Schoenberg Database of Manuscripts, 167–69, 171–74, 181–82
    data model, 169–70
    Group tool, 175–77
    historical integrity of, 171
    and legacy data, 171

Schoenberg, Larry (*continued*)
  special collection research tool
Schoenberg Institute for Manuscript Studies, 168, 177
scholars of the Victorian era, 96
schollars, 16, 17
Schomburg Center for Research in Black Culture, 14, 113
Schoolcraft, Henry Rowe, 12
science fiction (sci-fi), 211, 237; *see also* Paskow Science Fiction Collection, SF Nexus
  data curation, 228–32
  digital research project at Temple University, 214–17
  genre's inception, 212
  New Wave era, 211, 217–23, 227
  pulp, 223–27
Science Fiction Research Association, 214
search engines, 95, 112–13, 117
search strategies, 121–22, 201, 262
secondary source material, 134, 172, 195, 253, 261
Semantic Web, 168
serendipitous information retrieval, 201
settler colonialism, 93, 93n2
SF Nexus, 215, 217, 223–27; *see also* science fiction
Shaw, Bernard
  letters of, 43
Singer, Ryan
  Chief Cthulhu (Great Old One), 102, *103*
Sketchfab, 186, 200
slaves, 8, 12, 120
Smith, Martin Cruz 98
  Stalin's Ghost, 98
social libraries, 4, 5, 6, 13–15, 18–20
  African American, 5, 14, 15, 18, 19, 21
Society of American Archivists (SAA), 130, 131, 132, 137, 140; *see also* Association of College

Society of American Archivists (SAA) (*continued*)
  and Research Libraries/ American Library Association
Society of Antiquaries, 33
software tools, 200, 201, 253, 262, 269
SPARQL Protocol, 181
spatial information, 185, 190, 194
special collections, 96–97, 106, 112, 113, 127, 132, 213, 217, 251, 257; *see also* libraries, Native American Literature Collection, Schoenberg Database of Manuscripts
  access to, 127–28, 130, 134, 136–40
  audience and outreach, 136, 138–39
special reference collections, 86
speculative fiction, 215, 217, 218, 219, 222, 223, 229, 231
Spencer, 2nd Earl of, 29
  Althorp
    library of, 29; *see also* Dibdin, Thomas Fragnall
    catalogues, 29
    Aedes Althorpianae, 29
    Bibliotheca Spenceriana, 29
Stanford Literary Lab, 215
status symbol, library buildings as, 84
structural racism of library systems, 94
"The Stuff of Science Fiction," 228
Sturgeon, Theodore, 218, 223
subscription lending libraries, 4, 5, 6, 12, 18, 19; *see also* Boston Athenaenum, Salem Athenaeum
  female access to, 4–5, 12–15
  summer schools for girls, 8
Sutherland, Ivan
  "Sword of Damocles" device, 192

T

Tate Gallery, 58
technological innovation and libraries, 128–30, 137–38, 186
Temple University, 213, 218
Temple University Library, 216
  Digital Scholarship Center/Loretta C. Duckworth Scholars Studio, 203, 213
  Paskow Science Fiction Collection, 213, 217
  Special Collection Research Center (SCRC), 213
text mining, 214, 227
  limitations of, 216
Thomas, Sheree R., 225
three-color printing, 32
3D models, 186, 193, 194, 197, 200, 201
3D printing, 257, 264, *265*
3D-scanning technologies, 185–86, 188, 190, 192, 193, 199, 202
Ticknor, George, 79
"total library," 218, 233–36
traditional circulation, 90, 246, 250
Traditional Knowledge Labels, 105
Trans-Atlantic Platform (T-AP) Digging into Data Challenge
  The Mapping Manuscript Migrations, 179–81
Transactional Records Access Clearinghouse (TRAC), 161
Treschel, Frank, 175
Triangle Research Libraries Network, 250
Trinity College, 33, 34
triplestore, 181
Trusted Digital Repository, 155
Turnbull, Gordon, 36, 44

U

UBorrow from the Big Ten Academic Alliance Libraries, 251
UChicago Text Lab, 215
Umbra Search African American History, 112–13, 117, 118, 119, 120, 123; *see also* Digitizing African American

Umbra Search African American History (*continued*)
    Archival Materials Across University of Minnesota Collections (DAAAUMN)
uniform codes of practice, 83
Underwood, Ted
    "The Life Cycles of Genres," 213
Union Army, 11
United States Government Publications Office (formerly *US Government Printing Office*), 154–60
    1993 GPO Access Act, 154
University of Calgary, 228
University of Illinois, 84
University of Kansas, 216
University of Manchester, 29
University of Michigan, 84
University of Minnesota, 112
    Archives and Special Collections, 112
University of North Texas, 161
University of Paris, 77
University of Pennsylvania, 160, 168
University of Virginia, South Carolina College, 84
University of Wisconsin, 84
US Patent and Trademark Office, 160
Using Primary Sources: Hands-On Instructional Exercises, 139

V

Vander Wal, Thomas 124
Vanity Fair, 53
Vesey, Elizabeth 43
video game industry, 199
virtual browsing, 201–02
virtual reality, 185
    in the academic library, 186, 195–96, 198, 201, 204
    and disabled users, 204
    hardware, 202

virtual reality (*continued*)
    and pattern recognition, 185, 230, 235
    role of librarians with, 202
    scholarly applications and benefits of, 194–95
    visual, aural, and haptic perception, 191
Vizenor, Gerald, 101

W

Waddell, Anne, 13
Waddesdon Manor, 39, 58
Walker, John, 53
War of 1812, 17
web-based data curation, 214
web-based tools, 229
web-based viewing of 3D models, 200
Wheatley, John, 3
Wheatley, Phillis, 3, 14
Wheatley, Susanna, 3
Whitehead, Colson
    The Underground Railroad, 222
Wilde, Oscar, 47
    Salome, 47, 47
Windows Mixed Reality, 186; *see also* virtual reality
Winston, Brian, 187
winter schools, 8
Wired, 198; *see also* Kelly, Kevin
Wolf, Edwin, 135
Wolfe, Patrick, 93
women's colleges, 19, 21
women's reading clubs, 8, 18, 19, 20
World Anti-Slavery Convention, 10
World War I, 128
world wide web, 236
Worldcat, 99
Wormsley Estate, 38, 55; *see also* Getty, Mark
Wormsley Library, 55, 56
Worth, Edward Edward, 34
Worth Library at Dr. Steevens's Hospital, 33, 34

Index

Wright, Richard
   Black Boy, 22
Wrightsman, Charles Bierer, 38, 52
Wrightsman, Jayne (née Larkin), 33, 38, 40, 52–55
   as benefactor of Morgan Library
   honorary member of Fairfax Murray Society for the Department of Drawings and Prints, 55
   Roxburghe Club member, 52, 54
   Placets de l'officier Desbans, 53, *54*; see also Desbans, Edme-Louis
Wrightsman Galleries, 38
written word, 76

Y

Yale University, 45, 46, 77, 84, 85
   Beinecke Rare Book and Manuscript Library, 26, 46
   library circulation data, 120
   Yale Center for British Art, 52
   Yale University Digital Humanities Lab, 232
      Pix-Plot, 232, *233*
      Robots Reading Vogue, 214
   The Younghee Kim-Wait (Class of 1982)/Pablo Eisenberg Native American Literature Collection, 97, 98

www.ingramcontent.com/pod-product-compliance
Lightning Source LLC
Chambersburg PA
CBHW081113160426
42814CB00035B/301